Edward Hayes Plumptre, Julius Charles Hare

The Victory of Faith

Third Edition

Edward Hayes Plumptre, Julius Charles Hare

The Victory of Faith
Third Edition

ISBN/EAN: 9783337762926

Printed in Europe, USA, Canada, Australia, Japan

Cover: Foto ©Lupo / pixelio.de

More available books at **www.hansebooks.com**

THE

VICTORY OF FAITH.

BY

JULIUS CHARLES HARE, M.A.,

ARCHDEACON OF LEWES, RECTOR OF HERSTMONCEUX, AND
LATE FELLOW OF TRINITY COLLEGE, CAMBRIDGE.

Third Edition.

EDITED BY

E. H. PLUMPTRE, M.A.,

PROFESSOR OF DIVINITY AT KING'S COLLEGE, LONDON; VICAR OF BICKLEY.

WITH INTRODUCTORY NOTICES BY THE LATE
PROFESSOR MAURICE AND DEAN STANLEY.

London:
MACMILLAN AND CO.
1874.

TO

THE RIGHT REV.

CONNOP THIRLWALL, D.D.,

LATE LORD BISHOP OF ST. DAVID'S,

IN WHOM

THE THREE WRITERS THAT ARE HERE BROUGHT TOGETHER

RECOGNIZED A FRIEND AND TEACHER

WHOM THEY ALL ALIKE HONOURED,

I 𝔇𝔢𝔡𝔦𝔠𝔞𝔱𝔢 𝔱𝔥𝔦𝔰 𝔙𝔬𝔩𝔲𝔪𝔢.

CONTENTS.

	PAGE
PREFACE. BY PROFESSOR PLUMPTRE,	ix

INTRODUCTORY NOTICES.

Essay on Archdeacon Hare's Position in the Church, with Reference to the Parties that Divide it. By Frederick Denison Maurice, M.A., . . . xvii

Archdeacon Hare. By Dean Stanley, . . . xc

SERMON I.

Faith, the Victory that Overcometh the World, . . 3

SERMON II.

Faith, a Practical Principle, ... 32

SERMON III.

Office and Province of Faith, ... 63

SERMON IV.

POWER OF FAITH IN MAN'S NATURAL LIFE, . . 103
                           PAGE

SERMON V.

POWER OF FAITH AMONG THE HEATHENS, AND AMONG THE JEWS, ... 151

SERMON VI.

FAITH IN CHRIST, THE VICTORY THAT OVERCOMETH THE WORLD, ... 189

PREFACE.

THE sermons on *the Victory of Faith*, by Archdeacon Hare, have for some years been out of print. They are now republished, in the belief that as they were the utterance of one who was in no small measure in advance of his own generation, measuring forces and watching currents of thought of which few then took account, so they are not yet altogether left behind by its advancing waves. Rapid as that advance has been, tending to an ever keener and more sharply defined antagonism between the schools of superstition and unbelief, clearing the middle ground and threatening to leave no room for those who belong to neither school, and enter their protests against each, there are still, it is believed, many who cannot accept either the theory of Ultramontanism or that of Secularism, who cannot even attach themselves to any of the 'parties in the Church of England, whose drift seems, consciously or unconsciously, to be sweeping them on to the one or the other issue. Seekers after truth, who, when they pray "Increase our faith," do not mean "Enlarge our capacity for believing without evidence or against it," who shrink from the thought that all man's knowledge of God is that there is nothing to be known, will find, it is hoped, something in the witness which this volume bears that may sustain and cheer them. Here was one who, though caring little for the ritual which symbolizes Romish dogmas, not anticipating, it may be, that because it does so symbolize it, it would have been deliberately revived within the Church of England, and therefore giving little heed to its history and meaning, had yet gone into the controversy with Rome precisely in the regions where it touches on the innermost depths of man's intellect and heart, and, as the result of that study, came forth with a profounder reverence for Luther, and a more assured conviction that the great movement of the sixteenth century, which we must still speak of as the Reformation, was, in spite of incidental drawbacks, a great gift from God. Here too was one whose knowledge both of the lower and the higher criticism which the scholars of Germany have applied to the documents of our faith was wider than that of any theologian of his own time, wider, perhaps, than that of any who are living now, and who yet cherished to the last the conviction that those documents contain the records of a divine Revelation given "in sundry times, and divers manners" to our fathers, and are still an instrument of priceless value for the education of mankind. Here, lastly, was one who had gone beyond the controversies between rival churches and questions as to the date or authorship of this or that sacred book, and had entered no less deeply into the systems of philosophy, which, at the time he wrote, were influencing the minds of those that were afterwards to be among the teachers of men, and who found rest in the belief that man is more than a highly intelligent and civilized animal, and has other sources of knowledge and other grounds of belief than those which come to him through the senses, other measurements of right and wrong than a quantitative standard of utility. Amid the confusions of our own time it may guide and comfort some who are wandering and perplexed to hear the clear tones of that voice bearing a renewed witness to the truth, and, as he points to the path which they have missed, bidding them walk in it, when, without that guidance, they would turn to the right hand or to the left.

It need not be concealed that another motive enters into this republication. The graceful and interesting *Memorials of a Quiet Life*, recently published by Mr. Augustus Hare, have brought the names and characters that were connected with that happy home at Hurstmonceaux, where so much of the "quiet life" was spent, before many thousand readers to whom they were before wholly or comparatively unknown. The writer of that book had a definite task before him, and has accomplished it with a consummate skill, which has made it one of the most popular of recent Christian biographies. But just in proportion as readers have been drawn to admire and reverence her life who is there naturally enough the centre of the group, have they, in not a few cases, wished to know more of those by whom her mind was more or less guided, who influenced her as much as, or more than, she influenced them, to whom she herself looked from the first day on which she learned to know them with reverence and admiration. What, they have asked, was the teaching in which that refined intellect and loving soul found rest? Was this peaceful and devout life the outcome of influences which have sometimes been described as "tending to the subversion of the faith?" Is our knowledge of that goodly company complete, so long as he who formed its true centre is known to us only at second hand—so long as we see him only by a reflected light with more or less of shadowy indistinctness? That this has been more or less widely felt, the inquiries which have been addressed (as I am informed by him) to the author of the *Memorials* as to the republication of his uncle's works is a sufficient proof. Circumstances having placed in my hands the responsibility of meeting or refusing to meet the want thus expressed, I have decided, as the appearance of the present volume shows, on the former alternative. It will be followed, in due course, by *the Mission of the Comforter*.

The volume bears, it will be seen, a somewhat composite character. No adequate life of Archdeacon Hare has as yet been written. I am constrained to add, however regretfully, that I see no prospect of any such life being written now or in the future. The lapse of years and the scantiness of materials make the work more difficult than ever. The memoir which I have prefixed to the last edition of the *Guesses at Truth* is, as was inevitable from the limits within which it was confined, hardly more than a chronological *résumé* of the chief events in his career, and of the chief writings which marked its several stages. There are, however, two studies of the man, his character, and his influence, which show, each of them, the hand of a more skilled master, working under happier conditions. One of these, the memoir by the Dean of Westminster, originally published as an article in the *Quarterly Review* for June, 1855, and lately reprinted in his volume of *Essays on Church and State*, appears here through his kind permission, and that of his publisher, Mr. Murray. From the other I venture, on my own responsibility, to remove the veil of anonymous authorship, which has till now shrouded it. When the *Charges* delivered by Archdeacon Hare were collected for publication in the year that followed his death (1856) there appeared with them a somewhat full Introduction, "explanatory of his position in the Church with reference to the parties that divide it." Those who read that *Introduction* would recognize at every step the turns of thought and phrase that characterized the style of one who, more than most men, was incapable of disguising or suppressing his own intense individuality, and would have no difficulty in discerning that the voice which spoke to them from beneath the veil was that of Frederick Denison

Maurice. But the readers of collected Charges are comparatively few, and the fact that the *Introduction* was anonymous left it to lie in almost entire obscurity. Readers who still hold in honour the names of the two writers will, if I mistake not, thank me for enabling them to see how one judged of the other, what estimate the scholar, who in his turn became a 'master of those who know,' formed of the teacher at whose feet he had himself once sat, and to whom he acknowledged, with all the large-hearted humility of his nature, that he owed much that was most precious to him in the growth of his own intellect and heart. It was natural, while he lived, that he should shrink from even appearing to measure and to judge the work of one, who had been not only his teacher, but his brother and his friend. Now that he too has passed away, there seems no longer any reason for maintaining the same reticence.

Hare, Maurice, Stanley, Thirlwall (I venture to add the name of the great prelate to whom I dedicate this volume), these are, I suppose, classed together in popular estimate, if not as the leaders of a party, at least as the representatives of a school. I am not sorry that the juxtaposition of writings by three out of the four should enable readers to judge how far that estimate is true—how far it is the exact opposite of the truth. They will see, if I mistake not, that though brought together as friends, having many points of sympathy, honouring and admiring each other, few writers could be named less cast in the same mould, more characterized, each of them, by special gifts and graces of their own. It is not so, as a moment's recollection will show, with those who belong to what are known as the great parties of the Church. There, in the books of either school, you find the same shibboleths intelligently or unintelligently repeated, you trace the same opinions. Their systems move as in a well marked groove along the same lines of curvature. That which the writers who are now brought together had in common was their refusal to run in those grooves, to be bound by those shibboleths. Each felt that it is not thus that men attain to the knowledge of the Truth, that history leads us to know both the strength and the weakness of contending schools, that their wisdom was to advance in the paths in which they felt that the Divine Teacher was leading them on to clearer views, or more vivid perceptions, or profounder thought. This also they had in common, that they disclaimed in speech and act the party character which men tried to thrust on them, wished for no organization, desired no representatives in the press or among politicians. Lastly, they had this in common, that the rule of being "ever strong upon the stronger side" was not their rule, that they never took up popular cries, or shrank from facing popular indignation, when justice or truth required it. Examples of that form of manliness are not so common that we can afford to forget those who in our own day have been most conspicuous for it. Of the two who have fought the good fight, and have kept the faith, we who remain behind and follow as afar off can but say, as we dwell on the memory of men whose gifts were greater and lives loftier than our own, "*Si natura suppeditet, similitudine decoremus. Is verus honos, ea conjunctissimi cujusque pietas.*"

E. H. P.

BICKLEY VICARAGE,
December 16th, 1873.

INTRODUCTORY NOTICES.*

ESSAY ON ARCHDEACON HARE'S POSITION IN THE CHURCH, WITH REFERENCE TO THE PARTIES THAT DIVIDE IT. BY FREDERICK DENISON MAURICE, M.A.

AN able and friendly critic,† in attempting to give an account of the religious parties which exist in England, connected Archdeacon Hare's name with one on which he bestowed the title of *the Broad Church*. So intelligent an observer must have had some clear apprehension of his own meaning, when he ventured upon the perilous experiment of coining a new nickname which was sure to be eagerly welcomed by hundreds, to whom it would serve the same purpose as the words Puritan, Methodist, Jacobin, Mystic, served their forefathers. The conceptions which have been formed of his meaning by those who have adopted his phrase have certainly been anything but clear and definite. It has

* Reprinted from the Edition of the Charges of Archdeacon Hare, published in 1856.
† Mr. Conybeare, in the *Edinburgh Review*, vol. xcviii, page 273.

been said, for instance, by one critic that the writer of these Charges belonged to the school of Archbishop Whately ; by another that he followed in the wake of Dr. Arnold ; by a third, that he himself aspired to form a school, consisting of restless spirits who were impatient of everything English, and cared only for German literature, German philosophy, German divinity. A still greater number of persons suppose that he was, by nature and inclination, merely a man of taste and letters ; that he took up theology in his later years as a professional pursuit; that he wished to introduce into the treatment of it the indifferentism and eclecticism which he had cultivated in another region ; that he was impatient of the accurate distinctions as well as of the fervent zeal which he found in each of our Church parties ; that he hoped out of them to construct one of a mild *poco-curante* character, which should be agreeable to refined and scholarlike men, and in which all the roughnesses that have made the Church displeasing to the world should be smoothed and pared away.

The following remarks are written to show how far any of these statements correspond with the facts.

Of all his eminent contemporaries, probably the one with whom he was most rarely brought into personal contact, and whose writings had the least influence in forming his opinions or his character, was the Archbishop of Dublin.* That distinguished man and Mr. Hare were educated at different universities; their pur-

* Archbishop Whately.

suits, habits of mind, objects of admiration, were most dissimilar. The one has devoted his great abilities, when they have not been turned in a strictly professional direction, to logic and political economy. Mr Hare's mind was formed and nourished by philology and poetry. He always professed the most fervent gratitude to Coleridge, whom Dr. Whately probably regards with feelings not far removed from contempt. The chasm between the Platonical and the Aristotelian intellects (which has been pronounced—perhaps too rashly, but not without considerable warrant from experience— to be impassable) separated theirs. That the English Church is "broad" enough to comprehend persons so unlike as these two; that she can claim their different talents and qualities of mind for her service; that those who very little understand each other may, nevertheless, help different persons to understand their relation to her better, by helping them to understand themselves better: this may be joyfully admitted. But the admission seems to go some way towards proving, first, that a Broad Church party, such as has been dreamed of, is impossible; and secondly, that if it were possible it would be unnecessary, seeing that a body has existed here for about a thousand years, which is considerably more inclusive than the new creation could ever become.

It is a far more reasonable supposition that Mr. Hare learned much from Dr. Arnold. He could hardly help doing so, for they were personal friends, and some of their pursuits and interests were similar. They both devoted much attention to Niebuhr's Roman History; they had a common affection for Niebuhr's distinguished pupil, Chevalier Bunsen. Moreover, Dr. Arnold, beyond all question, *was* the head of an illustrious school, in which he both acquired and communicated all that was strongest and most vital in his ethics and divinity, and through which he acted powerfully on his country. But as Mr. Hare had completed his college course, and had become a teacher himself, before Dr. Arnold was called to be the Master of Rugby, he certainly did not study under him there. Their acquaintance was made when the minds of both were full grown; and in a characteristically frank letter of Dr. Arnold's, published by Mr. Stanley, he tells Augustus Hare that it was a long time before he liked his brother at all. When they came to appreciate each other, their intercourse was maintained on the only footing upon which the intercourse of two men of independent characters and different duties can be maintained—that of exchanging each other's treasures, and respecting each other's peculiarities. Mr. Hare probably reverenced Dr. Arnold as nearly the most useful man in England, and as having gifts in high exercise, in which he felt himself to be deficient; but there is not the slightest indication in his writings that his theology or his philosophy had been materially affected—of course neither had been originally shaped—by this influence. On one question of religious politics, that of the admission of the Jews to Parliament, Mr. Hare certainly accorded with Dr. Arnold's opinions, perhaps adopted them; but as they were at one on that question with five-sixths of the religious world, and at variance with some of their own most intimate friends, it was scarcely a basis for a school, certainly not for a Broad Church school, to rest upon.

It is a far greater temptation, however, to call a party into existence, than to join one of which the colours and watchwords are known. There was a time in Mr. Hare's life, as the writer of the kind and cordial article upon him in the *Quarterly Review* has observed, when he had the opportunity of influencing a certain number of young men. He was for ten years one of the Classical Lecturers in Trinity College. Only one "side" of the College attended his class—he worked under the tutor of that side—and he had few of the opportunities which the master of a public school possessed of knowing the characters and tendencies of his pupils. The field, therefore, was a comparatively narrow one, but it was here, if anywhere, that he must have scattered the seeds out of which his party afterwards developed itself. What seeds he did scatter at that time, and how they germinated, may, perhaps, be gathered from a paper of reminiscences which has been communicated by a clergyman who attended his class rather more than thirty years ago. For a biography, his eminent contemporaries who adorned the college then, and many of whom adorn it still, could supply much more valuable materials; but in reference to the point under consideration, the testimony of a pupil who knew him at Cambridge only in that capacity may be of more direct use.*

"You ask me whether I can recal any of the impressions which were made upon me by Hare's lectures? Such a question would sound very singular to most persons whose Freshman's year was passed so long ago as 1823-24. Probably nearly all their remembrances of that time would be more vivid than that of their regular teacher, especially in classics. The mathematical instruction being more new to them, and more directly connected with the place, might have left some traces in their minds; the words of an eminent professor like Sedgwick, who found (and finds still) something much more living than sermons in stones, still deeper traces : yet I should suppose the first look of the College buildings, perhaps the face of the first old schoolfellow who greeted him, would recur more naturally to a man who was looking back over so many years even than these. I cannot, however, offer this excuse for silence. I *do* recollect Hare's class-room exceedingly well. I am often surprised how clearly all the particulars of what passed in it come back to me, when so much else that I should like to preserve has faded away.

"You will suppose, perhaps, that this was owing to some novelty in his method of teaching. You will inquire whether he assumed more of a professional air than is common in a College, and gave disquisitions instead of calling on his pupils to construe a book? Not the least. We construed just as they did elsewhere. I do not remember his indulging in a single excursus. The subject in our first term was the Antigone of Sophocles. We had Hermann's edition of the play, which had not long come out; his entire edition of Sophocles was not then published. We hammered at the words and at the sense. The lecturer seemed most anxious to impress us with the feeling that there was no road to the sense which did not go through the words. He took infinite pains to make us understand the force of nouns, verbs, particles, and the grammar of the sentences. We often spent an hour on the strophe or antistrophe of a chorus. If he did not see his way into it himself, he was never afraid to show us that he did not; he would try one after another of the different solutions that were suggested, till we at least felt which were not available.

"You will think that so much philological carefulness could not

---

* The pupil whose testimony is here given was, it need hardly be stated, Mr. Maurice himself.

have been obtained without the sacrifice of higher objects. How could we discover the divine intuitions of the poet, while we were tormenting ourselves about his tenses? I cannot tell; but it seems to me that I never learnt so much about this particular poem, about Greek dramatic poetry generally, about all poetry, as in that term. If there had been disquisitions about the Greek love of beauty, about the classical and romantic schools, and so forth, I should have been greatly delighted. I should have rushed forth to retail to my friends what I had heard, or have discussed it, and refuted it as long as they would listen to my nonsense. What we did and heard in the lecture-room could not be turned to this account. One could not get the handy phrase one wished about Greek ideals and poetical unity; but, by some means or other, one rose to the apprehension that the poem *had* a unity in it, and that the poet *was* pursuing an ideal, and that the unity was not created by him, but perceived by him, and that the ideal was not a phantom, but something which must have had a most real effect upon himself, his age, and his country. I cannot the least tell you how Hare imparted this conviction to me; I only know that I acquired it, and could trace it very directly to his method of teaching. I do not suppose that he had deliberately invented a method; in form, as I have said, he was adapting himself exactly to the practice of English Colleges; in spirit, he was following the course which a cultivated man, thoroughly in earnest to give his pupils the advantage of his cultivation, and not ambitious of displaying himself, would fall into. Yet I have often thought since, that if the genius of Bacon is, as I trust it is and always will be, the tutelary one of Trinity, its influence was scarcely more felt in the scientific lecture-rooms than in this classical one;—we were, just as much as the students of natural philosophy, feeling our way from particulars to universals, from facts to principles.

"One felt this method, without exactly understanding it, in reading our Greek play. The next term it came much more distinctly before us. Then we were reading the Gorgias of Plato. But here, again, the lecturer was not tempted for an instant to spoil us of the good which Plato could do us, by talking to us about him, instead of reading him with us. There was no *résumé* of his philosophy, no elaborate comparison of him with Aristotle, or with any of the moderns. Our business was with a single dialogue; we were to follow that through its windings, and to find out by degrees, if we could, what the writer was driving at, instead of being told beforehand. I cannot recollect that he ever spoke to us of Schleirmacher, whose translations were, I suppose, published at that time; if they were, he had certainly read them; but his anxiety seemed to be that Plato should explain himself to us, and should help to explain us to ourselves. Whatever he could do to further this end, by bringing his reading and scholarship to bear upon the illustration of the text, by throwing out hints as to the course the dialogue was taking, by exhibiting his own fervent interest in Plato, and his belief of the high purpose he was aiming at, he did. But to give us second-hand reports, though they were ever so excellent—to save us the trouble of thinking—to supply us with a moral, instead of showing us how we might find it, not only in the book but in our own hearts,—this was clearly not his intention.

"Our third term was spent on one of the early books of Livy. My recollections of these lectures are far fainter than those which turned on Greek subjects. I have often been surprised that they are so; for the translator of Niebuhr must have devoted, even at that time, great attention to all questions concerning home history. Some of the remarks he made have since come to life in my mind; there was the same abstinence here as elsewhere from disquisition, and from whatever was likely to hinder us from learning by making us vain of what we learnt. But he had not, or at least he did not communicate to us, that vivid sense of locality which seems to have formed the great charm of Dr. Arnold's historical teachings, and which is united with much higher qualities in Carlyle's magnificent epic of the French Revolution. I should fancy, therefore, that his readings on poetry and philosophy would always have been the most interesting and valuable.

"I believe that Hare gave some lectures on the Greek Testament to the students of the second year, but I never heard any of them; nor had I ever any conversation with him on theological subjects. In fact, I had very few opportunities of conversing with him on any subject. I had no introduction to him. I had never heard his name when I entered the College, and I availed myself of the kindness which he was disposed to show me, in common with others, less than I should have done, if I had been older and wiser. When we met again many years after, my theological convictions had already been formed by a discipline very different, I should imagine, from any to which he was subjected; they were not altered in substance, nor, so far as I know, even in colour, by any intercourse I had with him. But to his lectures on Sophocles and Plato I can trace the most permanent effect on my character, and on all my modes of contemplating subjects, natural, human, and divine. How hard it is in these days—in this commercial England—to believe that all ideals of excellence are not mere pretences—mere shadows which men have dreamed of and followed, till they woke up to the dismal pettinesses of actual existence ! How history seems to favour the conclusion— what a record it is of the failures and disappointments of great men in the pursuit of honour, patriotism, beauty, truth! How confidently men of the world pronounce that only boys hope to find the end of the rainbow, or the good which cannot be measured and is not the work of fancy ; stamping their warning against such vain efforts with the awful warrant of their own past experience ! How continually do theories which assume selfishness as the basis of all actions and life, start up and scare us with the suspicion that they are putting into form what we are holding, but do not like to confess ! What enormous weight religious men throw into the scale of that practical unbelief,—how they sustain even the dogmas of Rochefoucauld and Helvetius—by their statement of the motives which uniformly govern mankind, with the exception of some inconsiderable fraction of it ! Above all, what an evidence, for awhile entirely indisputable, in support of these conclusions, is brought home to the heart of him who has had a revelation of his own evil, who has discovered that in him dwelleth no good ! I know for myself, that there have been times of inward strife and horror, when I have hated all ideals and all teachers—Hare among the rest—who had ever spoken of them as if they were not delusions. But I am certain that if I had continued in that hatred, I should have lost altogether the sense of my own evil, and should only have retained St. Paul's words as the utterance of a dogma, not of a fact. Thanks be to God who has forced me to acknowledge that there is an ideal, in which and after which man is created ; an ideal which explains and justifies all the ideals men have perceived, and followed, and found themselves unable to reach ; an ideal which tells us what our sin is; an ideal which can lift us out of it ! And thanks be to God for any teachers He has raised up to uphold that faith in a generation particularly inclined to abandon it, and so to sink lower, as it might rise higher, than all which have gone before it. Hare, I believe, had this vocation. He must have been prepared for it by some special discipline, which we who profited by it may not be exactly able to understand. We have a hard enough battle, but I have sometimes thought that theirs must have been in many respects harder, whose boyhood was passed in the stirring years between Trafalgar and Waterloo ; and who in their

C

manhood, when they might have expected to see the fruits of the seeds which had been sown by Spanish and German wars of independence, found themselves amidst the flatness and foppery which lasted to the end of the reign of George IV. Then, when it was bitterness even to think of foreign politics ; when domestic politics were absorbed in the one question, whether a few Roman Catholic gentlemen should or should not be allowed to add their quota to parliamentary loquacity and electoral corruption ; then, when the spiritual movement of Methodism had subsided, and seemed to have left behind it only a cumbrous religious machinery; then, when so genial a writer as Sir Walter Scott, so free from the affectations of his own time, so full of sympathy with past times, could only maintain his ascendency over his contemporaries on the condition that he never affronted them with a single type of heroical excellence ; then, when so acute and charitable an observer as Miss Austen, scarcely introduced into her exquisite sketches one being, lay or clerical, male or female, who had ever breathed, even in dreams, any air purer and freer than that of the pump-room ;—in such a time there must have been an unspeakable sinking of heart, and a terrible questioning whether all which had been told in other times of a good that the senses could judge of, and that gold could not buy, did not belong wholly to those days. The Bible surely might have satisfied that demand ; but how possible is it for a mercantile age to find in the Bible nothing but the endorsement of certain accommodation-bills that it has drawn, the worth of which rests not on a real faith, but on an imaginary credit ! I have spoken as John Bulls and clergymen are wont to speak of the German literature and philosophy in which Hare is supposed to have taken a great interest; have spoken of them, I mean, with much fear and little knowledge. But if that literature and philosophy were instrumental in sustaining him against the influences of English society, if they prevented him from becoming the slave, or, which is the same thing, the leader, in some one of its circles, he may have owed it to them that he did not lose his fervent love for the thoughts and language of Shakespeare, Hooker, and Milton ; that the Old and New Testament became dearer and dearer to him every year that he lived.

"Before I finish these hasty and trifling memoranda, I ought to say that Hare's Plato lectures did me another service, closely connected with that of which I have spoken. They taught me that there is a way out of party opinions ; a principle which is not a compromise between them, but which is implied in both, and of which each is bearing witness. Hare did not tell us this. If he had, he would have done us little good. Plato himself does not say it; he makes us feel it ; and his interpreter was only useful as he led us to his author, and did not put himself between us and him. But Hare's mind was clearly penetrated with the conviction,—his after life, to whatever work he was called, must have been the acting out of it. If he tried to form a party afterwards, we who were his pupils could not have become members of it till we forgot all that we had learnt from him. If it was an eclectical party or school, *that* we could have less sympathy with than with either of those of which it must have been the negation. I have known very few of those who attended his classes at Trinity, so that I am not the least able to speak of the influence he exercised generally. Those few were men singularly unlike in their opinions, belonging to different sections of the Church, most of them suspicious of Hare's theology. They retained, however, a fervent affection for him, and I think they had so far suffered from their training, that no one of them could be recommended to the editor of any religious journal as a safe roadster, who would run without danger of starting and gibing in a party harness."

If Mr. Hare did not seek to be the founder of a new school in England at all, it is not necessary to prove that the school was not an Anglo-Germanic one. But as the writer of the above notes has alluded to the influence which German books and German thinkers may have had over his mind, in the interval between his leaving College as a pupil and returning to it as a teacher, a few words on that subject seem to be called for.

From very early youth till he left this world, he felt this influence, and rejoiced to confess how much he owed to it. He was taken to Weimar by his parents when he was a child ; and during a winter which he spent there, when illness hindered him from attending to other studies, he first learnt German. Weimar had other associations . for him besides those which have

made it inseparable from the names of Göthe and
Schiller. He had reason to know that the Duchess
who honoured them, and whom they honoured, was
not merely a friend of great men ; she paid the kindest
and most soothing attentions to his mother during a
period of sickness and blindness which preceded her
death. His eldest brother, who gave him his first
initiation into Greek, was also an excellent German
scholar, and no doubt used his knowledge of that as of
other modern literature, to make his lessons more
lively. Indeed, it would not have been easy for Francis
Hare, who combined the rarest literary accomplish-
ments with the most agreeable social qualities—who
was equally popular with scholars, men of the world,
and children,—not to inspire one whom he loved with
interest in everything in which he took interest
himself. Julius Hare, therefore, could scarcely have
avoided German studies, even if he had desired to avoid
them. But he could not feel such a desire, because
the more he engaged in those studies, the more clear
and intelligible his English books and his classical
books became to him. He learned from these foreign
teachers the intrinsic worth of the national treasures
which so many of us value only for some *extrinsic*
peculiarities, or for the food that they supply to our
vanity. He learnt to prize the bequests of the old
world as helps in understanding the changes of times,
and in apprehending that which does not change and
is not of time; so escaping from the pedantry and
frivolity of the merely antiquarian or dilettante scholar.

His readings at this time were chiefly among those
German poets who had fought their way through a
great many opposing tendencies, from each of which
they had derived some lessons: through the French
habits of the age of Frederick; through the book-learn-
ing of their own professors; through the wild and rhap-
sodical sentiment which was the reaction against both.
These writers had felt and confessed that there is an
order and harmony somewhere, which men's confusions
have not been able to destroy, and that Art and Letters
are precious only as they help us in discovering it.
The other class of writers, the pure philosophers, he
honoured because they appeared to him to have grap-
pled honestly and earnestly with the question in which
all men are interested,—whether the spiritual world is
merely a fantastic world, or whether it is the substantial
ground of that which our senses tell us of.

No doubt there were perils in both these kinds of
study. The one may lead a man to build what has
been called a palace of art, and to inhabit it, till some
rough blasts of actual sorrow shake it to pieces. Those
who engage in the other task may receive such delight
from the process of seeking for an invisible kingdom,
as to lose all care whether they find it, till at last
weariness overtakes them, and they are content to rest
in any plausible theory about the object of their strivings, as if that *were* the object of them. Hare may
have been liable, at different times of his life, to each
of these temptations, but he had much to assist him in
overcoming them. His aunt, the widow of Sir William

Jones,—worthy by her clear sense, unusual cultivation, and firm principle, to have shared the affection and labours of such a man,—had great influence over his mind and character. She told him distinctly that she wished his German books were burnt. He regarded her opinion with the deference which an imaginative and impulsive nature pays to one of sterner stuff, even when there are no strong bonds of affection and gratitude between them; but this was a point which he could not yield, because he was convinced that he should be transgressing the spirit of her advice if he had conformed to it in the letter. He explained to her that his patriotism and his faith were in danger, from the materialism which in England was claiming every domain of thought, and even religion itself, as its subject, and that the Germans, whom she dreaded, had at least preserved his intellect, and in some degree his conscience, from this infection. He wrote to her in January, 1820 —"As for my German books, I hope, from my heart, that the day will never arrive when I shall be induced to burn them, for I am convinced that I never shall do so, unless I have first become a base slave of Mammon, and a mere vile lump of selfishness. I shall never be able to repay an hundredth part of the obligations I am under to them, even though I were to shed every drop of my blood in defence of their liberties. For to them I owe the best of all my knowledge, and if they have not purified my heart, the fault is my own. Above all, to them I owe my ability to believe in Christianity, with a much more implicit and intelligent faith than I otherwise should have been able to have done; for without them I should only have saved myself from dreary suspicions, by a refusal to allow my heart to follow my head, and by a self-willed determination to believe, whether my reason approved of my belief or not. This question has so often been a subject of discussion, that I have determined, once for all, to state my reasons for remaining firm in my opinion."

But, perhaps, the counsels which he could not follow were not without their use. They may have reminded him of a truth, which he became deeply sensible of afterwards, that an Englishman, though he need not be a materialist, must be a practical man; that no education can be good for him which does not develop his practical qualities; that though he becomes a very miserable creature when he acts without thinking, he becomes even more feeble and contemptible when he aspires to think without acting.

These lessons were also deepened by the influence of relations nearer to his own age. His fourth brother, Marcus, to whom he was most fondly attached, though he did not share much in his literary tastes and pursuits, had that kind of character which was sure to act most powerfully upon him: the clear manly sense, warm heart, and resolute purpose of an English sailor and Christian gentleman. And if intercourse with this brother were not a sufficient protest against un-English tendencies and literary self-indulgence, that protest came in another form from the one who shared all his thoughts and aspirations. Augustus Hare, who was a fellow of New College, had known and felt some of the perils of a life among books. He triumphed over them, and devoted himself to the work of a tutor, before he felt himself qualified for the work of a parish priest. He was thoroughly loyal to Oxford; an admirer of Aristotle's ethics; full of reverence for the past; capable of speculation, but esteeming it for the sake of action; reverencing all forms of beauty, and moral goodness as the perfection of beauty; chivalrous, even military in his tastes; exercising a powerful influence over young men, even more through the nobleness and gentleness of his character, than by any words which he spoke to them; eager for the well-being of all countries, especially of that lovely one in which he was born, and in which he found a grave; but connecting all with England, counting those happy whom God called to fight for her in the field, and those highly honoured whom He permitted to work in any lowly office for the peasants in her villages. If his mind and that of Julius had not had an original difference of structure, and if they had not been quite differently trained, they would, probably, not have blended so well together. The book* which contained the result of

---

* *The Guesses at Truth* was not, however, the first literary undertaking in which they worked together. Augustus Hare had been scandalized by an ignorant attempt to throw doubts upon the fact of our Lord's resurrection. He answered the book in *A Series of Letters by a Layman:* the part of those letters which referred to German authorities was written by Julius. It is worthy of record that this book, which was an able specimen of the books of evidence most popular in England—which was expressly in

their common meditations was called by a name which showed how little they aspired to lay down decrees upon any questions of which they spoke. But in escaping from that charge, they have fallen under another, which would have appeared to them still heavier. These writers, it has been said, suppose truth to be mere guess-work. An observation more curiously inapplicable to the spirit and character of both brothers was certainly never hazarded. Because they were so confident that truth is fixed and eternal—that it is not the creature of men's notions and speculations—that a man must seek for it as hid treasure, not refer it to his own narrow rules of judgment—therefore they thought it an exercise useful in itself, certain of reward, to trace the vestiges of it in every direction, to grasp even the skirts of its garment, and if they missed it still to testify that it was ready to declare itself to more faithful inquiries. They believed that there was a ladder set upon earth, and reaching to heaven; that the voice of God may be heard in the calm midnight, nay even in the open day, by those who are at the lowest step of this ladder, who have only a bed of earth with a stone for their pillow, if they will reverently apply their ears to listen, and ask to have it dis-

answer to German neologians, or their English imitators—which was praised at the time in the *British Critic*, and might have procured for either brother a good ecclesiastical reputation, was published anonymously when both were laymen. When Julius afterwards wrote books which were less likely to recommend him to the religious public or to the ecclesiastical authorities, his name appeared at full length on the title-page.

tinguished from the noises of which the air is full, and which try to drown it or mock it. These guesses have cherished this conviction in the hearts of many who have needed it, and who would have suffered infinite loss if they had been without it. And they have led not a few to look further still; to ask whether there is not a Centre of all God's revelations, one in whom He created the world, one in whom He has enlightened men, one in whom He has made himself perfectly known. The words, "I am the Way, and the Truth, and the Life," have come to them as at once the encouragement and the satisfaction of their guesses. If this result is not what our doctors of the law, our masters in Israel, desire, it may nevertheless be one which He does not disapprove, who in every part of nature and in every human relation found parables of his kingdom, and openings through which his disciples might have glimpses of it.

In this book, especially in the later editions of it, in which Julius Hare is the chief spokesman, German authors are largely referred to. But the book is essentially and characteristically English. The language is singularly pure of foreign admixtures. English authors are evidently those in which the writers most desire to interest their readers. Burke, with his strong national conservatism, is one of their chief favourites. Among their contemporaries, they indulge their private affection, and show what is the habit of their mind, by praising Landor, less for his exquisite scholarship and his Italian lore, than for his pure and beautiful English.

Wordsworth, who disliked German poetry, and is in general despised by those who admire it, they speak of with fervent affection. He was dear to them, because he had taught them to love better their own soil, and the peasants who work on it; to believe that, for us, Westmoreland has more poetry in it than Arcadia.

And the sympathies of both brothers were awake to mediæval forms and virtues, though they honoured Cervantes, and held that the nineteenth century, as much as the sixteenth, has a work which is altogether different from that of the thirteenth or fourteenth. Augustus expressed an almost passionate admiration for the *Broad Stone of Honour*, which exhibited a type of character essentially like his own. Julius knew and loved the writer of that book, who he found had the best possible right to speak of Bayard and St. Louis, because he had drunk into their spirit, and would have been what they were. He never ceased to remember with deep gratitude his intercourse with Mr. Digby, and the lessons he had learned from him; yet at the very time that he had most opportunity for cultivating that intercourse, he was translating a book of severe critical history with another friend, whose clear, penetrating intellect and resolute spirit of investigation he appreciated as highly as he possibly could the ardour of the believer in all legends of knightly heroism.

Catholicism of *this* kind will seem to some most alien from that Catholicism which they demand of a divine; they will say that a man, whose sympathies were so general, could not hold the definite faith of a Churchman. And another class will ask with displeasure, what a Protestant was good for, who could derive strong impressions from a writer like Mr. Digby—a writer whose heroes were always drawn from what he called the Ages of Faith, and who came at last to regard the Reformation as the disturber and subverter of faith. Such Catholics and such Protestants will therefore probably agree in the opinion that Hare loved Madonnas and old buildings, and therefore the times which produced them,—Philology, and therefore the age and country in which it has been most vigorously pursued ; that his Theology was merely an accidental graft upon these, his proper and original, though sometimes rather discordant, taste. This opinion will, no doubt, be strengthened in many minds by the fact, that he always spoke of Samuel Taylor Coleridge as one of his chief teachers, not in human studies only, but in the one which chiefly concerned him as a clergyman. He cannot be suspected, as many have been, of resorting to Coleridge because, at his *restaurant*, German cookery was adapted to weak English stomachs, not yet prepared to receive it in its genuine forms ; for Hare knew the taste of German dishes and had partaken of them fearlessly. But a more plausible reason has been assigned for the language in which some clergymen as well as laymen learnt to speak of a man whose name was ordinarily tabooed in literary as well as in religious circles. They had acquired, it has been said, something more of philosophy than their contemporaries; they had discovered that there are certain principles which cannot be set aside even by the longest tradition of the highest authority. There were, however, certain dogmas received by tradition, sanctioned by authority, the rejection of which was on many accounts inconvenient. To procure a reconciliation of the apparent contraries was highly desirable. Coleridge—so these reporters say—in windy harangues, addressed to all who visited his chamber at Highgate, announced the possibility of such a reconciliation; and even gave hints, which answered the purpose of his hearers the better for not being understood, about the method of effecting it. These hints, it is added, vague and unsubstantial as they were, yet acquired consistency and solidity when they were combined with the various motives which induced Englishmen, studious of ease and respectability, to arrive at the sage's conclusion. He himself, in the meantime, we are told with considerable exultation and unquestionable truth, gained little by his orthodox eloquence. Devout men heard of it with more fear than satisfaction; the pension of a hundred a year which had been conferred on him by royal bounty was withdrawn; he owed more to the generosity of an unknown London surgeon than to all the nobles and prelates in the land.

No doubt there have been, and are, persons who greatly desire to find in some ingenious philosophical scheme a justification for opinions which they have taken by inheritance, and which they think it safer not to abandon. No doubt some of this class did frequent Coleridge's soirées occasionally—nay, even put them-

selves to the trouble of reading passages from his books.
But it is certain also that every one of them returned
from him with disappointment, even with indignation;
for they discovered that he made the rudest demands
upon their conscience and reason; insisted upon their
feeling the ground at their feet, and not assuming upon
hearsay that there ought to be such ground; made it
his very business to bring into discredit the kind of
security which they had expected him to endorse.
What use could be made of such an oracle? How
absurd to consult it, when clever men like Le Maistre
were at hand, who could bring forward the most plausible apology for every opinion that had ever been held
under priestly sanction since the world began; sure to
leave behind them disciples more advanced than themselves, who would find apologies for every crime that
has been committed under priestly sanction till now,
or that may be committed till the world shall end.
How continually one hears the compassionate, patronizing exclamation, " Poor Coleridge !" from persons
who have found the seller of the genuine article which
they had vainly expected to obtain from him. And
though this phrase is joined, of course, with others
about " transcendental, mystical stuff," it is clear from
the faces of the speakers, that they could well have
endured what they did *not* understand in his discourse
or his books; but that, now and then, a phrase or
passage made itself painfully intelligible to them, and
produced a half-awakening in souls which preferred to
be asleep.

There were spirits of a different order altogether from those who also experienced ultimately a discontent from intercourse with Coleridge, which was bitterer than theirs, because far nobler. They had felt for him the passionate devotion which earnest and generous minds always feel towards one from whom they have received great spiritual benefits; their devotion had become idolatrous, and they demanded from the idol that which it could not bestow. In that crisis of painful uncertainty, when these disciples were reluctantly confessing to themselves that the seer had not cleared up all doubts, and solved all mysteries, if any one of the kind friends who are always at hand for such services, brought forth weaknesses which the worshippers had resolved not to see—if it should be suggested to men full of energy and strong will, and eagerness for action, that in all these qualities, the being to whose intellect they had done homage was sadly deficient, —who cannot predict the result? The kind friends did a necessary work. The idols of a man, as well as the idols of an age, whether they be of clay or of gold, must be utterly abolished. But let him who is in haste to undertake the task of an iconoclast, either on the small or the great scale, wait at least till he has read and pondered that essay on Voltaire—full of the deepest wisdom and the solemnest warnings—which he will find in Mr. Carlyle's Miscellanies.

There were, however, some whom these arguments and insinuations could not affect; because they neither resorted to Coleridge in hopes of obtaining a philosophical excuse for being Christians and Churchmen, nor wished to find in him a perfect guide. They had been led by strange paths into the belief that man is not an animal carrying about a soul, but a spiritual being with an animal nature, who, when he has sunk lowest into that nature, has still thoughts and recollections of a home to which he belongs, and from which he has wandered. They had felt as if these were especially the discoveries of their own time, as if they had arrived at them by processes which their fathers did not know. But these discoveries stopped short just at the point where they became most interesting and personally important. Where is that home of which we have these reminiscences? how can we ever come to it? They heard from some teachers eloquent words about abysses and eternities. The assurance that these are about us all, made them more eager to know if man's home is in them, or if there is nothing in them but darkness. They heard from others that the age of Theology had passed, and the age of Science begun. If Science has become Omniscience, can it not interpret that cry for a living God which still goes up from human hearts whether there is a Theology or not? It was not, therefore, because these weary seekers wanted a compromise between the old and the new, because they were afraid to follow truth whithersoever it led them, but because they were sure that, unless they pushed their inquiries further, they should be obliged to retrace their steps, to unlearn all they had learnt, to sink back into materialism, to believe in Mammon

—though they believed nothing else—that they welcomed the voice of a man who said to them, "What you are feeling after is that Father's house which the men of the old time spoke of. It was not a cunningly-devised fable of theirs, that their Father and yours is seeking to bring back His children to Himself: these struggles and failures of yours confirm their words." Beneath all strange mystical utterances—beneath those tetrads which might or might not be useful as scientific expositions of a truth lying beyond the senses and the intellect—they heard this practical message from his lips, they saw that he could not have received it or proclaimed it unless the whole man within him had passed through a tremendous convulsion. If, when they obtained a more accurate knowledge of his history, they discovered that it was not merely his reason which had demanded God as its foundation, but that he had been compelled by the feebleness of his will, by the sense of moral evil, to cry out to that God, in the old language, "Be merciful to me a sinner," this information could not make them reject either the lore or the teacher; it united both more closely to their own bitter experiences and brotherly sympathies.

This, or something like this, was the reason of that unshaken attachment which Julius Hare felt for Coleridge while he was in the world, and after he had left it; this was the reason why he so thankfully acknowledged him as a theological teacher. Unless he had found such a teacher, all his *Guesses after Truth* in various directions would have wanted that object and centre towards which they were always pointing; there would have been no blessing from his strivings for himself or for his country. When that help had been given, he was bound to unceasing gratitude; but he was not bound to take Coleridge as a pope—he was bound to reject him and every man in that capacity. As a philological critic, even as a commentator upon Scripture, he did not esteem him very highly; from many of his conclusions on divinity, as on other subjects, he entirely dissented. But he owed it to him, probably more than to any other man, that he was able to trace the path which connects human learning with divine, the faith of one age with the faith of another, the sense of man's grandeur with the sense of his pettiness and sinfulness. He did not learn from him that the Middle Ages might be pardoned for their idolatries because they produced magnificent Gothic cathedrals, and because the thoughts that were born in them found their expression in the pictures of Raffaelle and Michael Angelo; but he did learn to recognize in all cathedrals, and all pictures, a testimony *against* idolatry; a witness that man is made in the likeness of God, and that he is not to make God in the likeness of himself. He did not learn to pardon the strifes and the unbelief which have followed the Reformation, because we owe to it our philology and our criticism; but he did learn that the Reformation has removed the great obstacle to unity, by holding forth the actual belief and knowledge of God as possible for all men; he did learn that philology and criticism, which become dangerous when they are not free, will, if they are honestly used, be found instruments—subordinate, but still most precious instruments—in restoring faith in God's word, and fellowship among His children.

The commencement of Mr. Hare's strictly theological career is marked by his Sermons on "The Children of Light," and "The Law of Self-sacrifice," and "The Sin against the Holy Ghost." The first was preached before the University of Cambridge, in 1828; the two others in Trinity Chapel, in 1829 and 1832. Any one who will be at the pains of reading these discourses, will perceive how naturally the line of thought in them all flows out of that which has been traced in the *Guesses at Truth*. There is no violent transition from the literature to the divinity, no effort to forget the one for the sake of the other. The Sermon on "The Children of Light" starts from the assumption that those whom the preacher addresses are spiritual beings, that the light is about them, that they have been brought into it, that to walk in darkness is to renounce their birthright. The writer had not been so long in Cambridge without knowing that some of those who were listening to him were living thoughtless, animal, sinful lives; that they needed to be *turned* from darkness to light. He was not the less eager on that account to apprise them of their true position. The strongest feeling on his mind at this time seems to have been, that a true life is a continuous life; that sin causes the breaks and dislocations which sever the child from the man; that a true conversion is not a disturbance of

order, but a restoration of it. He may have seen the
need, in a later part of his life, of bringing out more
strongly the other side of the truth—that which our
popular and exciting preachers often seem to regard as
the whole of it; but he never retracted or even modified
the doctrine of this sermon. That on " The Law of Self-
sacrifice" is even more characteristic of him, and a better
commentary on his previous, as well as his subsequent
writings. Here he encounters the selfish theory of
morals in no partial, half-hearted way. He at once
announces the opposite law as the one which binds
together all things in earth and heaven, as that which
affords the only explanation of all the great facts of
history, of all that has produced any real effect upon
mankind in poetry, art, science. Selfishness he traces,
indeed, everywhere: but as the disturbing, destructive
force; the enemy of the order of the world, not its principle; that which the Son of God by His sacrifice came
to subvert, because He came to renew and restore all
things. Theology is here, as elsewhere, the necessary
climax as well as the necessary foundation of all his
other thoughts; he does not want to reconcile them
with it; it is the reconciliation of them. The Sermon
on " The Sin against the Holy Ghost" is in strict harmony with these, inasmuch as it connects the common
daily life of the English student in the nineteenth century with the principles set forth in Scripture, even
with the most awful sentences in it. These are not used
to produce a fearful impression upon the nerves, but to
keep the conscience alive to its continued peril, as well

as to its mighty treasures and responsibilities—to the truth, that all true and righteous deeds, by whomsoever they are enacted, are the work of the Holy Spirit, now, as in other days; so that, in attributing them to an evil source, we are committing a sin of the same kind with that of the Pharisee, when he said of the Son of God, "He casteth out devils by Beelzebub, the chief of the devils."

There is no occasion to contrast these Sermons with others which are wont to be delivered in College pulpits: but they may be referred to as affording a hint of that union of human and divine knowledge of which one could wish that the students in the English halls of learning should be perpetually reminded; no effort being made to warp the one into consent with the other, but each unfolding itself naturally out of the other, as they must do if it is true that the Son of God is also the Son of Man. And they serve also to show that the preacher had not sunk the man in the collegian; that he was in sympathy with the world of nature and the world of human beings; that he never liked to regard the *cloister* as something set up in opposition to the *crowd*.

It was after he had preached these Sermons, and before he had entered upon the duties of his parish, that he visited Rome for the first time. Some of his Protestant friends, who knew his love of art, his affection for Mr. Digby, and the personal sympathy which he had with the Eternal City, trembled for the effect that it might produce upon his mind. Their fears were groundless. Rome was all, and more than all, that he had imagined. It was made still dearer to him than it would have been for its own sake, because he formed in this visit his friendship with the Chevalier Bunsen —a friendship which was as close and hearty as those which men begin in their boyhood, and proved more lasting. But the splendid vision left him a stronger Protestant than it found him. "I saw the Pope," he used to say, "apparently kneeling in prayer for mankind; but the legs which kneeled were artificial; he was in his chair. Was not that sight enough to counteract all the æsthetical impressions of the worship, if they had been a hundred times stronger than they were?" Of course, those who are used to such ceremonies would have regarded this one with perfect calmness; a skilful apologist would probably have been able to prove that artificial legs contain a moral and mystery which are quite wanting in the natural legs. This Mr. Hare fully believed. The moral and mystery of the whole system came out, it appeared to him, in that one characteristic symbol. He was told, no doubt, that while he stood outside of the Church these things, and many others, must seem incomprehensible to him; that if he were once received within it, his eyes would become used to its lights, and his lungs to its atmosphere, and that all discords would be felt as parts of the harmony. He did not dispute that prophecy— reason and experience were both in favour of it. Those whom he regarded as far superior to himself— such men as Frederick Schlegel, and others still more honoured and dear in his own land—had become habituated to falsehoods which they once abhorred. He had no right to give himself credit for a moral sense which they had not exhibited. Therefore he said to himself, asking God to strengthen and defend the resolution, "My soul, enter not thou into their secret; unto their assembly, mine honour, be not thou united." He did not, however, come back to England with any purpose of making speeches against the artificial legs which Romanism requires. He did come back with the hope and prayer that, whatever artificial legs we are leaning upon in our Church, whether they are of home or foreign manufacture, might be cast away, and that we might be taught to worship Him who is a Spirit in spirit and in truth.

It was while he was dwelling upon this thought in reference to his future work, that the character and writings of Luther became his especial study. Some have expressed their astonishment that a man with an ardent love of beauty, whose tastes and education must have inclined him to the æsthetical side of religion, should have become the passionate admirer of the coarse Reformer of Saxony. The few hints which have been given respecting the course of his moral and spiritual discipline may diminish their wonder. His love of beauty had always been connected with the pursuit of an ideal which man is meant to seek, and which raises him above himself. He had learnt and proclaimed the doctrine, that he cannot be raised above himself unless he renounces himself. Luther had cried aloud, "We have no righteousness of our own; to claim any is our wretchedness—the secret of our guilt, the cause of our despair. Christ's righteousness is the only righteousness we can have; by believing in that we become clothed with it, it is in the truest sense ours; by believing in that we rise out of our evil, we become justified before God, we have peace with Him." Here Mr. Hare discovered the great practical divinity which unites the ideal and the actual; which proves that the giving up of self is the deliverance from sin—the beginning of that resurrection which is only attained, the Apostle affirms, when a man casts away his own righteousness altogether, and is found in Christ. Mr. Hare could never admit that Luther was too vehement in the assertion of this principle, that he did not surround it with sufficient limitations. The danger to morality lay, it seemed to him, in any qualification or half-statement of it, in permitting any loophole through which self-seeking or self-glorying might creep in. That there had been a multitude of such loopholes in all the systems which had attempted to formalize the Lutheran doctrine—that the very phrase "justification by faith" may become one of the widest of them, if it is disjoined from belief in a person,—this he fully admitted. But the remedy, he conceived, lay not in what are called guarded statements, or middle ways, but in the bold, full proclamation of the doctrine as it presented itself to Luther, when he rose from his anguish and learnt to say, "I believe in the forgiveness of sins;" as it stood out in

his Lectures, when he was exalting Paul above Aristotle
and Aquinas; as it embodied itself in the theses, wherein
he laid the axe to the root of Indulgences, and affirmed
that it was good for a man to have his sins punished
and damned, that he might be delivered out of them;
as it broke forth in simple, burning words, when he
was rousing the heart of Europe, not with the tidings
of a new gospel, but of an actual Christ, in whom they
might believe as their fathers had done. In these great
facts of history he saw the beginning of the emancipation of the nations and of the Church laid in the actual
emancipation of the consciences of those who entered
into the Reformer's meaning and accepted his good
news. Holding this belief, what signified it if even
some of the best of Luther's contemporaries—such men
as Sir Thomas More, whom Hare specially loved—
counted him a heretic and disturber of the peace? What
signified it if contemporaries of his own, whom he highly
respected—the ablest representatives of the scholastical
and the ecclesiastical learning of other days, as well as
of the learning of the Renaissance—such men as Sir
William Hamilton, Dr. Mill, Mr. Hallam—agreed in
disliking the man of the people, and believing all
calumnies against him? What was credit with
scholars and divines to the interest of scholarship, of
humanity, of divinity, which he thought were involved
in the defence of Luther and of his principles?

If his zeal in this cause showed how readily he could
cast away all care of personal reputation, it showed
also how highly he prized all distinctions which were

not in the inventions of the schools, but had their ground in the being of man and in the relation of man to his Creator. The distinction of the flesh and of the Spirit, of the Law which condemns, and of the Gospel which speaks freedom and peace, of the man according to the law of death, and the man according to the spirit of life in Christ Jesus,—these are the subtlest which divinity presents to us. The materialist laughs at them, the mere intellectual man thinks they can have nothing to do with practice, and at all events must not be presented to the multitude. But, seeing they belong not to books and to formulas, but to man, he found in these the deliverance at once from materialism and from technicalities; he held that every beggar has an interest in them, and that the Spirit of God would teach every beggar to apprehend them. In *this* theology he believed there lies the best prospect for the illumination of all our faculties, as well as the groundwork of a true human morality, not depending on accidents of times and seasons—not receiving its shape from circumstances, but compelling circumstances to receive their shape from it.

The Lutheran doctrine may not be all that we need; it may concern our personal life more than our life as portions of a commonwealth; it may appear to interfere with the unity of the body, by the immense worth with which it invests each member of the body. But Mr. Hare was convinced that if we lose it, we lose all hope of rising to a higher level,—we must certainly sink to a lower one, that though Christ may seem to be proclaimed in it only as the emancipator of the individual conscience, He is implicitly recognized in it as the centre of the whole fellowship in heaven and earth. And it should be observed, that in the Sermons on the "Victory of Faith," and the "Mission of the Comforter," which present these *human* distinctions in a living and practical form, they are always grounded upon those deeper distinctions in the *Divine* nature which are the subjects of the Catholic creeds. In no discourses, though they may profess ever so much exclusive orthodoxy, are the persons of the Father, the Son, and the Spirit, and their essential unity, more constantly assumed as the foundation of moral order and of Christian love.

It would appear, then, that Mr. Hare's claims to be a "Broad Churchman," in any of the senses which that name has been supposed to bear, were more than questionable. He did not seek to conciliate men of letters by rejecting theological men and theological principles that were obnoxious to them. He defied men of letters by asserting the importance of the principles which they most stumbled at—by upholding the champions whom they most disliked. He did not choose the objects of his affection among his contemporaries, or, in past days, for their softness; he preferred those who had strong and definite purposes, even if they expressed them vehemently and passionately. He retained, indeed, his reverence for the gentleness which belongs to the true knight, and which is the best characteristic of the bravest Englishman. He believed a perfect Christian must be a perfect gentleman; but the man who speaks roughly, almost savagely, from the burning spirit in him, had, it seemed to him, more of the elements of this character than he who, under a surface of the most polished marble, hides a cold and hollow heart. Mr. Hare, therefore, had at least as much temptation to become a partisan as an adjuster of parties. Why he was not the first—in what sense he coveted, in what sense he utterly repudiated, the other character—a few remarks on the circumstances of the English Church, at the time he became one of her working ministers, may help to explain.

During the years he passed at college there had been a lull in the ecclesiastical world. Many influences— that of Bishop Heber was perhaps the most widely felt —had contributed to bring the "Evangelical School" and the "Old Church School" into a better understanding with each other. The language which had been denounced in the beginning of the century as enthusiastical or methodistical, was beginning to mingle with phrases of another kind, if it did not supplant them, in the discourses of dignitaries; the rector who had the temper of the last age often industriously selected his curate from the ranks which supplied the popular and exciting preachers to this. There was a change perceptible even in the persons who kept their places in those ranks most faithfully. They spoke much more than they had been used to speak about the importance of a State recognition of Christianity. Without absolutely renouncing the fellowship of Dissenters in the

Bible Society and elsewhere, the alliance became cold and suspicious. Under the pretext of keeping aloof from political Nonconformists, those who belonged to what was called the "Low Church School" showed an evident inclination to exalt the bonds which united them to the National Establishment, above those of spiritual sympathy which they had once exclusively prized. This truce was broken by the sudden apparition of a set of men who were evidently as strong in their reverence for institutions as Englishmen usually are, but who proclaimed that *ecclesiastical* institutions do not depend upon the authority of kings or parliaments, and should not be meddled with by them. This doctrine, touching so closely at one point upon that which had been held by the Puritans of old, and has passed from them to a large body of Scotch Presbyterians and English Dissenters, was nevertheless united with a passionate denunciation of Puritanism, and of all that has sprung from it. The English Church had suffered, it was said, terribly from a mixture with Puritans, and from the infections of their notions; but its ministry was Apostolical, its doctrines were those of the time before the separation of the Western and Eastern Churches, it renounced the pretensions of the Romish Bishop, because they interfered with the authority of other Bishops, and were not supported by the testimony of the first ages. It adhered to the tradition of those ages more faithfully than any branch of the Church did. By this tradition it explained the nature and force of its Sacraments; it justified the authority of the true Catholic Church; it interpreted the Scriptures.

Mr. Hare became a rector in the diocese of Chichester just when these doctrines were putting on their first phase; when they were awakening the indignation of the most moderate Dissenters, whom they seemed almost to exclude from the pale of salvation; when they were alarming Conservative Churchmen by their scorn of the State and of Establishments; when they were arousing the half-slumbering conviction of the Evangelical school, that inward faith and not outward institutions must be the ground-work of a spiritual society. At the same time these teachers were winning proselytes at least as rapidly as they were creating opponents; enlisting the sympathies of young men, wearied by the heartless tone of statesmen who seemed to regard religion only as an instrument for keeping the lower classes in their due relation to the upper—weary of the mere individualism of some Evangelical teachers, and of the compromise between State religion and individual religion in others —or merely weary of themselves, and longing for some new excitement. This last class, who found plentiful gratification in repeating the scornful jokes of the Oxford Tract writers against their different opponents, were somewhat staggered by finding that a specially severe asceticism was demanded by these writers, and that the most awful language was used by them respecting the sins of baptized men. But if not a few were alarmed by this tone of speaking, or deemed it so severe that they might pass it by altogether, and busy themselves with more attractive aspects of the system, quite as many welcomed it as corresponding to doubts and terrors in their own minds, as proving that the new doctors were falsely accused of substituting the external for the internal, as an escape from certain convictions about Justification by Faith, which had been demanded of them in the Evangelical School, and which they had found it difficult to reconcile with their experience, and with other lessons coming from the same quarter.

From what has been said of the previous discipline of Mr. Hare, and of the results to which it had led him, it may be conjectured that there were parts of this teaching, and those some of the radical parts of it, which would cause him more pain than they caused to any of the persons who uttered the most vehement imprecations against it. He who had been learning to reverence Luther more than all doctors in divinity, was suddenly told that he must prove his devotion to the English Church, by renouncing fellowship with him, and by acknowledging that the principle which he spent his life in defending, though it might have a right interpretation, was, as *he* meant it, as *he* preached it, subversive of morality and of theological truth. And this was not all. To uphold Christ as the present living Head of the whole body of the Church, had appeared to the writer of these Charges the only hope for its unity. Now he was instructed that the promised Presence was only with the Clergy as the successors of the Apostles, he could scarcely help thinking that it was not in any real sense a presence of Christ at all, but rather a delegation of functions to men who were supplying His place in His absence. Much of the language which was used by the partisans of the Tracts went this length; if followed to its principle, it seemed to him to involve all the vices of Romanism, and at last a kind of denial which has not yet been fully developed, though it shortly may be, in Romanism itself.

Accordingly, his first sermon preached before the clergy of the diocese of Chichester on the text, "Lo, I am with you always, even unto the end of the world," was expressly a vindication of the words from what he regarded as the perilous limitation which had been forced upon them. The sermon excited considerable attention at the time. The School, whose interpretation it combated, received it as a sign that the preacher intended to commence a polemic against them. And if to assert Justification by Faith in the broadest Lutheran sense; to maintain that the Church cannot be contemplated apart from its invisible Head, and has no powers except in Him; to claim for all its members an actual knowledge of the truth, and not the second-hand knowledge which is derived from tradition; to affirm that the function of the English Church is not, as some affirmed, to steer its course between "the Scylla of Rome, and the Charybdis of Geneva,"—there being as many spiritual as geographical obstacles to such navigation;—if this was to engage in polemics with the Anglican divines, their expectation was not disappointed. His sermons at Cambridge, which have been alluded to, were implicitly, if not in words, an assault upon all these maxims and habits of thought.

But he had no notion of joining in the cry against the new teachers which some were raising. There was in them, he was sure, a real craving after unity; a desire to make English clergymen more aware of their responsibilities to God, and of the powers they might use for the good of the people; an impatience of secularity; a willingness to endure obloquy and loss for the sake of a conviction. To such tempers as these his inmost heart responded; he was sure the English Church needed them, and could not afford to be without them. He could not help seeing that it had profited and was profiting in many ways by their exertions; that they were doing more than any class or school for education, and were stirring others who differed from them to labour for it also; that they were encouraging better and less visible modes of giving than the one which the subscription-list offers; that they were helping to break down the barriers between rich and poor in churches. Nor could he doubt that they had awakened deeper thoughts in the minds of many laymen, and a greater disposition to study theology, and subjects that illustrate theology, amongst the clergy. He could not withhold his assent from the sentiment which his honoured friend the Bishop of St. David's had courage to utter in one of his early Charges, that this movement had given rise to more valuable writings in theology than had appeared for a very long time previous to it. However, therefore, his blood might boil at many of the statements of these writers, respecting the truths which were dearest to him, and, he believed, most precious to England, he dared not look back upon the quiet which they interrupted with any regret. He was glad that the clergy had not been allowed to settle upon their lees; he desired earnestly that he might be an instrument in preventing their relapse into a dangerous and deceitful repose.

Could he be such an instrument, by endeavouring to keep alive a party excitement? All experience showed him that he could not. This excitement must die away through its own violence; when it was strongest, any clear-sighted man might perceive that it was subsiding, and that the usual reaction of indifference and coldness was at hand. Not that the bitterness of strife could depart with the zeal which concealed and seemed to justify it. Parties are never so cruel as when the real battle is over; then comes the hour of proscriptions and confiscations. In our day, the attachment to a chief, which of old gave a party something of the cordiality of a clan, can scarcely be maintained. For an invisible Newspaper Pope summons both leader and disciples to its tribunal, and absolves the latter from their allegiance, if the former rebels against its authority. To make a principle the bond of party union under such conditions is equally difficult. The Newspaper declares what principles are *not* to be held, what are to be denounced. Opposition to them becomes the watchword. What is *believed* is a secondary question altogether.

Mr. Hare had reflected on these observations, which bear directly upon our religious parties. Were they not illustrated and confirmed by events in the political world? Who ever defended party so ably, so much upon principle, as Edmund Burke? Who was more attached to his own? Who clave to quite another party with more tenacity, or could prove more eloquently the necessity for it, than George Canning? Yet each of these eminent statesmen broke up his party. No men could less resemble these in temper of mind and education—no two could less resemble each other—than Sir Robert Peel and the Duke of Wellington. Yet they also twice consolidated and led large parties, and twice destroyed them. Could these successive events be attributed to accident? Was there not a Divine necessity in them? Were they not a handwriting on the wall, declaring to States that the old doctrine of ruling by faction had been weighed in the balance, and found wanting—that unless there was some other to fall back upon, government would become impossible? And ought not the handwriting to be deciphered, and interpreted, and applied to themselves by Churchmen? Should *they* not be able to declare in words, and to show by example, what the higher principle is, and in whose strength it may be carried out?

The writer of these Charges certainly thought so. He believed that if the clergy are to be zealous and energetic in action, vigorous in defending the truths which are given them to keep, they must understand that they are united in other and higher bonds than those of a school. He did not believe that it was an easy thing to put on those bonds, and to cast away the others. The way of party—the defenders of it say so, for they plead that it is an inevitable evil, one to which "poor human nature" must yield—is a *broad* way, in our Lord's sense of the word,—one readily found, smooth to walk in. The other way is (in His sense) a strait and narrow one, not visible always to the naked eye, difficult to persevere in after the opening into it has been detected. But if the first is a downward path, leading societies and individuals to death—if the second is the upward path to life, the search must be worth all the earnest effort that can be bestowed upon it.

This search is quickly concluded, if we may assume that in wavering statements—a perpetual equipoise of affirmations and negations—lies the secret of reconciliation. Mr. Hare, the reader will have perceived, hoped nothing from that method. All the experiments he saw of it had tended to exasperate animosities rather than to heal them—to drive earnest men into the arms of the factious, from sheer despair of extracting any meaning or any practical help out of the counsels of the moderate. Nor could he admit the application of the precedents upon which the advocates for this system rely. He had known and loved Bishop Heber, and he was sure that it was not the moderation of his opinions, but the heartiness and generosity of the man, his freedom from professional formality, his possession of all the qualities which belong to the Christian gentleman, which gave him his power over his contemporaries.

These noble gifts were exhibited to Mr. Hare continually in his own diocese, and he could perceive what effects they were producing. Dr. Otter became Bishop of Chichester at a time when the religious strife was at its height, and when political strifes were mingled with it. He himself must have been suspected by many of the clergy, because he owed his appointment to a Whig minister. By a courtesy which made itself felt in all his words and acts, and which evidently proceeded from a divine root within, he caused men of the most opposite opinions to understand that they were parts of the same family, and that he was their spiritual father. No earnestness which belonged to any of them, as members of a school, was weakened by the feeling of this higher relation,—it contributed as much to the increase of their activity as of their charity. What a duty was laid upon every clergyman, who witnessed such an example, to endeavour in his own sphere to show that a life has a more healing and elevating influence upon men than any theories! But how much was this obligation increased in the case of one whose early studies had led him to the conclusion that there is a living Truth, in which opposing theories have their meeting-point, and that this truth may be found, if, instead of acquiescing in either of the theories, or violently contradicting it, we will patiently question it to see what is meant by it, what is in the heart of him who is cleaving to it! And what light fell upon both these lessons,—how they were translated to a new ground,—by a devout meditation on the Gospels, which proved that the spirit of sectarianism in the opposing Jewish schools hated the Son of God, because He witnessed for the truth which each was denying, and for that which each was distorting; and that the men of each of these sects who really loved the principle in which they had been nurtured turned to Him because they saw all that they believed embodied in Him, and saw that it was united with truths which they had not yet been able to believe! It was so then, must it not be so now? Is not the Son of God still the enemy of all parties, as parties— still the refuge for the members of every party who really hold those principles in the love of them, for the sake of which it has been allowed to exist? And may not those who can proclaim Him in this character be instruments of a reconciliation which is not identical with compromise, but the direct contradiction of it?

No one can entertain such a conviction as this, without longing for some opportunity of showing that it is emphatically not a paper notion; that it is applicable to human beings in all circumstances, with all their varieties of temper, with all their infirmities and sins; that it never was needed by any age more than by ours; that it may be better appreciated by our age than by any which has preceded it. The office of an archdeacon is in many respects peculiarly favourable for such an experiment. It never can be regarded by the most ill-natured looker-on as a prize for ambition or covetousness: the sphere in which it is exercised is limited and humble; it does not involve the necessity for that reserve in the statement of opinions which is often almost imposed upon the Bishop; its holder cannot for an instant be thought of as separated by any external accidents from fellowship with his brother clergy. A more felicitous position for a person with the objects which Hare was aiming at can scarcely be conceived. He probably felt so himself; and it was with reluctance that he told Bishop Otter, when he offered him the Archdeaconry of Lewes, that he considered his first sermon in the diocese was a disqualification, because it had given offence to a very estimable portion of those among whom he would be called to labour. His objection was kindly and decisively overruled by the Bishop, who expressed his own sympathy both with the principles of the sermon, which had procured for Hare a party reputation, and with his desire to prove that he did not deserve it. Dr. Otter was confident that if he took the office the impression would soon be removed altogether.

From that moment he devoted himself to his work with the ardour of a boy, and the deliberate purpose of a man. He seemed to think that he had found the task for which he had all his life been preparing. His fine collection of books, with the unusual knowledge he possessed of their contents, all the experience he had acquired in the world, all that he had suffered in mind or body, were gifts which would enable him to perform the task of an archdeacon, as he had conceived it, more honestly.

His first duty was to claim all his clerical brethren as fellow-labourers. There were some, of course, who were ready to hail him as a champion of Justification by Faith, and of their champion. With them he could fraternize heartily on the ground of their positive belief; their friendship he valued for its own sake ; he was eager to learn from them. But he did not share their animosities; he met them on the ground of common love, not common hatred; if they demanded the sacrifice of any other attachment, as a proof of the sincerity of his attachment to them, he must submit to be considered insincere. It is scarcely necessary to say that those who were most strenuous for their own convictions, and had given the greatest pledges of their adherence to them, were the least likely to impose any such condition.

With members of the party which had an excuse for thinking him their enemy he acted on the same principle. He found abundant points of sympathy with them — into many of their plans of practical reformation he could enter heartily. He abhorred the pew-system, and all that is connected with it, and all that it represents, as much as they did ; and since this subject especially concerned his office as Archdeacon, it was one of the first which he brought under the notice of his clergy. He could join in their schemes for education, believing them to be often sound and comprehensive, though he was not the least inclined to denounce the State, the Evangelical school, or the Dissenters for those which they originated.

Some of these schemes were suspected; who could prophesy whether they might be tending? He certainly could not, and he did not fancy that he had any call to prophesy. What was wrong was not to be done, because it was wrong; what was right was to be done whatever might come of it: God would see to that. He did not expect to escape suspicion himself, and he was certain that he had no business to cherish it towards any one else, seeing that experience shows it to be the best means of promoting the acts which afterwards are thought to justify it. Was it not a simpler thing to tell his friends to their face, when he thought they were taking a bad course; to listen to their explanations; to say, if they did not satisfy him; to proclaim it openly, if they did? If he hated all the practices which are associated with the name of Jesuitism, he was bound to avoid every approach to them in his own intercourse. "Beware of that man, he is a Jesuit." Is he? Then it is a point of common prudence not to try our hand at weapons in which he is confessedly master; to use only those which he does not understand—plainness of speech, straightforward acts, open-hearted trust. Those who follow this course probably meet on the whole with fewer designing men than their neighbours; sometimes they foil them when they do meet with them; sometimes they may call forth out of the covering in which he was buried a human being, who had never discovered himself before, and who is charmed by the voice of Truth from its very strangeness.

All his clergy must have seen that Archdeacon Hare's nature was vehement, that his convictions were strong, and that he took no pains to disguise them. But these qualities seemed to win him the regard of men whom coldness would have alienated There were some, of course, in his archdeaconry upon whose aid he could calculate, some who had themselves won the confidence of opposing parties. It was no wonder that the two Mr. Andersons of Brighton should have given him their friendship, for that was never withheld from any person who was trying honestly to labour in the cause of Christ, and was never withdrawn in good report, or in evil report. But he could also reckon among his friends his old fellow-collegian, Mr. Henry Venn Elliott, and many besides, who, if they had trusted more to what they heard of him than to what they saw, might have deemed him quite unworthy of their confidence. He valued also exceedingly the regard of Mr. Woodard, the hard-working and disinterested founder of the schools at Shoreham and Hurstpierpoint, who was ordinarily classed in the other school. All these excellent men might differ from him in a hundred points, and not understand him in a hundred more; so much the better, if, in spite of those differences, and that want of understanding, they could yet perceive that he had the root of the matter in him, and that the nearer they got to that root—the less they dwelt on the surface—the closer their sense of union with him became

In all the work which he did in the diocese, he had not only the hearty and generous co-operation of the successive bishops, whose kindness to him was unvarying, but also for several years the advice and assistance of his dear friend Mr. Manning, the Archdeacon of Chichester. How valuable he considered that advice and assistance; how thoroughly he believed—while they were working together, and after they were separated—that Mr. Manning's plans were wise; that his love to the Church which he left was true and profound; that he had rare gifts of head and heart; those knew best who knew him best. The secret of their friendship, and of any success which attended their fellow-work, consisted in this, that they dealt honestly with each other. Hare never concealed from Mr. Manning his repugnance to the system which had been announced with so much clearness and logical precision in the book on *The Unity of the Church*. Of course the objections to the *Victory of Faith* and the *Defence of Luther* were stated as frankly. When Mr. Manning, in one of his Charges, appeared to identify Unity with Uniformity, or at least to treat them as inseparable, Hare announced publicly, in a dedication to a sermon he preached at Brighton, his entire dissent from that proposition; his conviction that unity is not only distinct from uniformity, but involves in its very nature and definition the existence of wide diversities of opinion and of external practice. He did not hide his opinion that nearly all the questions of our time are connected with this; that Mr. Manning's doctrine of unity involves conclusions which would be fatal to the existence of any national church, *because* utterly inconsistent with the idea of a Catholic Church. To many a logician of Mr. Manning's school, to many a stout partisan of the opposite school, a statement made so openly might have appeared to determine their future relations with each other. Probably they laboured together more happily, and with more freedom after than before its publication. Mr. Hare was certain that the formal conclusion to which his friend had come expressed most inadequately the belief concerning unity which was struggling in him. He did not change that opinion—it was strengthened—when he saw how heavily the chains of system pressed upon a spirit that was born for freedom. If ultimately it put on heavier chains as a way of escaping these, he owned the honesty which had led to so intensely painful a resolution. He regarded this event as one of the saddest and most stirring admonitions to the English Church respecting her sins, and the captivity with which God may punish them; he longed more for the time when Christ shall be revealed as the real centre of that Unity, which men are trying to create by substitutes and counterfeits of Him. But he never drew *this* lesson from the event which caused him so much sorrow; it never drew from him one wish that he had been less cordial, less open, with one who deserved all cordiality and openness. If the years which he had passed through had been given back to him, with the knowledge how they would end, he would not have changed his course. The stings of conscience we feel in recalling hours of fellowship, which death or something worse has robbed us of, are not for any too frank and generous outpourings of the heart, but for the dryness, distance, reserve, suspicion, which has defiled so many of them, and made them unfruitful.

But if he held intercourse with men of high cultivation in different sections of the Church, his main desire was to use their wisdom, as well as any opportunities of study and reflection that might have been granted to himself, for the help of those labourers who are teaching in out-of-the-way neighbourhoods, without much money to buy books, or much time for reading, but for whom God has provided another kind of education,—in poor men's cottages and beside sick beds,—who need to be admonished of the greatness of that work, and need to connect their local interests with those of their country and of the Church. It may seem to many that his Charges were not addressed to this portion of the clergy. He felt differently. He thought that those whose work is in danger of becoming a drudgery, whose faith may degenerate into a mere repetition of words, whose zeal may be turned into impotent fury against men or opinions that are almost unknown to them, especially require to be encouraged, to be reminded of high and eternal principles, to hear questions which had been resolved for them by some oracular journalist thoughtfully and earnestly examined; to be shown how they may encounter the thoughts which are disturbing the minds of their flocks ; to discover how dead words may acquire vitality when they are used to meet new perplexities, to interpret the world in which we are moving. For this purpose, a friendly official, who had a right to speak, but not to command, might be more useful even than one whose authority was greater; provided he spoke manfully and deliberately; was indifferent about committing himself; was very careful of uttering rash words which should exasperate the passions of his hearers, or cold words which should check any honest enterprise they might be engaged in, any good hope they might be cherishing. It seemed to him, that if he set himself to speak of the sins which he and they had to confess, before he commented on the sins of other men ; if he spoke of the position which God had given them, as a reason for not trusting in it, but in Him; if he showed them what high ends they might pursue, and what low ends they were often tempted to pursue; he should do justice to the deepest and strongest conviction of each school in the Church, while he fought with the tempers in each*which were weakening it and keeping them asunder. A few instances will show how he fulfilled this intention.

No subject has given rise to so much contention in our times as the privileges of the Church. Every statesman hears the word with alarm ; he suspects that some claims will be put forth which will interfere with the peace of the nation, with his own work, with ordinary notions of justice and truth. Nor is he only afraid of one party in the Church. One, indeed, talks most loudly of the independence of the Church—of the powers of the clergy, which are derived straight from Heaven; but the other forbids him to do acts which his conscience often tells him he must do—appeals to Scripture to settle questions which he feels must be debated in Parliament—declares that there is a moral standard for religious men which he cannot in the least understand.

Now, Archdeacon Hare grapples with this subject, nominally in one Charge, really in all. He recognizes the high privileges of the Church; he refuses to consider it in any sense as the creature of the State. He urges the clergy to look upon themselves as the ambassadors of God, not as the servants of men; he would have them not only believe in their powers, but assure themselves that they have powers by using them. If they say, "We have the powers, because there has been an apostolical succession in our Church," without the least denying the fact, he would ascend higher still; he would claim more for the Church than the mere believers in a succession dare to claim; he would assert the living and continual Presence of our Lord with it; he would not allow that we can ever be *satisfied* with a descent of treasures, though we may be thankful if any have come to us in that way. But if he is asked to say, "The clergy have such and such powers *exclusively;* they do not represent the Church, or act as her ministers; these powers are given to them to set them apart from the laity—to constitute them a separate caste or order"—he does not mutter a doubt, or choose a middle way; he is at once distinctly and unhesitatingly on the side of those who assert the rights of the laity, who maintain that Christ is with the whole Church. Nor does he make some uncertain answer to the question, whether, because we have such and such powers, foreign Christians are to be unchurched and Nonconformists excommunicated. He denounces such doctrines, not as partially true, but as utterly wrong and dangerous; intrusions upon Christ's office of a Judge; practical denials of His work as a Universal Redeemer. There are no compromises in any of these statements; sentences are not balanced against sentences; a second clause in a sentence is not introduced to nullify the first. But he throws himself heart and soul into the earnest practical faith of the writers of the Oxford Tracts, while he asserts how high, and from what source, our gifts are; how great the responsibility, not to man, but to God, for the use and abuse of them. He vindicates the earnest faith of the Evangelical, which rebels, on the ground of Scripture as well as experience, against the exaltation of a mere order; he shows how in work the convictions of both may find a meeting-point, and may be realized to the very utmost.

But will not this work clash with that of the State? He answers, No; our high privileges are given us on purpose that we may perform duties. And these are just the duties which the true statesman wants to get done, but cannot do. This is a very obvious proposition, and a very old one—implied in the Constitution of England, repeated again and again by her best sons. But it requires to be brought out in reference to the circumstances of each age; the common-place must cease to be a common-place, by being acted out. Men who believe they have a Divine commission talk ignominiously of being hampered by the State. How can that be? If they fulfil their commission, by making Englishmen nobler citizens, what does the State care how they were enabled to do it that unspeakable service? But here comes in the moral confusion. *Is* that exactly what Churchmen are appointed to do? Are they not to make citizens of the kingdom of Heaven? Will those who are best in the one character be the best in the other?

To show that this *is* exactly what the Churchman has to do—that he is to teach a higher morality than the civic morality, but not one which is different in kind from that—that he is to lay the foundations of morality deeper than those who are merely aiming at right acts can lay them, but that his foundations are utterly false and rotten if any acts can be built upon them which a true English gentleman would think dishonourable, which the conscience of a simple Englishman would revolt at—consequently, that the citizen of the heavenly kingdom must be the best citizen of the earthly—this was Hare's aim: a plain, vulgar one, perhaps, but not needless in any day—most needful in ours. And he felt that he could appeal on behalf of this sound and practical principle, not only to the English heart which dwells in the clergy of the old school, but to the Christian heart which there is in the clergy of both the newer schools. If the Evangelical dreads Romanism, he must resolutely abjure that tenet which lies at the root of every Romish corruption, that there can be a religious end which is not a moral end; that truth and righteousness may ever be sacrificed in the cause of a true and righteous God. If the High Churchman condemns what he calls the fanaticism of the Puritans, he ought to see that the fanaticism which they can be justly accused of, and which corrupted what was very noble and great in them, arose from the false notion, that the servants of God are obeying a mere arbitrary Ruler, and not a just King. And before he takes a mote out of the Puritan's eye, he must see that there is not a beam in his own; that, in the name and cause of his Church, he is not sanctioning the same separation of human and divine maxims which shocks him when it is turned to the opposite use.

With this moral question the political is closely involved—"What, is not our polity higher than the national one? Are we to submit to it? Are we to receive our tone from it?" By no means, he would answer; prove how much higher your polity is, by giving a tone to the State. But what tone? Statesmen want to believe—they are very slow to believe—that a just and righteous God is ruling in the earth, and therefore that they must be just and righteous. Proclaim that truth to them; call them to account, as the prophets of old did, when they forget righteousness and justice in any of their dealings with any of their subjects. But if you have this trust from God, do not be talking as if there were some special questions in which the Church is interested, and in which the land at large is not interested; as if you were always to be on the watch lest the State should intrude upon *your* rights, should rob you of your revenues; as if this was the way of proving that you have a Divine commission from a Master who pleased not Himself, but was the servant of all. This petty jealousy for itself makes all the protests which the Church might bear against the neglects and ill-doings of rulers totally ineffectual. To discourage this kind of suspicion is the way to awaken the true godly vigilance of which it is the counterfeit—a vigilance which is impossible till the clergy assert the sins of their rulers to be their own—till they confess that no men are so responsible for the low standard of thought and practice which is amongst us as they are. To kindle a Church feeling, which should be at the same time a national feeling,—to change the uneasy consciousness of certain undefined rights which exists in Churchmen into a conscience which shall be alive to their obligations, social as well as individual—is one great object of these Charges.

The question, viewed in this way, has reference to ecclesiastical pretensions, therefore, to the temptations of the High Church School. There is another aspect of it which more directly concerns the other School. In one of the Charges, he grapples with the question of the Maynooth Grant, and, as usual, delivers himself upon it fearlessly, yet with much deliberation. It was a subject, he thought, on which the good feelings of the Clergy were peculiarly likely to lead them astray, and make them the tools of rash declaimers. Leaving the question open, what course it was best for the Legislature to adopt, he contends that it was clearly a case in which the Legislature was not barred by any Divine laws from exercising a discretion. They had a right, he thinks they were bound as men holding a trust from God, to determine what it was best for the whole land that they should do; they were bound to disregard any one who stopped them by a preliminary appeal to God's hatred of idol worship. How deep that hatred is, how fatal such worship is to the life and order of nations, what danger there is of our falling into any—even the worst—forms of it, no one felt more strongly than he did; but he believed that those who leapt at once from this premiss to the conclusion that it is a wicked thing for the nation to contribute to the education of Roman Catholics, play most unwarrantably with God's word; get credit for maintaining a principle in name which they cannot carry out in fact; and lead religious men away from their real dangers to fictitious dangers.

Another very important question is involved in this. The politician is apt to worship expediency, as if there were no fixed law of right; the religious man denounces expediency, and endeavours to set up a fixed law for all cases. By different routes they come to the same result. There is *not* a fixed law for all cases; we must consider the application of laws in each case. Because he refuses to do so, the religious man is driven to exalt an expediency of his own,—*his* judgment of what will serve or what will hinder a particular end. This judgment he canonizes and worships; but it is a poor, flexible, human judgment after all: while it lasts, it interferes more with fixed morality than the politician's expediency, because it assumes a title to which it has no claim. Therefore he conceived that it was a duty to the eternal truths of morality to show what is the province of expediency, and how it may be made subservient to them. His brethren might differ from him in his conclusion; he believed that they would see that he was not indifferent to principle, but was fighting for it; or if any causes hindered them from doing him that justice immediately, they might recollect his words, and turn them to profit, after his voice had ceased to be heard among them.

The Contest with Rome, which is the subject of the longest and one of the latest of his Charges, is intimately connected with the questions that have been spoken of already. He was preparing for that contest by leading the clergy to purify their minds of those ethical and political notions which have made the Romish system immoral and anti-national. So long as they tolerated in their minds confusions about the difference between religious and secular duties; so long as they regarded the State as an enemy, or merely claimed it as a servant to do their works; so long as they thought any wrong act might be done for a good end, any false argument resorted to, or any evidence strained, to justify the best cause or confute the worst;—so long he was sure they were in danger of Romanism, they were doing much to hasten its restoration and its triumph in their own land. He desired to make the clergy feel that this terrible calamity, if it is in store for us, will not be owing to any acts of the State, but to themselves; and that one party has no right to reproach the other as the leader to this abyss: that all are leading to it who are doing anything to weaken the national heart, to confuse the national conscience, to keep alive national divisions. In fact, what is more fatal than these very accusations? this habitual disobedience to the solemn words in the Sermon on the Mount, "Judge not, that ye be not judged"? this habitual commission of an act which our Lord pronounces to be the act of a hypocrite? If there is one proof more than another which the writer of these Charges gave that he was seeking the peace of the Church, it was in his perpetual call to the members of it to own their own sins first, and to feel their brethren's sins as their own. And these were not idle words. He felt, when he was speaking to his brethren, that he had more to answer for than any of them had, and that he was truly standing forth for that time as their representative, to bear their offences and infirmities with them. So he was led to understand our need of One who has borne the sins of the whole body, and is making intercession for it.

The last of the published Charges in these volumes is on the subject of Convocation. Archdeacon Hare believed, with the majority of the High Church party, that questions affecting the clergy ought to be discussed in a body where they are fairly represented; he believed, with a number of the Low Church party, that the deliberations of such a body must be ineffectual unless the laity also are represented in it. It is not necessary to argue here whether he was right or wrong in either of these opinions. They cannot be passed over, because they occupy such a prominent place in the Charges, and because they illustrate the purpose and spirit of those in which they are not directly referred to. Everywhere he shows the same desire that the clergy should work together as a body; should meet and compare their thoughts; should bring their local experience to bear upon the common weal, in order that they might not work in hostile sections, under the dominion of hostile party-organs. Everywhere he shows the same wish that the clergy should not be divided from their lay brethren by any artificial barriers. Everywhere he indicates his anxiety that the Church should have a free action of its own; that it should be one which assists the national action, not impedes it. And it is also characteristic of him, that though he saw innumerable imperfections in the existing form of Convocation, though he set no great store by its traditions, he yet preferred to make use of what we have, as a means of obtaining something better, than to cast it aside. In the hard task of imparting to that body some vitality, he had the great pleasure of finding himself working by the side of persons from whom he differed upon almost every subject; and of some, as Dr. Mill, whom he had known, and for whose character he had a deep respect, but with whom he had been in direct controversy. Nothing gave him better auguries for the future than the discovery that it was possible for men so unlike in their opinions, and so little disposed to smother them from any motives of policy, to labour for the same end, when they believed that end was the consolidation of the Church and not of a School.

The notes to Archdeacon Hare's Charges will perhaps surprise the reader more than the Charges themselves, not so much for the amount of erudition which they exhibit, as for the reasons which could have induced the author to conceal his erudition in such corners. The parts of them which contain documents illustrating events that were passing in England, or illustrating English history generally, civil or ecclesiastical, may justify themselves by the fact, that few clergymen have access to large libraries, and that if they have, they may not be sorry to see some of the results of the reading of a thoughtful and accomplished man brought to bear on the subjects on which he had already addressed them. "But what," it may be asked, "is the intention of the long translations from German divines which frequently occur? How could parish priests be profited by these? Do they not indicate a purpose of introducing German divinity covertly among our young English divines? Do we not see here the fine end of the wedge, which is gradually to be pushed further? Were not these extracts to familiarize us with a way of considering Holy Scripture, which is subversive of the belief and doctrine of our fathers, a way which will unsettle still more, as it has unsettled already, the religious mind of England?" When this question has been considered and answered, this Preface will have done all that it was designed to do, and the reader may be left to gather much better instruction from the Charges themselves—

It is true that these translations were not made without an object, and that that object had a direct reference to the feelings with which many clergymen regard, and teach their flocks to regard, the Holy Scriptures. It is true also that the writer had especially in his mind some of the younger members of his own profession. In the days of Luther men were wont to speak of the Word of God as quick and powerful, and sharper than any two-edged sword; they not only said it was so, but they found it to be so. A text of Scripture came to them as if it proceeded from the mouth of the Lord; it entered into them,—they bowed to it. In our days, we speak of the Bible as being the Word of God; often signifying nothing thereby, but that a certain book containing a certain number of letters is stamped with the Divine authority, and that any doubts concerning it are sinful. This is not the old Protestant, the old English, belief. That may be often hidden beneath the hard dogmatical Pharisaical worship of letters; it may come forth in hours of sorrow in its old strength. But they are not the same; one is stifling and killing the other; people do not feel that God's voice is speaking to them, that God himself is among them. The young men are beginning, many of them, to ask whether the notion of such a Voice is not altogether a delusion; whether the Book, which used to be considered Divine, is not a composition of mere mortals; whether all modern criticism is not leading us toward this conclusion. Those who are shocked at such inquiries, nevertheless appear to admit the truth of the suspicion. "In Germany," they say, "there is most criticism about the origin of the books of Scripture, and there the very notion of any divinity attaching to them is utterly discredited." "Well, then," replies the youth, "the further we search, the less plea there is for this old fancy; if we go on, we shall get rid of it altogether." What reply is given, but some moral about the danger of meddling with forbidden books, a moral which is not heeded, unless circumstances should make it prudent to feign a conviction, or some great heart struggle should bring forth the *real* conviction that there must be some message from God to man, that He cannot have left us to grope our way through the darkness without a guide.

Now Archdeacon Hare was inwardly persuaded that modern criticism has shaken *an* opinion: but that that opinion is the new one, not the old; the doctrine which has supplanted the Lutheran doctrine, not that doctrine itself. All in Germany have been shaken who mistook letters for life; or, to put the thing in another form, who did not believe in a Word of God, but only believed in the evidence that vindicates the authority of certain documents. Such faith can never sustain a soul; it is not the faith of God's elect; and, therefore, if we have nothing better than this, we must expect that God will show us, as He has shown them, that we are building on the sand.

Having this conviction, and not having adopted it lightly, or without a considerable knowledge of the history of German divinity, he thought it was the right and the safe course, to show the clergy, young and old, that German divines who have passed through the struggles of this age, who understand all the maxims of modern criticism, who do not shrink from any examination into the history of the Scripture books, do nevertheless believe, not only that God spake in times past by the prophets unto the fathers, but that He *is* speaking in these latter days to us by a Son. He did not pledge himself to any of their particular conclusions (for the conclusions of those whom he quotes on questions of criticism are different from each other); but he did pledge himself that they had, so far as it was possible for man to judge, such a faith in God's Word as we might be glad to share with them, or if that could be, to borrow from them. He had no notion, however, that borrowing was possible or desirable. He believed that no German ought to be an Anglican, and that no Englishman should affect to be a German. He believed that we have a work to do, which is altogether different from that which they have to do; that if we forget our own, and try to do theirs, we shall prove ourselves clumsy and stupid craftsmen; that the very opposition of our habits of mind may make us both help in bringing out the truth, which will be mangled if either tries to imitate the other. A cross between the two he held to be monstrous. "I can never advise any English parent to send his son to Germany for education," he said to a friend who consulted him on behalf of a gentleman who meditated such a step; "that boy must be an Achilles who can bear to be brought up by a Centaur." It was not to encourage any such mixtures that he made his countrymen acquainted with some passages of German theologians which were probably new to most of them. It was that ignorance of the Christianity of other men might not involve them in a perilous conceit of their own. It was that their Christianity might not rest upon a loose, insincere, half-conviction. It was that they might not live in an ignominious, cowardly, Godless dread, that if they knew more they should find everything in earth and heaven insecure and rotten. It was that they might feel Christ to be still that Rock of Ages on whom their fathers stood, and the Church stands, and against whom it is promised that the gates of hell shall not prevail.

It was impossible for one who had studied the conditions of English parties as he had, not to perceive that in this instance again both were contributing to weaken the Church's doctrine by their very strifes.

That plausible counterfeit for our old faith in God's Word, which assumes to itself the character of reverence for Scripture and its inspiration, derives strength from the eagerness of one party to maintain the necessity of tradition and Church authority in the interpretation of the Bible; from the eagerness of the other to prove that it stands apart from all human books. Both, unawares, degrade it into a mere document—a book which is divine because it is not human—although all its statements are grounded on the assertion that man is made in the image of God; although the centre of its revelations is the God-man. But the faithful and devout member of the Evangelical School always carries in his inmost heart a witness against this shocking perversion. He means what his fathers meant, even when he uses the phraseology of the newspapers. Instead of exaggerating the importance of the history, he is often apt to depreciate it, and to think only of the message which is carried to his own heart and conscience; to receive *this* as the only evidence that the book has come from the Father of Lights. And the faithful and devout High Churchman clings so earnestly to the belief of a Spirit dwelling in the Church through all ages, that he in his best moments feels and confesses the Book to be not chiefly a legacy from the past, but to contain for this day— for the peasants of England—a clearer, more intelligible testimony than all the commentaries upon it. Archdeacon Hare therefore could, in this case, as in all others, confidently believe that there was in these better, holier convictions, a living substance which would make itself manifest through the crust that conceals it. He did not deal rudely with the crust, but he laboured earnestly that, if it is broken, no part of the precious treasure within may be lost.

To those who knew him, any vindication from the charge of not being national will seem particularly superfluous. He was national all his life through, most so in his latest years. He hoped much that the present war, in spite of its miseries and horrors, would be an instrument of restoring the national spirit among us, not only by helping to cast out the money-getting spirit, but quite as much by the blow it would give to that other enemy and curse of England—its religious party-spirit. No efforts and no sorrows seemed to him too tremendous, if they aided in delivering us from the mad pursuit of material objects, which enslaves—from the mad pursuit of factious objects, which rends asunder —the heart of a country. And in thinking of the war, he could not of course separate English interests from the interests of mankind. He did not dream that it could do us any good, unless we felt that it had been undertaken as a witness that the God of Righteousness and Truth would not have the nations united under any despot, military or ecclesiastical; that He would have them bound together in one family in His Son. This was his idea of a Broad Church. To be an aider and abetter in setting up a new party in the land, with whatever specious name it might be adorned, whatever pretensions of largeness and liberality it might put on, he would have regarded as an act of treason against the sovereign of England, and against the King of kings. To aid and abet, even within the narrowest sphere, in making England a united country under its Queen, in making the Church feel its own union in Christ, he regarded as the highest honour which could be bestowed upon a clergyman, as the highest duty which he could fulfil. All the polemics he engaged in had reference to this end. He did not vindicate the decision of the Privy Council in the case of Mr. Gorham against some of his most valued friends, because he wanted any qualified statements on the subject of Baptism for the relief of his own conscience. He accepted the words on the subject in the Prayer Book and Articles without reservation; he prefered them to any that he or any one else could have substituted for them. Nor did he withstand those who wished to procure an ecclesiastical sentence upon Dr. Hampden, because he had any personal acquaintance with that prelate, or because he approved the judgment of the Ministry which selected him. But he felt himself called to bear a continual witness against those who confound the crushing of opponents with the assertion of principles; he believed that every party triumph is an injury to the whole Church, and an especial injury to the party which wins the triumph; he was thankful when the authorities of the Church, through love for its peace, thankful even when the State, through impartial care for its subjects, defeated by delays or by direct interference even a well-organized religious conspiracy, and rescued its victim. He well knew that his words would not please those who pleaded for toleration on the ground that all theological conclusions are indifferent and unimportant; he knew that he was encountering one faction just when its appetite for the prey was most ravenous; he knew that the momentary gratitude of the faction whose cause he espoused would be exchanged for a directly opposite feeling when its turn of power arrived, and it found that the maxims to which it had once listened with pleasure would, if acted upon, oblige it to quench its own thirst of vengeance. That they would treat the vexatious Marplot as a common enemy must have seemed extremely probable to any man of ordinary experience. That probability would have kept Mr. Hare silent, if he had adopted the popular opinion, that the acts of a servant of God are to be determined by a prudent estimate of the consequences that will follow from them.

. . . . .

His business was not *first* to reconcile schools and parties; their separation has caused another separation, upon which God has pronounced a more dreadful curse. The hearts of the fathers are turned from the children, of the children from the fathers. Much of our popular religious literature is perpetuating and deepening this estrangement; stimulating the terrors of the old respecting the seeds of popery or infidelity which are at work in those who are to take their places; encouraging *them* to think that faith and freedom are natural enemies. To counteract these poisonous suggestions; to convince men of his own generation that their suspicions were dangerous, not prudent; godless, not Christian; to sympathize in the thoughts, conflicts, perplexities, of those who were groping their way into truth; to assure them that God was guiding them, though they knew it not; to save them from casting away the inheritance they had received in their desire to increase it,—this was the great purpose of Archdeacon Hare's life. For this reason he was spoken of with reverence and affection by some of those from whose humility, fidelity, and wisdom, England has most to hope in the days that are coming. Those who are proud of their own orthodoxy or of their own liberality, those who despise others for their want of orthodoxy or their want of liberality, will join in dislike, probably in contempt, for him. But those who in their theology, as in their human studies, esteem depth a more important dimension even than breadth; who, however widely they may extend the area of their knowledge or their charity, seek first of all to build both upon a rock; those who suspect themselves and trust their fellow-creatures—who are led, equally by the discovery of their own weakness, and of the good which they had not looked for in them, to believe in God as the one Source of good to all; they have accepted the writer of these Charges, not as the dictator of their opinions, but as their Counsellor and their Friend.

ARCHDEACON HARE.*

How difficult it is for foreigners to understand the institutions of England! What a mass of contradictions is involved in our constitution, in our Church, in our universities! But it is, in fact, a part not only of "the system," as it is called, but of our character, of our situation. It is at once our curse and our blessing. Its dangers can be guarded against, its advantages may be made the most of; but its root is deep in our very inmost being—we cannot lose it or change it without ceasing to be what we are or have been.

To no point does this apply more truly than to our literature and theology. Go to France or Germany, and no man will be at a loss to tell you where the most learned, the most enlightened men of the country are to be found. They are members of the Institute; they are lecturers in the College of Henri IV.; they are professors in the universities. Here and there they may have risen to be ministers of state. But

* *Quarterly Review*, July, 1855. For further details of Archdeacon Hare's life, see the memoir of him by Professor Plumptre, prefixed to the last edition of the *Guesses at Truth*.

such a rise has been through their literary eminence; and that eminence is illustrated, not superseded, by their new position. Every one knows where is the oracle at whose mouth he is to inquire. In England it is far otherwise. Now and then it may be that a great light in theology or history will burst forth at Oxford or Cambridge, and draw all eyes to itself. But these are exceptions. Look over the roll of our literary heroes in ancient times or in present. Engaged in the distracting labours of the school-room, serving the tables of a bank, in the back room of a public office, in the seclusion of a rustic parish, are too often planted the men who in France or Germany would have been enthroned on professorial chairs, addressing themselves to the rising historians, philologers, or theologians of the age. The evil has been pointed out in the Report of the Oxford Commission, and may, we hope, be remedied to some extent by the Legislature; for an evil undoubtedly it is, that Archimedes should be without the standing-place from whence he might move the world. But there is a brighter side to this state of things which is not to be overlooked. It is a good that light should be diffused as well as concentrated; that speculation and practice should be combined and not always isolated; that genius should be at times forced into uncongenial channels, and compelled to animate forms of life which else would be condemned to hopeless mediocrity.

We have made these remarks because we are about to enter on a remarkable instance of their applicability.

If any foreigner landing in England in 1853 had asked where he should find the man best acquainted with all modern forms of thought here or on the Continent—where he should find the most complete collection of the philosophical, theological, or historical literature of Germany—where he should find profound and exact scholarship combined with the most varied and extensive learning—what would have been the answer? Not in Oxford—not in Cambridge—not in London. He must have turned far away from academic towns or public libraries to a secluded parish in Sussex, and in the minister of that parish, in an archdeacon of one of the least important of English dioceses, he would have found what he sought. He would have found such an one there: he would now find such an one no more. For such was Julius Hare, late Rector of Herstmonceux and Archdeacon of Lewes.

Julius Charles Hare was born on September 13, 1795. He was the third of four brothers, all more or less remarkable, and all united together by an unusually strong bond of fraternal affection—Francis, Augustus, Julius, and Marcus. Of these the eldest and the youngest have left no memorial behind; but the two nearest in years and nearest in character cannot be mentioned together without noticing the one as well as the other. Augustus Hare will long be remembered by all who can recall the lofty and chivalrous soul, the firm yet gentle heart, which was so well represented in his bearing and countenance. He will be long remembered by those who never knew him through the two volumes of *Sermons to a Country Congregation*, which will probably be handed down to future generations as the first example of the great improvement of rural preaching in the nineteenth century—as a striking proof of the effect which a refined and cultivated mind may have in directing the devotions and lives of the most simple and ignorant populations. But he will be remembered also by the undying affection of his younger and more celebrated brother, expressed many a time and oft with a fervour and simplicity unusual in our countrymen—nowhere more strikingly than in the revised edition of the *Guesses at Truth by Two Brothers*, in which they first appeared before the world.

"In truth, through the whole of this work I have been holding converse with him who was once the partner in it, as he was in all my thoughts and feelings, from the earliest dawn of both. He too is gone. But is he lost to me? Oh no! He whose heart was ever pouring forth a stream of love, the purity and inexhaustibleness of which betokened its heavenly origin, as he was ever striving to lift me above myself, is still at my side, pointing my gaze upward. Only the love which was then hidden within him has now overflowed and transfigured his whole being, and his earthly form is turned into that of an angel of light."

In his early training he owed much to his mother, a woman of great strength and beauty of character, daughter of Dr. Shipley, Bishop of St. Asaph, and his aunt, Lady Jones, widow of the famous Orientalist. A large portion of his boyhood and youth was spent abroad; and to this must be in some measure ascribed the foreign tinge which appeared, as well in the simplicity and impulsiveness of his character, as in his literary predilections. "In 1811," he playfully said, "I saw the mark of Luther's ink on the walls of the castle Wartburg; and there I first learned to throw inkstands at the Devil." This, as we shall afterwards see, expressed, in a fuller sense than that in which he had intended it, the origin of much of his future labours—the influence exercised over his mind by Germany and its great Reformer. His regular education was begun at the Charterhouse, and he there fell in with one of those golden times which at successive intervals crown the harvest to schools and colleges as well as of the natural world. The same generation of schoolboys numbered on its roll, besides his own, the names of the two Waddingtons, and of Grote and Thirlwall, the future historians of Greece, not to mention others less known to fame, but whose strong practical abilities, or whose fresh and genial natures, long retained a hold on the respect or the affection of their fellow Carthusians.

From the Charterhouse he went to Cambridge in 1812. His academical career was terminated by his election as Fellow of Trinity College in October, 1818; whither, after a short study of the legal profession, he returned in 1822, and entered on the office of Assistant Tutor of the College. In the honoured succession of those who have occupied the princely chambers which open on the long green avenue of limes—the glory of the Trinity Gardens, Julius Hare will always fill a distinguished place. To the twenty years which he passed at Trinity College he owed, as he says himself, "the building up of his mind."* Not only as a teacher, but as a student, he entered with all the ardour of his mind into the philological learning in which the University of Cambridge has always been pre-eminent. There, too, he laid the foundation of that German library which has now returned once more to the walls within which it was first begun. With his friend and colleague, now Bishop of St. David's, he there made accessible in an English garb the great and truly inspiring work of Niebuhr. With the same eminent man he set on foot the *Philological Museum*, which shared the usual transitory fate of such learned periodicals, but which during the period of its existence furnished more solid additions to English literature and scholarship than any other of the kind that has appeared.

But it was not from the intellectual atmosphere of Cambridge that his mind received its most lasting influences. There was the circle of his numerous and most distinguished friends. It has sometimes struck us that there was a strength and permanence in the youthful friendships of that generation which we hardly find in our own. How far more strikingly does Arnold stand out from the background of his generation by reason of the group of faithful and loving equals—equals not in character or genius, but in age and sympathy—with whom he is surrounded from first to last! So too it was with Julius Hare. Removed by distance, by occupation, perhaps by

* Dedication of *Sermons on the Victory of Faith*.

opinions, from almost all of them, he never forgot or was forgotten by them. Of Thirlwall we have already spoken, in his exquisitely polished Essays on philology and his history giving the promise of that calm, comprehensive, imperturbable judgment which has made his Episcopal Charges the chief oracles of the English Church for the last twenty years. Sedgwick was there, awakening, as his friend well expresses it, "an almost affectionate thankfulness"* for the delight which his genial wit and eloquent conversation afforded; yet more for the free and generous sympathy which, unchilled by time, he is still as ready as ever to pour forth. Less known, but not to be forgotten, was the author of *The Broad Stone of Honour*, and of *The Ages of Faith*, to that generation the chief representative of the admiration for mediæval times which has since spread so wide, and so far overshot the legitimate reaction which was then unquestionably needed in their behalf. Perhaps the one to whom he looked back with the chiefest portion of gratitude was his powerful and vigorous colleague, Dr. Whewell—afterwards the head of that illustrious College—through whose urgency he was mainly induced to exchange a legal for an academical course, a lay for a clerical profession.

There was yet another and a more intimate circle which grew up round the Tutor of Trinity—the exceeding great reward of every one sincerely engaged in the work of education, and, in the sense in which

* *Guesses at Truth*, First Series, 4th ed., p. 53.

we here speak of it, the peculiar blessing of a college tutor—the circle of his pupils. Many there must be who look back with interest to the stores of knowledge which streamed forth in only too abundant profusion in that well known lecture-room; many who cherish a grateful and affectionate reverence for the memory of him who delighted to be not only the instructor, but the friend of those young and aspiring minds with whom he was thus brought into contact; in whose very aspect they read a rebuke to all suggestions of evil, an enkindlement to purity and goodness. Three, however, require especial notice—three who to their connection with him would probably have gladly confessed that they owed a great portion of that cultivation which has given them a place in the literature of their country, and on whom he in return looked with a love, and in one instance at least with a reverence, which almost made one forget that the superiority of years and station, to speak of nothing more, was on his side, and not on theirs. There was the bold and generous, it may perhaps be added, the rash and eccentric, spirit of one whose story, with hardly any incidents worth recording, has had the singular fate of being told by two of the most gifted men* of his time, and who certainly left an impression

---

* The allusion is to the two biographies of John Sterling, by Archdeacon Hare and Mr. Carlyle. Each is to be reckoned amongst the most interesting of its author's writings. It would be presumptuous to adjudicate between two such men. But it may perhaps be pertinent to observe, that whilst the Archdeacon has probably understated the amount of Sterling's doubts in his later

on all who ever heard his converse, such as can hardly be conceived by those who only know him through the far inferior medium of his written words. There was the accomplished author of the *Notes on the Parables*, who has the merit of having first recalled the course of English theology from patristic to exegetical studies, after the decline and fall of the Oxford school, and who, more than any other of Hare's pupils, imbibed from him the accurate discrimination which has produced the series of delightful little volumes on *Words*, *Proverbs*, and the *English Language*. There was finally the noble-hearted man, who, whatever may be thought of the obscurity of his style, the insufficiency of his arguments, or the erroneousness of some of his conclusions, is perhaps the best example that this age can show of that deep prophetic fervour, of that power of apostolic sympathy which awakens not the less because it often fails to satisfy—which edifies not the less because it often fails to convince. We may not be able to go along with the vehement expressions of admiration for Mr. Maurice's works which fill the Archdeacon's pages, but we can well understand and honour the genuine enthusiasm with which he

years, on the other hand, he was right in ascribing Sterling's original abandonment of the clerical profession to the simple cause of ill health, which Mr. Carlyle believes to have been a mere pretext. It so happens that I had unusual opportunities of observing the working of Sterling's mind at the time in question, and I am persuaded that, as his interest in his parochial work was intense, so his reluctance to abandon it was deep and unfeigned. The description of his conversation is equally powerful and exact in both the biographies. My recollection of his sermons is hardly less vivid.

laboured to bring all the world to agree with him in his estimate of his friend and pupil, and, as was afterwards the case, his near and dear kinsman.

In 1832 the family living of Herstmonceux in Sussex became vacant by the death of his uncle, and his elder brother Augustus declining to leave the scene of his happy labours at Alton, the Rectory of Herstmonceux was offered to Julius. He at once accepted the charge, though we can easily imagine the pain with which the Fellow of Trinity exchanged the studies and society of Cambridge for the active ministration and the retired life of a country parish.

It was in the interval between the acceptance of the living and his entrance on its duties that he enjoyed a year's absence on the Continent, mostly with his friend and ardent admirer, Walter Savage Landor, whose *Imaginary Conversations* he had himself been mainly instrumental in introducing to the English public. In the course of this journey he first visited Rome, always an epoch in the life of any man who can think and feel, more especially to one whose Cambridge studies had necessarily drawn him into the careful study of the beginnings of Roman history, and whose love for art amounted almost to a passion. One there was too, then living in the Capitol, whose presence stirred the thoughts and warmed the hearts of many an English traveller, and lent an additional charm even to the glory of the Seven Hills and the treasures of the Vatican. It was the beginning of his lifelong intimacy with Bunsen; an intimacy confirmed and cemented when in after years the Prussian minister took up his residence in the parish of the friend, whose name stands prominent on the roll of those with which the elaborate work on *Hippolytus and his Age* is connected by its illustrious author.

One curious incident is worth recording, which marked his stay at Rome. Whilst there he preached a sermon in the English chapel—treating of some of the feelings with which travellers ought to be animated —on the characteristic text, "What went ye out into the wilderness for to see ? A prophet ? yea, I say unto you, and more than a prophet." We will give the anecdote in his own words :—*

"From the subject it came home to the heart of a part of the congregation, and in compliance with their wishes I endeavoured to obtain the consent of the Papal censor to its publication at Rome, having received a hint that that consent would not be withheld. For I had been misunderstood—as was natural enough—in the passage where I termed Rome this *fateful* city, and had been supposed to have called it this *faithful* city; whereupon, while some of my Protestant hearers were offended by the expression, rumour was busy in reporting that a sermon had been preacht at the English chapel speaking very favourably of Romanism. . . . . The *imprimatur* which I applied for was not refused—but proceedings at Rome are so dilatory, that months passed by and I came away before it was otained. Perhaps the delay was a civil substitute for a refusal."

He returned from Rome in the spring of 1834, bringing with him many costly works of art to adorn his new home. One of these, a Madonna of Raphael, which he bought at Florence, in a characteristic access of enthusiastic tenderness, he insisted on carry-

* Preface to *Victory of Faith*, p. xii.

ing in his own hands over the long ascent of S. Gothard.

And now he settled in the sphere of duty from which he never afterwards moved, and in which was afterwards associated with him the beloved and honoured partner of his later years, sister of his friend and pupil Frederick Maurice. Let us pause for a moment on a scene which became so much a part of himself and of his writings, that for all who knew him during the last twenty years of his life the recollections of Herstmonceux and of Julius Hare were almost inseparable.

On the edge of the long sweep of high land which incloses the marsh of Pevensey Level stretches the parish of Herstmonceux,* so called from the "weald," "forest," or "*hurst*" of Anderida, which once covered the hills of Kent and Sussex, and from the Norman family of Monceaux, who first appear as the owners of the property. The church stands at the extremity of the parish, on an eminence immediately overlooking the flat plain on whose shore the Conqueror landed, with the bright line of sea and the bluff promontory of Beachy Head in the distance. Immediately beneath the church are the ruins of Herstmonceux Castle, commonly said to be the oldest brick building in England since the time of the Romans; the ancient seat of the

* Every particular respecting the history of Herstmonceux has been carefully collected in a valuable paper in the Sussex Archæological Collection, vol. iv., pp. 125-208, by Mr. Venables, for several years curate of Archdeacon Hare, now Canon of Lincoln. It embodies many interesting and minute remarks of the Archdeacon himself.

Fienneses, Dacres, and Naylors, from whom, in the reign of Anne, it passed by marriage into the hands of Francis Hare, Bishop of Chichester, well known as chaplain of the great Duke of Marlborough, and ranked by his contemporaries on a level with Bentley for his critical sagacity and learning. The castle was dismantled by the Bishop's descendants; in the last generation the property was sold; and the only connection which the Hare family retained with the place was the benefice, which still remained in their gift. The rectory stood far removed from church, and castle, and village; and in its tranquil retreat Hare's remaining years were spent. Of all peculiarities of English life, none perhaps are so unique as an English parsonage. But how peculiar even among English parsonages was the rectory of Herstmonceux! The very first glance at the entrance-hall revealed the character of its master. It was not merely a house with a good library—the whole house was a library. The vast nucleus which he brought with him from Cambridge grew year by year, till not only study, and drawing-room, and dining-room, but passage, and antechamber, and bed-rooms were overrun with the ever-advancing and crowded bookshelves. At the time of his death it had reached the number of more than 12,000 volumes; and it must be further remembered that these volumes were of no ordinary kind. Of all libraries which it has been our lot to traverse, we never saw any equal to this in the combined excellence of quantity and quality; none in which there were so few worthless, so many valuable works. Its original basis was classical and philological; but of later years the historical, philosophical, and theological elements outgrew all the rest. The peculiarity which distinguished the collection probably from any other, private or public, in the kingdom, was the preponderance of German literature. No work, no pamphlet of any note, in the teeming catalogues of German booksellers escaped his notice; and with his knowledge of the subjects and of the probable elucidation which they would receive from this or that quarter, they formed themselves in natural and harmonious groups round what already existed, so as to give to the library both the appearance and reality, not of a mere accumulation of parts, but of an organic and self-multiplying whole. And what perhaps was yet more remarkable was the manner in which the centre of this whole was himself. Without a catalogue, without assistance, he knew where every book was to be found, for what it was valuable, what relation it bore to the rest. The library was like a magnificent tree which he had himself planted, of which he had nurtured the growth, which spread its branches far and wide over his dwelling, and in the shade of which he delighted, even if he was prevented for the moment from gathering its fruits or pruning its luxuriant foliage.

In the few spaces which this tapestry of literature left unoccupied were hung the noble pictures which he had brought with him from Italy. To him they were more than mere works of art; they were companions and guests; and they were the more remarkable from their contrast with the general plainness and simplicity of the house and household, so unlike to the usual accompaniments of luxury and grandeur, in which we should usually seek and find works of such costly beauty.

In this home,—now hard at work with his myriad volumes around him at his student's desk,—now wandering to and fro, book in hand, between the various rooms, or up and down the long garden walk overlooking the distant Level with its shifting lights and shades,—he went on year by year extending the range and superstructure of that vast knowledge of which the solid basis had been laid in the classical studies of his beloved university, or correcting, with an elaborate minuteness which to the bystanders was at times almost wearisome to behold, the long succession of proofs which, during the later years of his life, were hardly ever out of his hands. Many, too, were the friends of his boyhood, and youth, and manhood, who were gathered under that hospitable roof; many the scholars, old and young, who knew that they should find in that copious storehouse knowledge which they would vainly seek elsewhere on British ground; many and long were the evening hours in which he would read aloud, after his wont, the choicest treasures of prose or poetry, truth or fiction, from the most ancient or the most modern sources of English literature.

We have dwelt on this aspect of his life, because we believe it to have been the most unlike to any other which could be named amongst his contemporaries. But it would be to overlook a very curious as well as important part of his career, if we were to forget to ask how this shrine of learning rose and flourished on what might have seemed the uncongenial soil of the Weald of Sussex—how the Cambridge scholar was united with the country pastor—what benefit the white-frocked peasants or the neighbouring clergy reaped from the appearance of a character or a home amongst them which could hardly have been more unlike all around it had it been transplanted from another hemisphere. Those of our readers who have turned over the pages of the very interesting volume lately published on the reorganization of the Civil Service, will remember the clever, though not altogether conclusive, objections urged against the proposed reforms by the Under-Secretary of State for the Home Department:*—

"It may be instructive as well as amusing to inquire what would be the effect were my two immortal friends [Grote and Macaulay] to descend from the clouds, and assume for a few days the humble disguise of Home Office clerks. I very much fear the public would not discover the change. The more exact knowledge of the composition of the Spartan 'Mora,' or the Macedonian phalanx, would not peep out in a letter fixing the permanent staff of a regiment of militia; the eloquence of the great historian of our constitutional liberties would not be recognized in a letter pointing out to a country magistrate that he had strained the provisions of the Vagrant Act. The gods would return to Olympus undetected, leaving no θεόσσυτος ὀδμή behind."

May we venture to ask the same question as to another of Mr. Waddington's former schoolfellows?

* *Papers relating to the Reorganization of the Civil Service*, p. 391.

would he, too, have returned undetected to his Cambridge Olympus, had the University thought fit to recall the most learned of her sons to occupy his fitting place amongst her professors? or was there, even in these distant wilds, a sense of worth and power which they would else have never known?

An active parish priest, in the proper sense of the word, he never was; not so much, perhaps, by reason of his literary pursuits as of his desultory habits. Constant, regular, vigilant ministrations to the poor were not his wont—perhaps they were not his call. Nor can he be said as a general rule to have accommodated his preaching to his parishioners. Compared with the short and homely addresses of his brother Augustus to the poor of Alton, his long and elaborate discourses will hardly hold their place as models of parochial exhortation, even to more enlightened congregations than those of Herstmonceux. But it would be a great mistake to measure his influence on his parish, or his interest in it, by these indications. Coming to Herstmonceux as he did—to the scene of his own early years—remembered as a child by the old inhabitants—honoured as the representative of a family long known amongst them—he was from the first bound to them, and they to him, by a link which years always rivet with a strength of which both parties are often unconscious till it is rent asunder. His own knowledge of their history, of their abodes, of their characters, perhaps in great measure from the same cause, was very remarkable; and although his visits to them might be comparatively few, yet theirs to the rectory were constant, the more so because they were always sure to receive a ready welcome. Whatever might be the work in which he was employed, he at once laid it aside at the call of the humblest parishioner, to advise, console, listen, assist. There was that, too, in his manner, in his words, in his voice and countenance, which could not fail to impress even the dullest with a sense of truth, of determination, of uprightness—yet more, with a sense of deep religious feeling, of abhorrence of sin, of love of goodness, of humble dependence on God. Such a feeling transpired in his ordinary conversation with them; it transpired still more in the deep devotion with which he went through the various services of the church. "If you have never heard Julius Hare read the Communion service," was the expression of one who had been much struck, as indeed all were, by his mode of reading this especial portion of the Liturgy, "you do not know what the words of that service contain." And in his sermons, needlessly long, and provokingly inappropriate as they sometimes were, there were from time to time passages so beautiful in themselves, so congenial to the time and place, that Herstmonceux may well be proud, as it may well be thankful, to have its name, its scenery, its people associated with thoughts and with language so just and so noble. Who is there that ever has seen the old church of Herstmonceux, with its yew-tree, and churchyard, and view over sea and land, and will not feel that it has received a memorial for ever in the touching allusions to the death of Phillis Hoad,* to the grave of Lina Deimling,† to the ancient church on the hill-top? Who that ever heard or read the striking introduction of the stories of Hooker's death, and of the warning of St. Philip Neri, in the sermons on the "Chariots of God,"‡ and on the "Close of the Year," will not feel the power and life given to the pastor of the humblest flock by his command of the varied treasures of things new and old, instead of the commonplaces which fill up so many vacant pages of the sermons of an ordinary preacher. Not seldom, thus, a passage of Scripture or an event of sacred history was explained and brought home to the apprehensions of his most unlettered hearers, when it seemed to those who listened as if the windows of heaven were opened for a flood of light to come down; and when the purest and most practical lessons of morality were educed with surprising force and attractiveness.

It was impossible but that Herstmonceux Rectory should have become the centre of the surrounding clergy. The influence which was gradually fostered by the mere fact of his presence amongst them received its legitimate sphere when, in 1840, he was appointed by Bishop Otter to the Archdeaconry of Lewes. This office he discharged with remarkable zeal and success. It is not too much to say that his

* *Parish Sermons*, vol. i., p. 159.
† *Ibid.*, vol. ii., p. 460.
‡ *Ibid.*, vol. i., p. 433; vol. ii., p. 497.

Archidiaconal Charges occupied, with the single exception of those of his distinguished friend the Bishop of St. David's, the first place in this field of ecclesiastical literature. They laboured indeed under the defects inseparable partly from his own style, partly from the circumstance that, including under their undefined range all subjects, from the pewing of a church up to the war with Russia, they were marked by a certain incongruity of composition amounting almost to grotesqueness. And for his audience, we can quite imagine that their inordinate length may at times have been calculated to produce the effect which we once heard ascribed to them by the good-humoured wit of Bishop Blomfield,—" If I had been one of his clergy, and been '*charged*' in that way, I should have been like a gun—I should have *gone off.*" But with all these drawbacks there was in his delivery and his style a kindling fire, a trumpet-call, which few could hear or read without emotion; there was in his arguments an accuracy of research, a calmness of judgment, a clearness of statement, which made them the best resource for any one who wished to know the rights and wrongs, the lights and shades, of the leading practical questions of the day. Take any of the topics which have been the nucleus of the most embittered and entangled controversies,—the marriage of a deceased wife's sister—Maynooth—the management clauses of the Privy Council—and the best answer to any questions you may have to ask concerning them will be found in the Charges of the late Archdeacon of Lewes. They for the most part turn on merely temporary questions, but the principles and the spirit in which he discusses them are eternal. They relate chiefly, as addresses of this nature must relate, to the externals rather than the essentials of religion; but no one was more aware of this than himself, or more carefully guarded against any misconception that might arise from it.

It may have been inferred from what we have said that we should regard, and that he himself regarded, his proper sphere to have been neither in the labours of a parish, nor yet in the management of an Archdeaconry, but in the guidance of the more ardent spirits, of the more cultivated minds, which he had once known, and which he always delighted again to meet within the walls of his own University. This sphere was not granted to him; but on two occasions he was enabled to show how deeply he valued the opportunity of recurring to it—how powerful the effect occasioned by even the temporary appearance of such a man in the Academic world. Those who were present at Cambridge in the winter of 1839, and the spring of 1840, will remember the strange apparition —as one might almost call it—of the Select Preacher of those two periods in St. Mary's pulpit. It was many years since he had stood in that place. A tradition floated in the undergraduate world, that on the last time when he had appeared there the sermon had rolled on its seemingly interminable length far beyond the usual limit of Academic afternoon discourses, and, what was more important, the time allotted to the early dinner-hour of the great College, celebrated for its rivalry with that to which the preacher belonged. Whether from ancient feud, or sheer weariness of spirit, or the natural pangs of hunger, the numerous members of this community are said to have manifested their impatience by the most unseemly and unequivocal signs, and the sermon on the "Children of Light" (it was afterwards published at the request of the members of Trinity College), was closed amidst the audible scrapings and shufflings of a multitude of invisible feet on all sides of the eloquent preacher. Very different was the scene during the delivery of the two noble courses of sermons on the *Victory of Faith*, and on the *Mission of the Comforter*. No doubt in the interval Academic prejudice had been abated—Academic roughness softened. But there had been a change in the preacher also: the long sonorous sentences were the same, and the vast range over the concentric spheres of philosophy and religion, but there was an earnestness of purpose—a breadth and depth of feeling—which seemed to fill the stream of his discourse with a new and irresistible impulse; and as he stood before the vast congregation—listening in breathless silence to his impassioned appeal—his eyes glistening, his voice deepening with the increasing vehemence of his emotion, it seemed indeed as it had been a prophet amongst them.

These sermons perhaps formed the culminating point of his fame. He never again appeared in so public a position before the world. But he took an energetic part in all the ecclesiastical questions of the day, until disabled by the repeated attacks of an internal disorder, which, amidst much pain and suffering patiently and cheerfully borne, brought with it the greatest of all trials to an active mind, the incapacity of sustained application and work. Alleviated as it was by the constant care and skill of Sir Benjamin Brodie, who took a more than professional interest in his patient's recovery, year by year the effort of writing and exertion became greater; and for months he was altogether prevented from taking any active share in parochial duty. In the autumn of 1854 he delivered with difficulty his last Charge to the Clergy of his Archdeaconry, and on the 20th of January, 1855, he expired at Herstmonceux Rectory, in the arms of her who for the last ten years had cast a steady sunshine over his life. One sign, eminently characteristic, broke the all but entire unconsciousness of his last hours. When asked to change his position, he only answered, pointing with his finger as he spoke, "Upwards, upwards."

On the 30th of January his remains were conveyed to their resting-place in Herstmonceux churchyard. From the Rectory to the church the body was borne at the head of a mournful procession, increased as it wound along through its three miles' course by the successive troops of parishioners and clergy who joined it at the several stages of its progress. It was a clear bright day, in the midst of the unusually cheerless and dreary winter of that period, so dark with public disaster and distress; and the features of the wide landscape of plain, and sea, and distant promontory, stood out in the sunshine as the mournful band were gathered around the aged yew-tree, on the verge of the rising ground beside the ancient church. Beneath that yew-tree was the humble cross which marked the grave of his brother Marcus. The two elder of that fourfold band slept far away beyond the sea—Francis at Palermo, Augustus in the Roman cemetery beside the pyramid of Cestius, hallowed by so many dear and illustrious recollections of the English dead. And now the last of the four brothers was laid in the dust; and as the mourners stood round, many a heart must have been struck with the melancholy thought that the last link of a long familiar story was in him broken and buried.

But it was not only the revered pastor of a country parish, or the last member of a remarkable circle of brothers, that was there interred. Round the grave might be seen clergy of many different shades of religious belief, from far and near, who were there to pay their tribute of affection and respect to one whose very differences brought out his union of heart and feeling with them. And not those only who were present, but many in various classes and stages of life, when they heard that Archdeacon Hare was no more, felt that they had lost a friend, an instructor, a guide.

Let us ask what this loss has been?

To use the somewhat antiquated language of the last century, Archdeacon Hare's career might be described as that of an eminent scholar and divine. It is true that the words as applied to him convey an erroneous impression. The two spheres in him were so closely fused together, and both were so truly the expression of the entire man within, that it is difficult to consider them apart. Still for convenience' sake we may do so, moving gradually from the outward to the inward as our story leads us on. The scholarship of Julius Hare was of the kind which penetrated the whole frame of his mind. Like all English scholarship, it was built upon a classical basis, and the effect of this, enlarged as it was by the widest view of the ancient writers, never left him. Greece and Rome were always present to his mind; and when he endeavoured to arouse the clergy of Sussex to their duties by the strains of Alcæus, it was only one instance out of many in which his deep delight in classical antiquity found its vent in the common occasions of life. To the older school of English elegant scholarship he hardly belonged, but in a profound and philosophical knowledge of the learned languages, he was probably second to none even in the brilliant age of his Cambridge contemporaries; and he was one of the first examples that England has seen not merely of a scholar but of a "philologer," of one who studied language not by isolated rules but by general laws.

This precision of scholarship showed itself in a form which is perhaps, to many, one of the chief associations connected with his name. Almost any one who has ever heard of Archdeacon Hare's writings has heard of his strange spelling. Every one knows that his sermons were not "preached," like those of ordinary mortals, but "preacht"; that his books were not "published" but "publisht." It is but due to his memory to remind our readers that it was not, as most people imagine, an arbitrary fancy, but a deliberate conviction founded on undoubted facts in the English language, which dictated his deviation from ordinary practice. His own statement of his principle is contained in a valuable and interesting essay on the subject in the Philological Museum; and it was maintained, in the first instance, not only by himself but by his two illustrious colleagues at Cambridge. But Bishop Thirlwall openly abandoned it in his History of Greece, and has never recurred to it; and Dr. Whewell has confined it to his occasional efforts in verse. It was characteristic of the man that Hare alone persevered to the end; and whether it were a hymn-book for his parish church or a monumental tablet, a German novel or a grave discourse on the highest matters of Church and State, he would never abandon what he considered the true standard of correct scholarship, or countenance the anomalies of the popular practice. We may justly smile at the excess to which this pertinacity was carried; but it was an index of that unwearied diligence, of that conscientious stickling for truth, which honourably distinguished him amongst contemporaries; it was an index also, we may fairly allow, of that curious disregard for congruity which, more than any other single cause, marred his usefulness in life.

The scholarship of Archdeacon Hare was remarkable for its combination with his general learning. Learning as an acquisition is not perhaps uncommon; but as an available possession it is a very rare gift. It is easy to accumulate knowledge; but it is not easy to digest, to master, to reproduce it. This, however, was certainly accomplished in the case of Archdeacon Hare; and when we think with regret of the giants of learning in former days, or of the superficial literature of our own, we may console ourselves by the reflection that we have had one at least amongst us who was sure to have consulted all the oracles, dead or living, within his reach, on any subject on which he ventured to speak. And this was the more remarkable from the width of his range. At the time when he first appeared as a scholar, he and his companion Thirlwall were probably the only Englishmen thoroughly well versed in the literature of Germany; and this pre-eminence, even in spite of the ever-increasing knowledge of that country in England, he retained to the last. His acquaintance with German literature extended to its minutest details; indeed his earliest publications were translations of some of the German romances of La Motte Fouqué and Tieck; and many who have never read any of his graver works have reason to be grateful to him for the delightful garb in which he first introduced to them *Sintram* and the *Little Master*. But it was especially in theology that this branch of his learning made itself felt. One other name for a time was more prominently known as the English student and champion of German divinity: Pusey's *Answer* to Mr. Rose's attack on German Rationalism, though now almost forgotten in the greater celebrity of its author's subsequent writings, must always be regarded as the first note of cordial salutation interchanged between the theologians of England and Germany. The Hebrew Professor has since drifted so far away from the position which he then maintained that he has long since ceased to be identified with the country to which he owes so much. Not so the Archdeacon of Lewes. Whatever he wrote or thought was coloured through and through with German research and German speculation. Schleiermacher and Nitzch, Daub and Lücke, were as familiar in his mouth as Tillotson or Secker, Mant or D'Oyly. He quoted them without apology; he used them without reserve. You could no more be ignorant of their presence in his writings than of their books in his library. To a great extent the German language, especially the language of German theologians, will always be to us a dead language —a tongue in which the learned will converse with each other, but not a medium of popular communication. This is, in some respects, a great convenience. There are always subjects in which it is impossible for the mind of a whole nation, or of two whole nations, to be simultaneously on the same level; and in such matters a separate language is the best means of intercourse between those who are really able to form a judgment on the questions at issue. For this reason, we confess that we can never look with much hope or favour on mere translations of German works on theology or philosophy. It is next to impossible that they should convey to the uneducated Englishman the impression which they received from the German author. Often, indeed, the mere fact of translation renders them utterly unintelligible.* The real interpreters of German thought are those who, receiving it themselves, and understanding by experience its strength and its weakness, are able to reproduce it in an English garb, or rather to develop and animate English literature by the contact.

This was eminently the work of Archdeacon Hare; for, though so deeply versed in foreign learning, he yet never lost the feeling or the position of an English gentleman and an English clergyman. No one of his time was less of a copyist. Few minds of his time were more thoroughly native and original. The influences of modern Germany were powerful upon him; and in his letter to the editor of the *English Review*, in reply to a calumnious attack

* We select nearly at random a sentence, from an English version, of a book obscure indeed even in the original language, but yet containing much valuable thought, and certainly nothing like the thick darkness of the following remarks (Nitzch's *System of Christian Doctrine*, § 103) :—"*Christian ponerology is divided into two leading sections—that of sin, or the bad participating in guilt ; and that of death, or the bad which has participated in the same. Sin and death are here understood in an extensive sense.*"

upon him contained in that journal, he has himself described with admirable discrimination the effect they have had, or ought to have, on this generation. But it was a loftier and broader position on which he took his stand. His academical youth had been cast in a time when the finer spirits of both Universities were opening to the thaw which broke up the frost of the last century. It was at Oxford the age of the Oriel school—of that volcanic eruption which left as its two permanent traces on the history of this generation the names of Arnold and of Newman. It was at Cambridge the age when in a higher and wider sphere, though with less direct and tangible effects, there was the same yearning after a better union between Religion and Philosophy—between things human and things sacred. One potent spirit swayed in this direction the mind of Cambridge, which at Oxford was hardly known.—" To the honoured memory of Samuel Taylor Coleridge . . . . . Who, through dark and winding paths of speculation, was led to the light, In order that others by his guidance might reach that light without passing through the darkness,"—Julius Hare dedicated in after years his chief work, as "one of the many pupils who had by his writings been helped to discern the sacred concord and unity of human and divine truth."*
" At the sweet sounds of that musical voice," as he beautifully expresses it elsewhere,† those who listened

* Dedication of the *Mission of the Comforter*.
† *Guesses at Truth*, First Series, 3rd e l., p. 245.

seemed to "feel their souls teem and burst as beneath the breath of spring, while the life-giving words of the poet-philosopher flowed over them." We do not here profess to unravel the strange contradictions of Coleridge's mind and character. Yet, in Cambridge at least, these words hardly overrate the importance of his influence. Of this combining, transforming, uniting tendency, Hare was undoubtedly the chief representative; and the more so because it fell in with a peculiarly congenial disposition: and it was the more strikingly displayed in him, from the fact that his profession and station were ecclesiastical. The clergy in the middle ages, as is well known, represented all the better knowledge of their time. In England, even after the Reformation, literature and theology were not entirely divorced. But they gradually drifted away from each other. Puritan austerity on one side, and indolent narrowmindedness on the other, seem to have forbidden a clergyman, unless perhaps for the sake of editing a Greek play or a Grammarian, to step or even to look beyond the set circle of ecclesiastical learning. It was as breaking through these conventional barriers—as bringing a large, free, and genial nature into this limited range—that Julius Hare, both by precept and example, rendered such good service to the Church of England. The great writers of antiquity, the poets and philosophers of modern times, soldiers and sailors and statesmen, in the world of men, had a charm and an authority for him as genuine and as powerful as in his profession is often felt only for Fathers and schoolmen among the dead, only for bishops and pastors among the living. Nor should it be forgotten that his delight in these and like auxiliaries to the cause of religion was mainly because they brought him into contact with fact and truth. Perhaps (if we may for the moment make a comparison to render our meaning intelligible), in mere copiousness of illustration, a page of Jeremy Taylor abounds with more allusions than in any theologian of our time to the various writers of the world. Yet, without disparagement of the exuberant powers of that great divine, it is clear that these references in his hands were mere flowers of rhetoric —that he had no care for the anecdotes which he repeated, or the persons whom he cited, except so far as they decorated the triumphal procession of his stately argument. And such on a lesser scale have been many displays of theological learning in later times. But Archdeacon Hare—though it may seem almost paradoxical to say so of one whose fancy was so rich, and whose affections were so powerful—rigidly adhered to such fact and detail as he had verified and appreciated for himself. He did not, it is true, follow out to their consequences many of the investigations or arguments on which he entered; but still, so far as he went, it was for positive and exact truth that he sought and contended. In this respect there is a wholesome atmosphere pervading the whole region of his writings, that more than any direct doctrine or theory has had a natural tendency to elevate the mind of his contemporaries. " When I turn," so he writes in speaking of Arnold, " from the ordinary theological or religious writers of the day to one of his volumes, there is a feeling, as it were, of the fresh mountain air, after having been shut up in the morbid atmosphere of a sick room, or in the fumigated vapours of an Italian church."* The same in its measure, and in a somewhat different application, may be said of himself. To pass from common clerical society, however able and instructive, to Herstmonceux Rectory was passing into a house where every window was fearlessly opened to receive air and light and sound from the outer world, even though for the moment unwelcome, dazzling, startling. " Children," he says, in one of his apophthegms, "always turn to the light: O that grown-up men would do likewise!"

With such influences at work, and with such a mind to be affected, he was no sooner placed in a post of practical authority and activity, than he found himself in a position peculiar, but most useful. He was able, in a time when the panic of Germany mounted almost to monomania in many excellent persons, to prove in his own person that a man might be deeply versed in German theology without being an infidel. He was able also, in an age of vehement party warfare, to take an active and beneficial share in all ecclesiastical movements without being a partisan. No party or sect of the Church could claim him as exclusively their own. His separation from some, his agreement with others,

* Preface to Arnold's third volume of the *History of Rome*, p. xii.

of the leading members of each would really disqualify him from representing any of them. Yet he did not therefore hold aloof from joint action. He did not feel, as at some periods of his life Arnold felt, that he had no man like-minded with him; that his hand was against every one and every one's hand against him. On the contrary, few men of his time worked more harmoniously with his brethren, and received more sympathy from them. In his advocacy of Convocation he fought side by side with the almost proverbial impersonation of the ancient High Church school, the late Dr. Spry. His strenuous opposition to the modern High Church never deterred him from lending the whole weight of his support to Mr. Woodard's college and school at Shoreham and Hurstpierpoint. With equal energy he strove against the intolerance of the partisans of Dr. Pusey and of the partisans of Mr. Gorham; and yet he won, with almost a solitary exception, the affectionate respect of men of all these various shades of opinion; and theologians may think themselves happy if they can carry with them to the grave as much grateful sympathy as fell to the lot of Archdeacon Hare.

What, then, were the special qualities and views which won this admiration? And, first, let us observe that it was not in his case an abstinence from attack on his opponents. It was, indeed, a remarkable circumstance that, with a heart so kindly and a sympathy so comprehensive, he combined an eagerness for polemics more like the old controversialists of the age of

Salmasius or of Jerome than of divines in modern times. The attack on Sir William Hamilton, in the notes to the *Mission of the Comforter*, and on Dr. Newman, in his *Contest with Rome*, are amongst the most vehement both in thought and expression that the literature of this generation can furnish. Neither was it any peculiar attractiveness of style. To the popular reader it was too abstract and elaborate; to the critical reader it was disfigured by violations of taste almost unaccountable in one who had so just an appreciation both of the excellences and defects of the language of others, whether in prose or poetry There are, indeed, passages, such as the catalogue of the Christian heroes of faith,* where the sustained and elaborate energy with which he supports the greatness of the subject rises into a solemn and dignified eloquence: there are others to which his personal feeling lends an exquisite pathos. But, on the other hand, there is hardly a page in which we do not meet some quaint comparison, some novel turn of expression, which not only offends the eye and ear, but actually diverts the attention from the main argument in which the blemish occurs. Neither was it the establishment of any one great truth, or the victory of any one great cause, such as extort admiration even from the unwilling, and homage even from the dissentient. His writings are all more or less fragmentary. His most complete work is in the form of "Guesses"; his most elaborate treatises are "Notes" to other works. To

* *Victory of Faith*, pp. 224-231.

some of these very works "Notes" were promised which never appeared. No special object which he pursued has been carried; no public cause in which he took especial interest will be identified with his name.

But in spite of these drawbacks to the completeness of his career, there were charms which have secured for him, we firmly believe, not only a place in the affections of his contemporaries, but in the interest of posterity. What he was will always be greater than what he did.

First, there was a simplicity of purpose and of style which gave to all his writings the charm of a personal presence—of a living communication. He wrote as he talked: he wrote, if one may thus apply Archbishop Whately's celebrated test of good preaching, "not because he had to say something, but because he had something to say." It was no style put on and off for the occasion, but the man himself who was addressing you. There needs no portrait, no biography of the writer, to tell you what he was like. As long as the works of Julius Hare survive, he will live with them. The book is the author. "The curtain," as the Greek painter said, "the curtain *is* the picture."

Secondly, whatever might be the eccentricity of his mind in detail, he was one of the few writers, certainly one of the few theologians, of this age who, in his practical judgment of men and things, could lay claim to the name of "wisdom." "The wisdom which is from above is first pure, then peaceable; gentle, easy to be entreated, full of mercy and of good fruits, without partiality and without hypocrisy." These are the words which are inscribed by pious gratitude on his gravestone. In some points they jar against the roughness of his natural temperament, as must always be the case in applications of abstract truth to individual characters. But in some points they are strikingly appropriate, and the general effect well harmonizes with the purity and peace and genuineness of his teaching. Take his less elaborate judgments on books, on men, on things, as they are given in the delightful *Guesses at Truth*, which, though nominally by the two brothers, were almost entirely the work of the younger. Or pass to his more deliberate treatment of general truths. We have already spoken of the Charges. But what we have said of the more immediately practical questions there discussed is true also of the more permanent and universal topics which fill his other writings. Where, for example, shall we find so just and full an award dealt out to the Fathers, or again to the German theologians, or again to Mr. Carlyle, as in the Notes to the *Mission of the Comforter?* There has probably been a stage in the life of every thoughtful student of the present generation in which his mind has been warped by an excessive leaning, or, what is equally dangerous, an excessive antipathy, to one or other of the tendencies there represented. Let such an one read these "Notes," and he will find words of counsel the most appropriate, the most cheering, the most salutary, because they are words which in great measure are the response, yet not the mere echo, to his own feelings. Or again, where in ancient times, or in modern, has the true contrast between unity and uniformity—the value of the one, the worthlessness of the other—been so beautifully set forth as in the dedication of his sermon on Unity to his colleague Archdeacon Manning? Or (to pass to a far less pleasing subject), where amongst modern controversies has the *Contest with Rome* been more ably sustained than in the polemical notes which, under that title, attack some of the main positions of Dr. Newman, not the less powerfully, or the less unanswerably, because they are often disfigured by a harshness of tone and a roughness of expression, which perhaps strike us the more from their contrast with the grace and polish of the style of his antagonist?

There is yet one class of Archdeacon Hare's works which we have not noticed, but which are perhaps the most peculiar and characteristic of all. It is not the first time that the chief celebrity of a scholar or divine has rested on his vindication of some illustrious person, dead or living. But probably no one ever published so many or so various. He used to say playfully that he should one day collect them all in one volume, under the title of *Vindiciæ Harianæ*, or the "Hare with many Friends." They were, in fact, the natural outbursts of two of the most powerful springs of his nature—his warm and generous sympathy, and his strong sense of justice. Most of the chivalrous encounters were, no doubt, to be largely ascribed to the former cause. Any attack on Luther, Niebuhr, Bunsen, Coleridge, would have called forth his sword from its scabbard under much less provocation than was actually given in the respective cases. Indeed, in some of these instances we almost wonder at the amount of energy and learning spent against charges which hardly seemed sufficient, either in quality or quantity, to need any refutation at all. And in each of these cases it is impossible not to perceive the glowing tinge given to all his statements by the depth of his personal affection. But even when the object of attack was his dearest friend, it was an outraged sense not so much of private partiality as of public justice that fired the train; and in one remarkable instance, he came forward on behalf of an entire stranger. The great Hampden controversy, which seven years ago threatened to shake the Church of England to its centre, has, like many similar dangers, been long laid to sleep, and we may be quite sure will never now be revived either by its victim or his assailants. But, if any like tempest should again sweep over the ecclesiastical atmosphere, we cannot imagine a more salutary lesson for the future agitators than to read Archdeacon Hare's *Letter* on Dr. Hampden's appointment to the See of Hereford. It was at the time of special importance, as tending, more than any other single cause, to allay the panic occasioned by that act, and was as such gratefully recognized by the Minister who had selected the obnoxious professor for the vacant bishopric. But it was still more instructive for the sight which it afforded of a noble and disinterested endeavour to defend one whom he had never seen, whom he knew only through his writings, whom he had no cause—either before or after he had thus stood forward in his defence—to regard with any personal predilections. Most instructive of all is it for the example of calm and dispassionate mastery of the subject; the more so for the contrast—now from the distance of years even yet more evident than when near at hand—with the partisanship, in too many instances, of those whom he was called to oppose.

For the reasons we have mentioned, the *Vindication of Dr. Hampden* is perhaps entitled to the first place amongst these labours (not of love but) of justice. But the one on which its author's fame will chiefly rest is the well-known *Vindication of Luther*, first published in a Note to the *Mission of the Comforter*, and now reprinted in a separate and enlarged form. It was receiving its final corrections when death cut short his labours. It may thus be regarded as his latest literary work, and, in truth, there is none which so well represents his whole mind—none perhaps which he would himself have so delighted to leave as his last bequest to the world. "I am bound," he used to say, "to defend one to whom I owe so much." It is true that in this, as in others of his Vindications, we cannot feel satisfied that he has always hit the main point of the objectors; we cannot avoid the conviction that, whilst he is in possession of every single out-work, the citadel of the argument often remains unconquered. For example, after all that he has said, there will still be left an impression that Luther's conception of faith when expressed in its dogmatical form was either something very different from that portrayed so beautifully in the *Victory of Faith*, or else that it was not so distinctively or exclusively his own as to entitle him to the eulogies heaped upon him as its champion. But, on the other hand, we think that no one can read Archdeacon Hare's Vindication without feeling that it is an important step gained in the right understanding of Luther's character. The unparalleled knowledge displayed of the Reformer's writings is not only most valuable as a mine of reference, but is in itself a testimony to the greatness of the man who could inspire, at the distance of three centuries, such a vast, such an enthusiastic research. The numerous explanations of expressions long misunderstood, and of falsehoods long believed, are amongst the most decisive triumphs of literary investigation that we have ever seen. And above all, the breadth and energy of Luther's genius, the depth and warmth of his heart, and the grandeur of his position and character, amidst whatever inconsistencies or imperfections of expression, are brought out with a force and clearness which must often be as new to his admirers as to his detractors.

"When we see men like Archdeacon Hare cut off before their time"—so writes an able observer* of our ecclesiastical world—"it is a natural superstition which tempts us to look upon their removal as a sign of coming judgment, and an evil omen for the Church

Conybeare's *Essays on Ecclesiastical and Social Subjects*, p. 144.

which they adorned." But let us take a more cheering view. His childlike outburst of affection, devotion, and faith; his burning admiration of good wherever seen; his indignant scorn and hatred of evil, noble even when misplaced or exaggerated; his entire freedom from all the littleness of vanity, or ambition, or self-seeking, which so often vex and haunt the path of authors and of ecclesiastics—these are gifts bestowed by Providence with a sparing hand. Let us make the most of what remains of them; let us not suffer the image of them lightly to vanish out of our recollection.

Let the example of such a career fill us with thankfulness that there is at least one Church in Christendom where such a career could be run as in its natural field—which gives scope for such a union of fervent piety with refined culture and masculine learning. His course has been compared by one who knew him well to that of a noble ship with her sails wide spread, filled by every gale which blew. Where, we may ask, would so many influences have been combined to propel the bark onwards as in the Church and country where his lot was actually cast? Let us remember also that the divisions which awaken so many dismal forebodings, did but serve, in his case, to bring out more clearly his power of overlooking and overruling them to the common good. In the lull of ecclesiastical controversy—hushed as it always will be hushed in the presence of the really great events on which human happiness and misery depend*—his voice may

* Written at the time of the Crimean war, 1855.

be heard more readily than at times when it would be more needed. But if the theological factions of a few months or years past should revive, there would be no "truer remedy for the evils of the age" than if we could hear more and more appeals to the contending parties in the spirit of that which in such a time of agitation, in the spring of 1850, was addressed by Archdeacon Hare to his brethren :—

"With both sides I feel that I have many bonds of common faith and love and duty: with both of them I heartily desire to work together in the service of our common Master. With each of the two parties, on sundry points, I differ in opinion more or less widely: but why should this cut me off from them, or why should it cut them off from me? May we not hold fast to that whereon we are agreed, and join hand to hand and heart to heart on that sure, unshakable ground, which cannot slip from under us, and wait until God shall reveal to us what we now see dimly and darkly? Shall the oak say to the elm, *Depart from me—thou hast no place in God's forest—thou shalt not breathe His air, or drink in His sunshine?* Or shall the ash say to the birch, *Avaunt! thou art not to stand by my side—cast thyself down and crawl away, and hide thyself in some outlandish thicket?* O my brethren! the spring is just about to clothe all the trees of the forest in their bright, fresh leaves, which will shine and sparkle rejoicingly and thankfully in the sun and rain. Shall it not also clothe our hearts anew in bright hopeful garments of faith and love, diverse in form, in hue, in texture, but blending together into a beautiful, harmonious unity beneath the light of the Sun of Righteousness?"

THE VICTORY OF FAITH:

AN EXPANSION OF A COURSE OF SERMONS,

PREACHT BEFORE THE UNIVERSITY OF CAMBRIDGE,

A. D. 1839.

SERMON I.

FAITH, THE VICTORY THAT OVERCOMETH THE WORLD.

1 JOHN v. 4.

"This is the victory that overcometh the world, even our Faith."

ONE of the first things which must needs strike every reader of the New Testament, even the most thoughtless and careless, is the perpetual mention that is made of Faith, the great and paramount importance attacht to Faith. Faith is there spoken of as the foundation, the source and the principle of everything that can be excellent and praiseworthy in man,—as the power by which all manner of signs and wonders are to be wrought,—as the golden key by which alone the treasures of heaven are to be unlockt,—as the unshakable indestructible rock on which the Christian Church is to be built. When our Lord came down from the mount, where the glory of the Godhead shone through its earthly tabernacle during the fervour of His prayer, and where his spirit was refresht by talking with Moses and Elias on the great work He was about to accomplish,—when, after this brief interval of heavenly communion, He returned to the earth, and was met by that woeful spectacle of its misery and helplessness, physical and moral, the child who was sore vext by the evil spirit, and whom His disciples could not heal,—and when, the cure having been wrought instantaneously by His omnipotent word, He was askt by His disciples why they had been unable to effect it,—He replied, *Because of your unbelief.* And then, having thus taught them what was the cause of their weakness, He tried to revive and renew their hearts by telling them how they might gain strength, and how great strength they might gain: *Verily I say to you, if ye have Faith as a grain of mustardseed, ye shall say to this mountain, Remove hence to yonder place; and it shall remove; and nothing shall be impossible to you;* thus encouraging them by declaring the infinite power that lies in the very least Faith, if it be but genuine and living. In like manner, when the wonder of the disciples is excited by the withering of the fig-tree, He calls away their thoughts from the particular outward effect, to the principle by which such effects, and far greater, may be produced: *Verily I say to you, if ye have Faith, and doubt not, ye shall not only do this which is done to the fig-tree, but also, if ye shall say to this mountain, Be thou removed, and be thou cast into the sea, it shall be done.* Passing on from the Gospels to the Epistles, we find the power and workings of Faith still more frequently urged, and still more emphatically dwelt on. The most inattentive reader can hardly fail to observe, how the justifying character of Faith, in its absolute exclusive primacy, forms the central point of St. Paul's preaching. And in the text we hear the Apostle of Love, joining his voice with that of him who is more especially the Apostle of Faith, and proclaiming that *this*, and this alone, *is the victory which overcometh the world, even our Faith*.

In the Old Testament, it is true, this great evangelical doctrine of the power of Faith is not often stated in the same broad, naked, abstract manner. Even there however we read the declaration of the prophet Habakkuk, to which St. Paul refers more than once, that *the just shall live by Faith;* words which have often upheld the soul of the believer, when it might otherwise have failed and sunk under the crushing weight of the world. And if we look beyond the letter, and search into the principles which pervade and animate the Old Testament, it becomes plain that they are the very same, which are merely brought forward more definitely and explicitly in the New; and that the whole history, as is set forth in that great chapter of the Epistle to the Hebrews, is a record of the warfare waged by Faith, of its victories, its triumphs, and its conquests. Indeed this accords with the main character of the Old Testament; where we see those very truths exhibited visibly and livingly, in type and symbol, in action and endurance, which were afterward to be proclaimed under the New Dispensation in their eternal aboriginal universality. Nor is this process different from that which has prevailed in the other provinces of human thought. Everywhere the thing exists, and is taken up among the objects and elements of action, long before the thought comes forward into distinct consciousness. The sun did not lie slumbering beneath the horizon, until man had made out the laws which were to regulate his course. States had sprung up, and spread far and wide, and had grown into empires, and had armed themselves with power and with knowledge, before any one dreamt of speculating upon the principles of government and of social union. For it is only the word of God, giving utterance to the law, that precedes the work; and it is through the work that the knowledge of the law comes to the mind of man, and by the work that it is awakened there. The word of God goes before; and no sooner has it issued from the Eternal Mind, than the work starts forth in the fulness of reality: the thought and word of man follow after, and are often centuries or even millenaries behind.

Hence however the reader of the Old Testament, not having his attention so immediately drawn to the point, will not be so much startled and surprised, as a person reading the New Testament for the first time must needs be, by the great and wonderful things which are there predicated concerning Faith. And though much is also said concerning Love in the New Testament, and much concerning Obedience and Purity and Holiness, though great weight and moment are ascribed to them, and precious and glorious things are declared of them, yet all this does not seem so strange and perplexing, so entirely at variance with man's ordinary notions and opinions, as the sayings with regard to Faith. For although Christian Love and Christian Obedience and Purity are totally different, not merely in degree, but in principle, and therefore in kind, from anything known or even imagined upon earth, before the wreck of fallen humanity was glorified by the taking up of the manhood into God, still there were already certain qualities which bore the same name in the vocabulary of the natural man; and these were prized among the idols of the heart and mind, as the guardian deities of his domestic and civic life. From the very condition and constitution of mankind, Love and Obedience were necessarily in some measure consecrated, by being embodied in outward institutions of the deepest interest and widest power, by being at once the foundation and the cementing principles of family and of national existence. Love is so inseparably combined with the primary instincts and necessities of our nature, that, had it wholly passed away, mankind would have sunk into a putrid mass of worse than brutish licentiousness, which in the course of a generation must have crumbled to atoms under the joint action of those two natural and indissoluble allies, Lust and Hatred. Obedience was establisht in families by the indefeasible authority of strength over weakness, of protection over helplessness, of kindness over affection; while in every social union the first principle must needs be the subordination and conformity of each particular will to the will of the whole body, so far at least as is deemed requisite for the preservation and support of that body. Thus, wherever men coalesced into communities, it became apparent that such communities could not be held together, except by some common bond of order, by rights, by duties, and by obedience. Nor was man without monitors to remind him that he should endeavour to purify his life, from the worst at least of the pollutions which beset it. His very pride called up the thought of his superiority to all the creatures, whether animate or inanimate, that he saw around him, and warned him that he ought to have nobler purposes and higher aims than any sensual or worldly gratification can yield. Conscience sounded through the wreck of his soul, like the wind whistling through the ruins of a city that once bore the sceptre of empire, Babylon, or Palmyra, or Egyptian Thebes, admonishing him that the edifices, of which he saw the fragments, had been built and held together by Law, and that the decay of Law had been their destruction. Different too as these dim and shadowy nations were from the heavenly realities which Christ had set up in their stead, there was still a resemblance in them, betokening a certain cognateness. The sons of God had indeed entered into a lawless union with the daughters of men; and their progeny for generation after generation had wedded themselves more and more closely to the earth, and had degenerated more and more from their heavenly stock. Yet still some traces of their higher parentage might be discerned in their features; and from these the moral sentiments and the affections derived that power and sanctity; which they still retain: so that, when the Gospel proclaimed its holier Morality and its godlier Love, its voice did not pass altogether unechoed over the earth, as it did when it declared the soul-hallowing, world-conquering might of Faith.

Moreover, since the Gospel has been set up on high over the heads of the nations, and has been acknowledged, outwardly at least, to be the one great and only pure source of wisdom and truth, the very language of men, and all the manifold currents of thought and opinion, have been so shaped and modified by it,—so much reflected light has been shed abroad by it, even upon those who have not been dwelling immediately under its rays,—so much has been effected by its holy precepts toward correcting and ennobling the notions and views, so much by its sacramental influences in the way of purifying and elevating the feelings and affections of mankind,—that whoever sits down nowadays in a Christian country to read the Bible, comes to it with a mind prepared to receive and assent to a number of its truths, as matters of unquestioned certainty and general notoriety, without being aware that they too are a portion of the boundless riches which Christ has poured out over the earth. Thus it comes to pass, that even those who turn away in self-complacent blindness from the more peculiar and essential doctrines of the Gospel, are still mostly ready to admit the excellence of its Morality, and the beauty of its Charity: and they are willing to receive these into their own code of life; though not till they have enfeebled and deadened them both, by cutting them off from that root of divine Faith, out of which alone can they grow in perennial vigour and bloom. Indeed, when a person is very forward in extolling either the Morality or the Charity of the Gospel,—when he is apt to single out the parable of the good Samaritan, and such texts as express the duty so beautifully enforced by it, or such as *God is Love*, for the main and only prominent objects of his admiration,—it will often be found, if we are led to look closely into his opinions, that his Christianity,—supposing him to make profession of it, —has been stunted and enervated, as it has been so generally in the last hundred years, into a sort of sentimental theophilanthropy. For although the Christian will continually bless God, from the inmost depths of his heart and soul, for that gracious revelation of Himself, yet the remembrance of the manner in which that revelation was made, of the Cross from which it was manifested to the world,—and the consciousness thereby awakened and kindled of his own unworthiness, and of the miserable return he has made for the privilege of being thus allowed to look into the innermost mystery of heaven,—will strike him with awe, will make him shrink from taking those sacred words in vain, from uttering them with unhallowed lips. If the angels themselves veil their eyes in the presence of God, how can we do otherwise than cast ours down in speechless shame, at the thought of the ineffable glory of the Mercy and Grace, the Holiness and Righteousness, through which they must pass, before they can behold the central throne of Love; and which are themselves only particular manifestations of God's Love in His dealings with His creatures! Hence we shall rather exclaim with the Psalmist (cxxx. 4), *For there is mercy with Thee; therefore shalt Thou be feared;* more especially when we bethink ourselves what deceitful notions men are sure to form of God's Love, in measuring it by their own deceitful standard, stripping it of its Holiness and of its Justice, without which it could have no substantial reality, and degrading it into little better than infinite goodnature and imperturbable indifference, which they may insult and mock at as long as they please. They who look in the first instance at what they call God's Love, will take the second commandment without the first, which alone can sustain and give life to it. For God, they say, in His self-sufficing omnipotence, holding the reins of all the worlds in His hands, and evermore turning the wheels of life and death, cannot need or care for the love of His creatures: and they know not how it elevates and hallows the heart, to have a Being of infinite perfection to devote it to. They will take the Morality of the Gospel, without its Righteousness, and without the principle of that Righteousness; apart from which principle Morality can no more preserve an equable path, than a planet could revolve in its orbit without the centripetal attraction. For in nothing else is the wisdom of the Gospel, and its thorough knowledge of that which is in the heart of man, of his readiness to fall into every snare, and to be beguiled by every delusion, more apparent than in this,—that, in singling out the primary power, through the exercise of which mankind were to become partakers of the glory ordained for them, it did not, like the Law, enjoin Holiness and Purity, or any moral observance, as the ground of justification: nor did it choose out Love as that ground; precious and inestimable as it declares Love to be, and exquisite as are the colours with which it portrays Love's surpassing excellence and beauty. The Gospel did not make Holiness the ground of justification: it did not make Love the ground of justification: but it shewed its wisdom, and its knowledge of man's weakness and of his wants, in this more especially, that it made Faith the ground of justification.

Hereby alone was it possible to ensure the building up of the Christian life to the measure of the stature of the fulness of Christ. It is only when that life is firmly rooted and grounded in Faith, that the straight stem of Righteousness will rise, and branch out into the manifold ramifications of Duty, and that it will be crowned with the brightness and the sweetness of the amaranthine blossoms of Love. When moral rectitude is disjoined from Faith, there is no trust in it. It may stiffen into pharisaical formality, or ossify into stoical severity; or it may be withered by the blight and cankerworm of expediency; or it may tumble into the sty of Epicureanism, and rot there. When Love is disjoined from Faith, there is no trust in it. Caprice may throw it to the winds; chance may nip it in the bud; pride may blast it; vanity may eat away its core; prosperity may parch it; distress may freeze it; lust may taint and poison it: the slights and neglect, which it must needs experience at times in a world of frailty and mutability, will assuredly sour and embitter it. Indeed, according to the true Christian idea of Love and of Righteousness, neither the one nor the other can exist at all, except as springing out of Faith. Whereas, when Faith is genuine and strong, in proportion to its genuineness and strength it will infallibly produce both Righteousness and Love; a Righteousness and Love, which, having a living seed within them, will be abiding. Hence, as it was reserved for the Apostle of Faith to set forth that glorious picture of Love, which he himself so nobly realized in his life, on the other hand the Apostle of Love, after inculcating the duties of Obedience and Love through the main part of his Epistle, and showing how they mutually support and twine round one another, proceeds, in the passage which I have chosen for my text, to declare what alone will enable them to stand, what alone will enable them to withstand and overcome the multitudinous temptations and harassing opposition which they must needs have to encounter in this world, even our Faith.

Such being the importance of Faith, it becomes a question of momentous interest, What is this Faith, of which such wonderful things are declared in the Holy Scriptures? What is it as a principle or power in human nature? and what relation does it bear to man's other gifts and faculties? With regard to those two great concentric spheres of human nature, the sphere of our affections, and that of our duties or practical life, we have seen that, excellent and pure and heavenly as are the principles of the new life brought down by Christ, there was something answering and to a certain degree analogous to them already existing among mankind, in those fragmentary relics of the divine image, which had not been utterly effaced; somewhat in the same manner as in every flower, when it opens its petals, there is a likeness, lying partly in its shape, partly in the brightness of its colouring, which bespeaks its affinity to the sun, as well as its need of the sun to enliven and enlighten it. When the Law summed itself up in the twofold commandment of Love, and when the Gospel uttered its new commandment of a still diviner Love, of a Love after the pattern of that Saviour, who came down from his throne of glory, and gave himself up to the weaknesses and infirmities of humanity, to a life of suffering and a death of shame, for the sake of mankind,—although it had never entered into the heart of man to conceive a Love like this,—yet men had a certain notion what was meant by Love. There was a feeling in their hearts, which, though its wings had been miserably clipt by selfishness, and though its life-blood had been poisoned by sensuality, was known to be of wondrous power, and to be the chief bestower of such happiness as man is capable of enjoying. Indeed under the form of Friendship, under which it is free from the taint of sensuality, it attained to such highths of heroic selfdevotion as have hardly been surpast: and the pictures of filial and fraternal Love, which the poets of old portrayed, still stand among the most beautiful of the exemplars set up by the Imagination in its gallery of glorified humanity. So again the idea of Law had risen long before above the intellectual horizon. It had been impersonated in sage legislators: it had been embodied in wise and lasting and time-hallowed institutions: it had been declared to have a royal and heavenly nature, not springing from the perishable breath of man, not liable to decay or oblivion. Many of the moral virtues had been openly recognized as the noblest and most ennobling aims of human endeavour. Justice, Temperance, Fortitude were objects of admiration, almost of worship: and they had been realized in men whose names are still proverbial, and who gave proof that the being, made a little lower than the angels, and crowned with glory and worship, was still capable, even in his self-incurred degradation, of displaying features betokening his high original, and of shewing that he was indeed designed to be the first and goodliest among the works of the Creator. A certain dim idea of Duty the ancients had; though neither its grounds nor its object were distinctly perceived. Even the idea of Sanctity had gleamed upon them, as of a thing admirable and desirable. The main deficiency in their Ethics was, that they wanted the idea of Sin, the consciousness of their own inherent sinfulness and infirmity. Hence the moral virtues were regarded by them as so many gems in the crown of human nature, as the constituents of its dignity and majesty, to be wrested from the world by fighting against it; instead of being sought humbly by prayer as graces and gifts from above, to be nurtured in the solitude of our hearts, and guarded with unceasing watchfulness against the enemy within. They wanted the idea of Humility: they wanted the idea of Godliness: or at least they had debased it to bodily and intellectual, instead of moral and spiritual excellence. Thus their Love was imperfect, because it wanted the Love of God; their moral speculations were imperfect, because they wanted the notion of their duty to God, and of their relations to Him. In a word, each wanted the groundwork and the consummating principle of Faith. In every part of the peopled earth, some sort of aspirations rose from the heart of humanity heavenward. In one country they might be rude and rugged and insulated, starting up from the midst of a dreary waste, like the pillars of Stonehenge. In another country they might be carved and polisht, and connected by figured friezes, and ranged in beautiful symmetry, and surrounded by a luxuriant cultivation, like the temples of the Greeks. But everywhere they were empty and roofless: no covering from on high had descended upon them: no headstone had placed itself at top of them, to turn them into a church.

Now after the analogy of these examples, we might naturally be led to infer that, as our Lord, when He came to set up the law of Love and the Law of Holiness among mankind, did not come to destroy man's nature, but rather to fulfill it,—to fulfill its deepest cravings, its inmost unconscious yearnings, yearnings of which it only became conscious when it felt His fulness within them,—yea, to fill it, as the light fills the hollow chasms and yawning abysses of darkness,— we might infer that, as in both these cases He came to strengthen and purify and hallow what, however frail and feeble and imperfect, were already the best things to be found among mankind, and almost the only things which preserved them from being trampled to the ground and crusht by the iron hoof of sin,—we might infer that in like manner, when He chose Faith as the chief motive principle of the new life which He desired to awaken in man, He would in this case also take a principle that had already been stirring within him. We might infer that in this case also the new graft, however superior its fruitage might be, would still be congenial to the original stock. We might infer that the power, which was to effect such wonders in the regenerate man, nay, which was to be the main instrument on man's part in the work of his regeneration, cannot possibly have been buried in total sleep till then, but must have already shewn forth some tokens of its greatness, even in the unregenerate heart. And yet Faith, as a principle of life and action, in any sense at all approaching to that which it bears in the New Testament, is scarcely heard of without the pale of Christianity. Even within that pale, if we listen to the language of men, when they are speaking of the springs and motives of their own conduct, or that of others, or if we look into the speculative treatises which profess to examine into those springs and motives, though we shall find many good qualities ascribed to man, and many evil qualities, it is rare to meet with any mention of Faith, except in certain peculiar limited senses. Hence we might conclude, as mostly appears to be implied, that Faith, as a faculty of much consideration and power, is the peculiar organ of religion; and that in this sense alone, as standing in the sight of God, can man be said to live by Faith. At the same time it must be borne in mind that, while Love and the various forms of Duty are continually propelling man to outward action, and manifesting themselves therein, whereby they force themselves into notice, the workings of Faith are mostly underground. It is the root, as it is commonly called, of the Christian life: and when it shews itself forth, it is mostly combined with some other principle, which, bearing a closer relation to outward things, must needs be more prominent than that power whose peculiar province is the invisible. For thus much everybody knows about Faith, that its objects are not the objects of sight, but the things that are unseen. The point, as to which there is not the same agreement, is, How does it deal with its objects? in what relation does it stand to them? Or, to express the question, which I have been led to select for our consideration in this Course of Sermons, more generally,—What is the Faith, to which such power is attributed in the New Testament? and is there anything at all analogous to it in the ways and workings of the natural man? What is the Faith which overcomes the world? and how, in what respects, by what means, is that great and arduous victory gained?

On these matters the time now left me will only allow me to say a few words: their fuller discussion must be reserved under God's grace for the following Sermons. At present it must suffice to remark, that Faith is often defined in some such manner as follows, —namely, as being an operation of the intellect, an intellectual assent to propositions received, not upon grounds of reason, but upon testimony. And they who regard Faith in this light, proceed to lay down that religious Faith is an intellectual assent to certain truths, beyond the reach of reason, concerning God, and His will, and His dealings toward mankind, delivered by inspired witnesses, whose inspiration is proved by the evidence of miracles. Now assuredly such a definition of Faith, instead of affording us any insight into its mighty workings,—instead of enabling us to conceive and understand how it can be ordained to act such a leading part in the moral and spiritual regeneration of man,—only makes the mystery still more mysterious, still more incomprehensible, and utterly repugnant to everything we know of man, whether from searching our own hearts, or from observing the conduct of others. Man's intellect has indeed great power over all outward things. This we are not disposed to question. In these days more especially we all take far too much pride in it, and make presumptuous boast of it, nay, are apt to fall down and worship it, as the one great miracle-worker, the true mover of mountains. But powerful as it may be, omnipotent as we may deem it to be, over the world around us, over the outward fields of Nature, there is one region where our hearts and consciences tell us, sometimes in half-muttered whispers, sometimes in cries of anguish and agony, that it is almost powerless: and that region is the dim, visionary, passion-haunted one within our own breasts. We all know but too well,—every one whose life has not flowed away in listless inanity, every one who has ever struggled against the evil within him, must have felt but too vividly, — too vividly, though very far from vividly enough,—that our intellectual convictions, clear and strong as they may have been, have never of themselves been able to shake the foundations of a single sin, to subdue a single vice, to root out a single evil habit. Ever since that severing of the heart from the intellect, which took place when man gave himself up to the lust of godless knowledge, the Passions have made mock at the Understanding, whenever it has attempted to controll them, and have only flattered and pampered it, when it was content to wear their livery, and to drudge in their service; while the Will has lifted up its head against it in haughty defiance and scorn. Moreover this lesson, which we learn from our own miserable experience, is confirmed by the evidence of all history; where, in example after example, we see how vain and impotent the enlightening of the Understanding has been to elevate and purify man's moral being; and how, unless that enlightenment has been working together with other healthier powers, and been kept in check by them, its operation on the character of nations has rather been to weaken and dissipate their energies, to crumble the primitive rock into sand.

It might be argued, indeed, that this exaltation of Faith tends to the humiliation of the intellect, as implying that the highest spiritual truths are undiscoverable by any exercise of man's natural faculties. Something too like a judicial retributive order may be discerned in the arrangement, that, as the attempt of the intellect to soar out of its proper sphere brought about man's Fall, so the abasement of the intellect should be the means of raising him again,—that, as its rebellion against God's declared law cut him off from God, so its submission to God's revealed word should be a preliminary step to his reunion with God. And doubtless this is quite true, so far as the intellectual process is undeniably a main constituent in every act of Faith. The subjection of the self-relying, isolating Understanding, which would fain draw all truth out of itself, is a portion of that sacrifice of our carnal self-centred nature, which must precede the birth of a higher spirit. But is this all? Can this be all that is meant by Faith? Is it possible that the Faith by which man is to be justified, the Faith by which the world is to be overcome, should be nothing more than the assent of the intellect to the truths revealed in the Scriptures? How is that assent to act upon the heart, to stir it, to new-mould it? How can this be, my brethren? What testimony do your hearts, do your consciences give upon this point? Do they not cry aloud,—*Time after time our Understandings have seen and acknowledged many of the truths of the Gospel; we have been thoroughly satisfied of their truth; we have not felt the slightest disposition to question it: but our convictions have availed us nothing: they have passed like wind through an archway: our conduct has been unchanged: our hearts have continued unmoved, torpid, dead... dead as the lifeless carcase in which Galvanism for a moment awakens a shadow and semblance of life?*

Can Faith, I ask, be nothing more than an operation of the Understanding? At least the word seems ill chosen. For even when we speak of Faith as manifested in our intercourse with our neighbours,—when we talk of putting Faith in one another,—the moral action of the Will is a stronger element in that Faith, than the judicial exercise of the Understanding. Indeed a Faith which is merely a belief founded on the calculations of the Understanding, would be no Faith at all. It would want that very quality which is absolutely essential to all Faith, and which makes it what it is. For in all Faith there must be confidence; there must be reliance, there must be trust. The intellectual conviction may be indistinct; the grounds for it may be feeble, may never have been duly examined: very strong Faith in one man may rest upon weak grounds; while that of another may be frail and tottering, though based on irrefragable certainty. But in proportion as our confidence, as our trust, is firm and stedfast, so is our Faith: wherefore this, and not the intellectual belief, is the formative principle in Faith. In like manner, if we examine the other worldly senses of the word, *Faith*, we shall find that the moral ingredient in them predominates over the intellectual. Can it be then, that the Gospel, the dealings of which are almost wholly with man's moral nature,—the aim of which is not to elevate and ennoble his Understanding, but his moral nature,— the doctrine of which is, that the way to the knowledge of spiritual truth lies, not through thought and reasoning, but mainly through action and endurance, —should leave out, nay, cast out the moral element in the faculty to which it addresses its primary appeal? That this cannot be so, becomes nearly certain, when we look at the word in the Greek original, which we render by *faith*. In that word, as every reader of Greek knows, the leading idea is that of confidence, of reliance, of trust. Only in a secondary sense does it come to be used for intellectual belief; and even then it mostly implies an admixture, greater or less, of moral confidence. The same too is the case with the Hebrew word answering to that which in the New Testament we render by *faith*, and by the corresponding verb, *to believe*. And this explains how it comes to pass that in our Version of the Old Testament we so seldom find mention of Faith. The idea is there, and of perpetual occurrence, though not spoken of under the form of a general abstract proposition. Nor could it well be wanting in a book treating of the relations between man and God; Faith being the only faculty whereby man is conscious of such a relation. The word, however, by which that idea is exprest in the Old Testament, is rendered in our Version by *trust*. I should have to repeat a large part of the book of Psalms, were I to cite all the passages in which we are exhorted to trust in God. *The Lord redeemeth the soul of His servants; and none of them that trust in Him shall be desolate* (xxxiv. 22). *Trust in the Lord, and do good: so shalt thou dwell in the land* (xxxvii. 3). *Commit thy way to the Lord; trust in Him; and He will bring it to pass* (5). *The Lord will save them; because they trust in Him* (40). It will hardly be questioned, that the state of feeling designated in these passages by the expression, *trusting in the Lord*, is very nearly akin to what under the New Dispensation bears the name of Faith. For trusting in God must needs imply a belief in Him: only this belief may be a more general one in His goodness and providential care; whereas the belief and the Faith of a Christian centre in the specific act of the redemption wrought for him by Christ. Hereby his belief becomes a more definite and prominent element in his Faith. Indeed it is a general characteristic of the scriptural view of man, that the intellectual part of his being is hardly ever regarded, according to the abstractions of human philosophy, as distinct and separate from his moral nature. Light in the Bible is life; and life is light. Knowledge there is indeed power: if true knowledge, it is power for good; if false, for evil: and one or the other it must be: for no act of a living responsible soul can be of a neutral, negative character: that which is not with God is against Him. This appears,—to refer to one proof among hundreds,—from the description of Wisdom, according to its twofold origin and nature, given in the Epistle of St. James; where the Wisdom which descends not from above, it is said to be *worldly, carnal, devilish;* while the true Wisdom, which is from above, is set forth in its heavenly beauty, as *pure, peaceful, gentle, easy to be entreated, full of mercy and of good fruits, without partiality, and without hypocrisy;* every quality ascribed to each being wholly of a moral and practical character.

Here perhaps it may not be altogether idle to remark,—at least it will not seem so to such as have reflected on the strange and almost capricious dominion which words have so often exercised over the thoughts and actions of mankind,—that the poverty and want of formative power in our language, in which there is no verb obviously belonging to the same family with *faith,* by leading us to have recourse to the verb *believe,* which in its ordinary acceptation expresses an act almost purely intellectual, has helpt to foster the erroneous notion, that in Faith also the intellectual act is all in all. The verb, *believe,* being far more widely spread and connected in our language, has drawn away the noun, *faith,* from its more appropriate meaning; instead of adopting that meaning, as it ought to have done. So likewise in the Latin verb, *credo*, which tended much in Christian writers to determine the signification of *fides*, the notion of the intellectual act is more prominent than in the Greek πιστεύω, the moral element in *fides* being exprest in its derivative *confido*.

Hence it was with the fullest right that Luther and Melanchthon, when the true idea of Faith and of its power was reasserted at the Reformation, were anxious to urge again and again that *faith is trust*, that *faith signifies trust : fides est fiducia ; fides significat fiduciam*. This was only to assert, that the faith required in the New Testament is a feeling of the same kind with the trust enjoined in the Old Testament; as is proved,—to take a single instance,—by the passage in the Gospels, where the disciples are frightened by the tempest, while their Master is asleep in the ship, and where, on being awakened by them in their terrour, He rebukes them for their want of Faith (Matth. viii. 26) ; that is, for their want of trust, for their want of confidence in Him. To the same purpose it is well observed by Calvin, that, " if theologians would attend to that passage in the Epistle to the Romans (x. 10), *For with the heart man believeth unto righteousness*, they would give over talking about their frigid fiction of a *fides formata :* for that, if this passage were our only argument, it should suffice to finish the dispute, proving that the assent of Faith is of the Heart, more than of the Head, and rather of the Affections than of the Understanding." Accordingly, in the *Apology for the Confession of Augsburg*, it is laid down with perfect truth, that "Faith is not merely a perception of the Understanding, but a confidence in the Will, that is, the willing and receiving what is offered to us in God's promise." And this agrees with the definition of Faith given by many of our own most eminent divines; in proof of which I will only refer you to Bishop Taylor's *Discourse on Faith*, where he says in so many words, that the "Faith of a Christian has more in it of the Will than of the Understanding."

To establish and illustrate this truth,—to set forth the kingdom and the power and the glory of Faith, so far as the Spirit of God shall enable me to look into its mysteries,—and to shew how Faith, under one relation or other, has always been the main agent in whatsoever man has accomplisht toward overcoming the world,—will be the aim of the following Sermons. At first thought indeed one might be inclined to suppose, that this elementary principle, lying at the root of all Christian life, no less than of all Christian doctrine, must needs have been fully elucidated long ago. Nevertheless I have deemed that, even in this place, it might not be inexpedient for him who is appointed to preach before you, to bring forth old things as well as new out of his treasure. Nay, this may be the more expedient from the manifold temptations which here withdraw us from common subjects to matters of abstruser speculation or more learned research. Moreover there are peculiar circumstances in the present condition of our Church, rendering it desirable that men should be reminded of the great truths concerning Faith, which were proclaimed in the age of the Reformation. Vital and fundamental as the question touching the true nature of Faith is, there are few questions on which greater and more mischievous errours have prevailed. From the Epistle of St. James we perceive that, even in those primitive days, a party had arisen within the Church, which had stript Faith of its living power, and held that a naked intellectual recognition of the truths delivered in the Gospel was the only thing requisite to salvation. When heresies sprang up, and it became necessary to define the doctrines of the Church by the promulgation of Creeds, as the reception of those Creeds was deemed indispensable to true Christian Faith, that reception, the belief in the doctrines thus ascertained and defined, was held to constitute this Faith, and was identified, or rather confounded therewith. This notion was further promoted by the objective use of the word *Faith*, to signify the sum of those doctrines which are the object of belief, as well as the act whereby the mind and heart receive them, Thus, Faith being narrowed to the intellectual operation, and thereby deprived of its moral power, the provinces of Faith and of practical life grew to be regarded as totally distinct; and good works, being disjoined from Faith, were held to require some other source, in Hope and Love; which yet themselves can only rise out of Faith. For how can we love, or how can we hope, unless we have already believed in Him, whom we love and hope in? The inevitable result of this severance was, that a dead Faith on the one hand was responded to on the other hand by dead works; inasmuch as neither can live, except in union with the other: cut them asunder, and they both die. Such was the dismal condition of the Church in what are called the middle ages; until Luther, arising with the spirit and power of Elias, lifted up his voice in the wilderness, which in those days was spread over Christendom, and preacht the doctrine of Justification by Faith alone. On this doctrine he rested wholly and solely, esteeming all other things of less account in comparison of Faith in Christ, and confident that all the graces of the Kingdom of heaven would spring up in those who have that Faith graven on the living tablets of their hearts. From this doctrine he derived his strength: and then again it was seen that Faith is indeed the victory which overcomes the world. The bonds and shackles of dead ordinances fell off from those who were baptized with this purificatory fire. But the progress of knowledge and civilization produced its usual effect. The pride of knowledge bred the lust of knowledge; and the lust of knowledge pampered the pride of knowledge: and again it became a very general opinion that the belief of the Understanding is one and the same thing with Christian Faith; and that this belief is to be grounded on testimony. Hence we were inundated with dissertations on the external evidences of Christianity; in which it was treated like any other historical fact, and witnesses were sifted and cross-examined; but without regard to the main witness, the witness in the heart of the believer himself, in his infirmities, his wants, his cravings,—the witness along with which the Spirit bears witness in groanings that cannot be uttered. This, the only witness on which a living Faith in Christ can be establisht, was left out of sight: and so it is little to be wondered at if the Gospel half melted away into a system of philanthropical morality. From another and a very different quarter also have erroneous notions concerning the nature of Faith been recently propagated with much ability and earnestness by one of whom no reverer of piety and holiness should speak without respect. The main force of the vehement attack which has lately been made on the great Protestant and apostolical doctrine of Justification by Faith,* seems to lie in a total misconception of the nature and power of Faith. Against this misconception, whenever and in whatsoever form it shews itself, it behoves us to keep diligent guard. It behoves us to write the declaration of St. Paul on the front of our Church, that *a man is justified by Faith, without the deeds of the Law.* It should be our inwrought conviction, that, as Luther says in the Articles of Schmalcald, after quoting these words of St. Paul, "From this article no true Christian ought to depart, or to make any concession or admission contrary thereto, although heaven and earth and all things be confounded."

* [The attack referred is that in the *Lectures on Justification*, published in 1838 by the Rev. J. H. Newman.—ED.]

Now to Him who in His infinite grace vouchsafes to justify mankind by Faith, without the deeds of the Law, whereby no man living could be justified,—to Him who justifies us by clothing us with the righteousness of His only-begotten Son, and who by the indwelling of His Spirit sanctifies those whom He has justified,—in the glory of the eternal Trinity, be all praise and thanksgiving and adoration for ever.

SERMON II.

FAITH, A PRACTICAL PRINCIPLE.

1 John v. 4.

"This is the victory that overcometh the world, even our Faith."

In my last sermon I endeavoured to shew that the Faith, which is here said to have the power of overcoming the world, and of which such great and wonderful things are declared in other passages of the New Testament, by St. Paul and by our Saviour himself, must be something very different from that mere intellectual assent to the truths of revelation, with which it has often been identified. One main, and, as appears to me, decisive proof that it must be so, is the powerlessness of the Understanding to produce any lasting renovating effect on the heart and soul of man. And are we not led to the same conclusion by those blessed words, so full of grace and love, in which our Lord gives thanks to His Heavenly Father, *because He has hidden His salvation from the wise and prudent, and has revealed it to babes?* Had the decision of the Understanding, the balancing of evidence, the cross-examination of witnesses, been the grounds on which

Faith is to be founded,—had the work of Faith been wholly a work of the Intellect,—were there not a moral blindness, which will often disable the keenest Intellect for discerning the true meaning and spirit of what it sees, and a moral openness of heart by which the simple are fitted for seeing things as they really are,— the wise and prudent, as they are the best judges in matters of earthly science, would also be the best judges in heavenly science. As they alone rightly conceive the true system of the universe, while the unlearned continue all their lives deceived by the phantoms of the Senses, in like manner should we have found a readier and fuller apprehension of the divine nature and atonement of Christ in the philosopher than in the peasant. Whereas the fact is very often exactly the reverse. The philosopher, beguiled by the phantoms of his Understanding, finds it difficult, if not impossible, to raise his spirit beyond the moral teacher, the man Jesus; while the poor and humble acknowledge and adore Him as their ever-present Saviour and God. One can hardly talk with the poor on any spiritual subject, without being sensible of this difference. They receive the truths of the Gospel, as young children receive what is said to them, not with their Understandings merely, but into their Hearts. The same thing is implied in our Lord's words to Thomas. Had the conviction of the Understanding been the one thing needful in Faith, the stronger and more immediate the evidence, the more valuable would the conviction have been. But inasmuch as it is the moral readiness to receive and embrace truth that renders Faith acceptable in the eyes of God, therefore did our Lord pronounce that those who believe without seeing are blessed, above those who will not believe until they see. Were not this so, what would be the meaning of St. Paul's declaration (1 Cor. i. 17), that he had been sent to preach the Gospel *not with wisdom of words, lest the cross of Christ should be of no effect?* Had the purpose for which he was to preach the Gospel been chiefly to convince the Understanding, the wisdom of words would have been the very means the best fitted for accomplishing it. Seeing, however, that the main seat of Faith is not in the Understanding, but in the Will and the Affections,—seeing that, according to the words already quoted, it is *with the Heart that man believeth unto righteousness,*—seeing that God, when He demands our Faith, calls upon us to give Him our Hearts,—therefore, as we often find that men of a subtile nature are feeble in their Affections, and ill-fitted for action,—as the earthly lights with which they surround themselves are apt to dazzle their eyes, and to keep them from looking out and beholding the light in the heavens,—St. Paul here warns us of a truth, which it is of great importance that, in this place more especially, we should be strongly imprest with, namely, that the wisdom of words may too easily hinder our Faith, that it may involve us in a glittering mist, which will prevent our discerning the Cross in its pure and heavenly glory. Thus it came to pass that the Cross of Christ was not only a stumblingblock to the

Jews, who were deluded by the phantoms of their Senses and of their carnal Affections, but also to the Greeks, who were equally under a delusion from the phantoms of their carnal Understanding.

Every one's recollection may supply him with other passages of a like purport. To refer to a different class, by which the same truth is establisht,—when our Saviour commends the Faith of the centurion at Capernaum, and that of the Syrophenician woman,—when He rewards that of the woman with the issue of blood, and that of the persons who let down the sick of the palsy from the roof into the court before Him,—surely it was not on account of the intellectual conviction apparent in those acts of Faith that He spoke of them so graciously. Rather was it on account of the power which the intellectual conviction exercised in each of these cases to produce conformable acts,—on account of the earnestness and energy with which these persons laid hold on the truth they had discerned,—on account of their confidence, their trust, their boldness, in striving, undeterred by doubts or fears, by hindrances or obstacles, to gain and appropriate the blessing, of which they had seen the prospect. In all these instances it is plain that the Faith, which finds favour with our Lord, answers much more nearly to trust or confidence, than to what we usually mean by *belief:* and that this is its true character, we have seen, is establisht by the usual meaning of the original Greek word, as well as by the corresponding term in the Old Testament. So that Luther and the other Reformers were fully warranted, when, in consequence of the ambiguity attached to the word *fides*, and of the errour which that ambiguity had helpt to propagate, they were not only careful to lay down that it meant and was equivalent to *fiducia*, but often in their ordinary language substituted *fiducia* in its stead. This too, it is needful we should keep in mind, is still the point of main importance,—not the intellectual assent to the truths of the Gospel, but the practical hearty apprehension of them, manifesting itself at once the constitutive and the regulative principle of our lives;—the going humbly to the Saviour, whom we have been taught to acknowledge, and beseeching Him that, unworthy as we are that He should enter into us, until we have been purified and sanctified by His Spirit, He would yet speak the word and heal us;—the being instant in entreating that He would at least feed us with the crumbs which fall from His table;—the pressing forward, in spite of everything that would check or hinder us, if so be we may touch the hem of His garment;—or, should our hearts be too palsied to take any step towards Him of our own accord, the beseeching of our faithful friends to carry us into His presence, that He may perchance be moved by their Faith to bid us arise and walk.

Hence we see that nothing can well be more fallacious than the notion that Faith is not a practical principle. So palpable indeed does the erroneousness of that notion appear to me, that I should scarcely deem it requisite to argue the point, unless that erroneous doctrine had been so broadly asserted in the recent *Lectures on Justification*,* to which I have already referred. When we call to mind how our Lord Himself tells us of Faith, that it can *move mountains*, and that *nothing shall be impossible to it*,—when we bethink ourselves of St. John's declaration, that it is *the victory which overcometh the world*,—when we cast our eyes over the long list of heroic exploits, which in the Epistle to the Hebrews are said to have been wrought by Faith,—it would seem almost inconceivable how so learned and thoughtful and pious a writer could deny the practical power of Faith; unless one knew, from the experience of one's own heart, as well as from observation of others, how easily we are beguiled into straining and warping the strongest evidence and testimony, for the sake of upholding a favourite preconceived opinion. Were Faith nothing more than the assent of the Understanding, then indeed we should be forced to grant that it is not a practical principle. But this consequence of itself is enough to prove how totally inadequate that definition of Faith must be. In truth, if we look thoughtfully through the history of the Church, or even of the world, we shall find that this, under one shape or other, has ever been the main principle and spring of all great and magnanimous action, even Faith. The persons in whose character Love has been the predominant feature, have not seldom been disposed to rest in heavenly meditations and contemplations. Unless too

* [By the Rev. J. H. Newman. See note, p. 30.—Ed.]

it be corrected and nerved by Faith, Love shrinks from giving pain, and giving offence. But the great stirring motive spirits in the history of the world, *the angels who have excelled in strength, and who have done God's commandments, hearkening to the voice of His word*, have been those who by way of eminence may be called the heroes of Faith, those who by Faith have dwelt in the immediate presence of God; in proof whereof I will only remind you here of those two great captains in God's noble army, Paul and Luther. Nor is it difficult to perceive why this is and must be so. For Faith, and Faith alone, gives us the very thing which Archimedes wanted, the standing-place out of the world, and above the world, whence the world is to be moved. He who lives in a spiritual world, will desire, in proportion to the vividness and fulness of his life, to realize that spiritual world in the world of forms and shadows which he sees around him. He will desire to impress others with the truths, by which he himself is strongly possest,—to rescue them from the debasement, from which he himself has been delivered, —to make them partakers in the priceless blessings, which he himself is enjoying. His faith will inspire him with courage, and will gain him fresh supplies of strength from above: and it will carry him fearless through all dangers, while he says to his heart in the sublime words of the Psalmist: *God is our Refuge and Strength, a very present Help in trouble. Therefore will we not fear, though the earth be removed, and though the mountains be carried into the midst of the sea; though the waters thereof roar and be troubled, though the mountains shake with the swelling thereof. There is a river, the streams whereof shall make glad the city of God. God is in the midst of her: she shall not be moved. God will help her, and that right early.* Thus, by giving a substantial reality to that which is invisible, to that which is no object of the Senses, or of the natural Understanding, and by animating the Heart with an unshakable assurance of that for which it looks in hope, Faith performs the task assigned to her of overcoming the world.

It has often been urged indeed, even by persons of great learning and authority, that the wellknown passage in the Epistle of St. James is a proof that Faith, in the Bible, means nothing more than mere belief, which of itself and by itself is quite powerless. That passage is the main, and almost the sole, Scriptural prop of the opinion I have been contending against: and some writers have even maintained that St. James expressly designed to limit and qualify the expressions used by St. Paul. Nay, it has been assumed that there is an opposition and repugnance between the two statements concerning the conditions of Justification: and one school of theologians has sided with the one Apostle, one with the other, according to their several predilections. Grievous would it be to believe that Christ was thus divided, and that His Apostles themselves should have set the example of rending His vesture in sunder. But it has been shewn, I think, satisfactorily, by the excellent historian of the Apostolical Church,* that the appearances, on the strength of which it has been held that the Bishop of Jerusalem where he treats of the relation between Faith and Works, must be speaking with reference to the Apostle of the Gentiles, or at least to some perversion of his doctrine, are fallacious, and that he was merely reproving certain mischievous errours with regard to Faith, which were then prevalent among the Jewish Christians. As their fathers under the Law had been so apt to assume that outward rites and observances, and an outward acknowledgement of the Law were sufficient to justify them,—nay, that the mere fact of their being the children of Abraham entitled them to the blessings of the promise,—and as they themselves, even under the law of the Spirit, clung pertinaciously to the same delusion, which all St. Paul's energy and wisdom could scarcely dispell,—they had the strongest national predisposition, superadded to the natural one which lies in every carnal heart, to turn the living act of Faith into a dead act of belief, and to assume that, if with their lips they confest Jesus to be the Christ, they might claim a share in His salvation. Hence St. James, writing to persons by whom Faith was regarded as nothing more than an intellectual belief, and who in their practice debased it still further into the mere outward profession of such a belief, deeming, or rather cheating their consciences with the fancy, that such a profession would gain them an entrance into the kingdom of heaven,—his aim and purpose, like that of his

* [Neander, *Pflanzung und Leitung*, p. 564.—ED.]

brethren, being, not to define terms philosophically, or to lay open the secrets of man's internal structure, but to enforce practical truth,—has in some measure adopted the usage of the persons he was addressing. This accords with the constant habit of the Sacred Writers. Their commission being to declare great moral and spiritual truths in the forms of thought and language already current among their hearers; even though their expressions might now and then be at variance with the subsequent more accurate discoveries of Science. Nor is it easy to see how they could have done otherwise. For, as has been well observed, even if God had granted them an insight into the whole framework and order of the creation, they would either have had to speak unintelligibly, when their language was repugnant to the notions then received; or it would have been necessary to charge them with a special revelation of those physical and metaphysical truths, which were lying coiled up in the heart of the universe, and which man was only to draw forth by a slow, gradual process of evolution. Such being the ordinary practice of the Sacred Writers, and the two conceptions, of a moral faith and an intellectual belief, being so apt to slide into one another, as the whole history of the Church has proved,—whence the same term has been habitually employed to designate the latter conception as well as the former,—St. James in one instance uses the verb *believe,* applying it to the spirits of evil, where it means little more than an intellectual conviction, or at least a conviction which does not exercise any controlling influence upon the Will. Yet even in this passage Faith is not represented as continuing in mere notional unreality. It does not lie like .... I know not by what image to express the inanimateness of a bare intellectual belief: for in the outward world there is nothing, not a dead leaf, not a straw, not even a grain of dust, which is not connected with the rest of the universe by manifold bonds of mutual action : there is nothing in the outward world so torpid, so insulated, as a conviction of the Understanding lying amid the lumber of a paralysed Intellect. Even when speaking of the devils, the Apostle does not say that they *believe* and remain unmoved, but that they *believe and tremble*. So that this passage itself does not altogether bear out the notion of an inanimate Faith ; while it utters an awful warning to those who allow their Faith to linger in shadowy spectral lifelessness, it warns them that their Faith also will hereafter be quickened : but the effect of this quickening will not be joy and peace and hope in believing: that Faith, which is not clothed with the righteousness of the Son of God, will start up in the likeness of the devil's faith, and tremble.

Even apart however from this thought, it is surely contrary to sound principles of interpretation, to make the meaning of the word *believe* in a passage, where it is applied to spirits of whose nature and essence and relations we know next to nothing, the canon for determining the meaning of Faith in that multitude of passages where it is applied to man, and where this peculiar meaning is inconsistent with the context, and can only be foisted in by assuming that the word *faith*, in the common language of the New Testament, is not used appropriately, but stands for a complex act, of which it is merely one, and not the most important element. Not that anything would be gained for the argument by such an assumption; the question being, not whether the word *faith* is used appropriately or inappropriately by St. Paul and in the Gospels, but what is the idea there exprest by that word, and to which such great moment is ascribed. Surely too we are not to measure the things which we know, by the things which we know not; but contrariwise to guess at the things which we know not, from the things which we know. The ladder of our human discourse and reasoning must rest on the earth: we cannot hook it into the sky. Even in speaking of Himself, God has clothed Himself in the attributes of humanity: nor can we conceive what those attributes mean in their heavenly exaltation, except by considering in the first instance what they mean in their earthly debasement.

Besides, even though we were to confine our enquiry to the Epistle of St. James, in endeavouring to ascertain the apostolical idea of Faith, that Epistle in itself contains ample evidence that Christian Faith is something far higher, something that lies far deeper, than any mere act of the Understanding. For what is the point on which the Apostle mainly insists? That Faith without works is dead. Faith without works is a dead Faith, not a living,—a nominal Faith, not a real,—the shadow of Faith, not the substance. And why is this? except because Faith, if it be living, if it be real, if it be substantial, is a practical principle, a practical power; nay, of all principles, of all powers, by which man can be actuated, the most practical: so that, when it does not shew forth its life by good works, we may reasonably conclude that it is dead; just as we infer that a body is dead, when it has ceased to move; or that a tree is dead, when it puts forth no leaves. Not that the works constitute the life of Faith, or contribute in the slightest degree to impart life to it; any more than motion constitutes or imparts the life of the body, or than leaves constitute or impart the life of the tree. On the contrary it is from the living principle of Faith that the works must receive their life; without which they would be utterly dead, and mere dross and scum and rubbish; nay, unless they spring from Faith, instead of fostering, they overlay and stifle it. But they are its indispensable tokens, its never-failing fruits, whereby alone its reality can be ascertained. They are no less necessary to its health, growth, and vigour, than motion to that of the body: and like leaves they feed and strengthen the life they spring from. The comparison, with which the Apostle winds up his discourse upon Faith,—*As the body without the spirit is dead, so faith without works is dead also,* —might indeed occasion some perplexity; unless we bear in mind that he is reproving the notion that the nominal profession of faith in Christ is sufficient to absolve the professor from every moral or obligation. When contrasted with hollow words, even outward actions have something like life in them. But it would be straining this illustration unwarrantably to infer from it that the Apostle meant to lay down, that the relation which Faith bears to works, is like that of the body to the spirit. Few sources of errour have been more copious, above all in the interpretation of the Scriptures, than the propensity to realize images, —which in fact is a main element in all idolatry,— and to deduce general propositions from incidental and partial illustrations. The whole tenour of the New Testament establishes, that Faith is the invisible living spirit, which pours its life through the body of works, manifesting itself therein, and striving to bring mankind to the obedience of Faith, to the end that they may be clothed everlastingly with the righteousness of Faith.

From what has been said, it will easily be seen how important and precious was the truth reasserted at the Reformation, that the main seat of Faith is not in the Understanding, but in the Will. Not that Faith is a mongrel principle, neither one thing nor the other, but a medley of the two. Were it so, it could never have the living vivifying power ascribed to it. Every genuine act of Faith is the act of the whole man, not of his Understanding alone, not of his Affections alone, not of his Will alone, but of all three in their central aboriginal unity. It proceeds from the inmost depths of the soul, from beyond that firmament of Consciousness, whereby the waters under the firmament are divided from the waters above the firmament It is the act of that living principle, which constitutes each man's individual, continuous, immortal personality. Here, as in so many other cases, much confusion has arisen from the necessities of the Understanding to distinguish, in order that it may apprehend, what it would else be unable to comprehend. To facilitate the conception of the manifold intellectual and moral workings of our souls, we ascribe them to distinct powers or faculties : and then, beguiled by our own craft, we take our ciphers for realities, and are apt to fancy that these powers or faculties are things essentially and substantially different, bundled and fagoted together for the occasion in the complex unit, man. Whereas they ought rather to be regarded as different manifestations of the same indivisible spirit, acting diversely accordingly to its various purposes and relations,—as different diverging rays of the same central star. It is true, this original unity of our nature seldom shews itself in our present fallen state. The primary stem having been cut down, the root merely sends up a number of lesser stems ; and instead of lofty forests mounting heavenward, we see little among mankind but thickets of underwood that just rise above the ground. Indeed this our divided condition is the main cause of our weakness. While our Conscience, our Understanding, our Affections, and our carnal Appetites are dragging us in opposite directions, the Will is torn and mangled, and almost dismembered: and from this misery nothing can save us, except the atoning power of Faith.

Bearing this in mind, we perceive how every act of Faith, as the act of a man's whole personality, will be single; and that there is no confusion of thought, no mixing up of incongruous elements, in saying that it is not the act of the Understanding alone, but of the Understanding, and still more emphatically and essentially of the Will. If it were the act of the Understanding alone, it would be the act of a fraction of man's being. Only as the act of the Will, mainly and primarily, is it the act of the whole man. Hereby alone is it an act for which we can feel and acknowledge ourselves accountable. Hereby alone does it become an act of such a kind, that we can conceive how by its exercise, when applied to its right Object, and thus endowed with a higher life and a supernatural power, the great and deadly wound in our nature should be healed,—how by it we should be enabled to cross the chasm which since the Fall has severed us from God. Nor will any one who is at all in the habit of reflecting on his own inward workings, —of considering what he does when he thinks, or when he gives the rein to any of his affections, or when he wills to realize any of his thoughts or feelings in action,—no one who is at all accustomed to observe himself in the mirror of his own consciousness, will scruple to allow that an act may be simple and single, although it require the coincident activity of several of what we are wont to regard as distinct powers. The same thing happens, for instance, in almost every act of thought. Almost every such act will involve processes of perception, of apprehensive imagination, of abstraction and generalization, of memory, of reasoning, too rapid, it may be, and evanescent to excite observation, but still indispensable preliminaries to the completion of the particular thought. In like manner every utterance of feeling toward an outward object must needs imply sundry processes of the perceptive and reflective powers. Nor can there be any action of the Will, except where the object it acts upon has been presented to it through the medium of the Intellect, and has at least awakened a ripple on the slumbering surface of the Heart. So that there is nothing beyond the specious shadow of an argument in the objection which has been urged against the account of Faith given by the Reformers, on the ground that its seat cannot be at once in the Understanding and in the Will. For how can the Will of an intellectual being ever act, except in some kind of consort, more or less, with his Understanding? How, as was just now observed, can it act outwardly, on outward objects, except where some notice of the objects has been conveyed to it by those faculties, which are the medium of its intercourse with the outward world? How can we believe, except in Him of whom we have heard, of whom we have been informed, in whom we have seen some grounds, more or less convincing, for believing?

We must hear of Christ with our outward ears, before the sound of His voice can reach our hearts. Thus *Faith*, as the Apostle says, *comes by hearing*. In a certain sense the outward act must be prior in order of time to the inward. In like manner, if we advance a step further, a certain kind of intellectual perception and recognition of Christ and of His work must be prior in order of time to the moral and spiritual apprehension of it by the Heart and the Will. Hence, as we are ever apt to confound antecedence in order of time with antecedence in order of causation, transferring the relations of one category to the other, it is often assumed, especially by those who are more conversant with intellectual speculations, than with the practical life and workings of Faith, that the intellectual act is the cause which produces the moral, that, as being the cause, it is of higher dignity and importance than the effect, and accordingly that it is the main point toward which our attention is to be directed.

In truth this itself was the bent and sway and warp, which our nature received at the Fall, that we were driven aslant from all spiritual things, and grew in everything to lean toward the material, the carnal, the objects of sense. Our thoughts are ever dwelling on outward things, and are mostly content to serve as clerks in the countinghouse of the Senses: and only with labour and difficulty, and after a long discipline and training, can we fix them steadily on the world within us. Our Affections have become the minions of our Appetites, cleave to the dust, nay, will feast and fatten themselves by feeding on the dead body of Sin. Even our Philosophy, with all its vaunted superiority to sense and to outward things, has often wasted its powers on the humiliating attempt to make out that the spiritual world is no better than an essence or elixir drained off from the material, that thoughts are merely the shadows and ghosts of sensations. While our bodily eyes are incessantly exercised, from morning till night, from the earliest dawn of childhood till everything becomes faint and dim beneath the dusk of old age, in looking curiously and anxiously about and around us, the inward eyes of Consciousness and Conscience require to be purged and unscaled before they will even open,—yea, to be " purged and unscaled at the fountain of heavenly radiance," before they can discern the true form and colour and value of spiritual objects. Hence Philosophy has ever been apt to forget the perceptive powers in the objects perceived; more especially in the later ages of intellectual culture, when those objects are so multiplied by the growth of luxury, the widening of experience, and the progress of science, as to overlay every other consideration. And even when it turns its attention to examine the perceptive powers themselves, it scarcely looks beyond the secondary, derivative, and subordinate ones, and paddles about in the waters which lie on this side of the firmament of Consciousness, without thinking of soaring into the waters above it. In this manner it has come to pass with regard to Faith also, that the outward act of intellectual belief,—outward with reference to that moral Will, which is the central principle of our being—has grown to be regarded as the main and most important part of Faith, nay, to be talkt of as the one sole principle, which, strongly as all experience and observation repell such an assertion, forms the groundwork of the Christian life.

Yet, even as to priority in point of time, if we look closely into the question, we shall see that the primary germinal act must be that of the Will, not of the Understanding. There must be some motion of the Will, however slight, which in the first instance directs the application of the Understanding to an object, before that object can be introduced through the Understanding to act upon the Will. The flower must open by an act of its own, before the sunbeams can enter into it: and though it opens under the warmth of those very rays, which, before they gain an entrance, lie fosteringly around it, still, unless there were a living principle in the plant, the warmth of the sun would no more unfold the blossoms, than it can open an artificial bud, or a painted one. So again every fresh operation of the Understanding requires a fresh exercise of the Will, determining, directing, prolonging, or diverting its attention: and the more definite and comprehensive the object, the greater effort of the Will is requisite to embrace it. Hereby we may be assisted in some degree to conceive how the influences of the Spirit should be of such momentous power in the work of our Faith,—in producing it from the very first, and afterward in nourishing and maturing it. Were Faith merely an act of the Understanding, it would lie without that region which is the peculiar sphere of the Spirit. At least His ordinary influences, those which are promist to every believer, and in which whosoever is baptized into the name of Christ has a share, do not seem to extend to the illumination of the Understanding; except so far as the Understanding is necessarily elevated and enlightened by the purification of the Heart, and the sanctification of the Will, by a singleness of view in pursuit of truth, an inward harmony with it, and an unhesitating readiness to adopt it. So far however as Faith is a spiritual act, so far as it is the act of the Will, which Christ came to redeem from the bondage of the flesh, we may feel assured that, in every act of spiritual Faith, in every act by which we evince a desire to become partakers in Christ's redeeming grace, to shake off the yoke of corruption, and to strive after the glorious liberty of the children of God,—in every such act, we may feel assured, the Spirit of God will be working along with our spirits.

Moreover a right insight into the nature of Faith, as depending far more on the Will than on the Understanding, will teach us the groundlessness and fallaciousness of a proposition, which has often been promulgated with great pretensions to philosophical candour and freedom of thought, that no man is accountable for his belief; for that it does not depend upon himself, but wholly on the evidence by which he has been led to form and entertain it. Sad would it be to think, that Truth is thus to vary with the accidents of condition and circumstance, nay, of chance and caprice in the mind of the receiver; sad would it be to think that there is no better and surer answer than this, which man is bound to render to Pilate's question; sad, that each man should return a different answer, and that there should be no criteria for deciding amongst them; sad, that the crowning result of all knowledge should be to run races blindfold in Chaos. But a very slight attention to the processes of our own minds, to the growth of our own opinions,—nay, even to the manner in which we arrive at our conclusions with regard to any one particular point, though no more than a mere question of fact,—might convince us that there is hardly anything wherein our volition exercises so decisive an influence, as in this very matter of the formation of our opinion and belief. Or we need only look at any controversy in which men's feelings, as political partisans, are engaged, to see how persons equally discreet and sagacious, and fancying themselves equally impartial, will habitually frame totally opposite judgments. For in every practical question the Will gives the mind its bias; and the Will is the archsophist, and is ever attended by a swarm of lesser sophists in its train. It in great measure determines the degree of attention which we bestow on the several parts of contradictory evidence, the weight which we attach to them. We dwell almost unconsciously on that which favours and flatters our prepossessions; we welcome such arguments like old friends, and entertain them with open-hearted hospitality; while it requires no little effort and struggle not to turn away and close our doors against that which thwarts or contradicts us. Hence even for our intellectual judgments we may justly be held responsible; the more so the more intimately those judgments are connected with our practical lives. What then? Is this warping bent, this squint of our Understandings, to be corrected and to pass away all at once, the moment we begin to employ them in the examination of religious doctrines? Are there no prepossessions in the heart, to rise up against these truths, and to draw us away from them? Do not our sins shrink from them? do not our passions scoff at them? Has the intellect forgotten its craft, and cast away its snares? has it escaped from the entanglement of its own sophistries? Is it set free from the slough, which confined it to crawl along the earth? Is the mystery of the Cross no longer a stumbling-block to the Jew, no longer foolishness to the Greek? Yet, shallow and baseless as this notion is, I doubt not there are many in these days, who buoy themselves up in their carelessness about their own Faith, and about the Faith of their brethren, by crying out that no man can be held accountable for his Faith; for that we believe what we believe, through the compulsion which the evidence set before us exercises on our Understanding, according to laws beyond our controll; that we can neither alter the character of the evidence, nor its power over our minds; and consequently that, if we go wrong, we cannot help it. Such a doctrine, even with regard to mere intellectual belief, implies the barest rankest necessarianism: and when applied to Faith, in its higher, more spiritual sense, it is utterly untenable, except in connexion with a scheme of opinions which undermines all morality, and would blot out the eternal distinction between right and wrong. It is a duty of charity indeed to refrain from pronouncing harsh judgement on the Faith of our neighbours; seeing that we cannot look into their hearts, and ascertain how far they may be truly accountable for it; we cannot know the manifold hindrances outward and inward they may have had to contend against; nor can we tell whether there may not be a living root of Faith striking deep underground, even where as yet there is little show of life aboveground. Therefore it is reasonable and just that we should refrain from condemning others for errours in Faith; provided that this toleration do not slacken our efforts to deliver them from their errours, lest perchance they should be accountable for them; as, if we do not endeavour to check them, we ourselves at least shall be. But into our own hearts we can look, —not indeed through and through them,—not so as to unravel all the network of falsehood and selfdeceit in which they are entangled,—not so as to pierce into all the hollow caverns of vanity and pride, into which our Consciences will skulk: to see all this we need to have our eyes purged and strengthened by the Spirit of God. So far however we can look into ourselves, as to discern much, very much that is wrong, much that is frail, much that is bloated, much emptiness, much self-indulgence, much sloth: and on this point I dare appeal to you all, confident that there is no one among you who will presume to assert, that he has done all he might have done, all he ought to have done,— might I not say, who has done a thousandth part of what he might and ought to have done?—in order to attain to a right faith in the Gospel. What may be the case with others, we know not : but with regard to ourselves, every one of us must confess, *Verily on this point I am guilty: verily I am accountable for my Faith, for its wants, for its weakness, for its errours.*

I have dwelt much longer than I had intended on this fundamental question of the practical nature of Faith; because the more one examines it, the more momentous its importance is discovered to be; and at every step some new mischievous fallacy or delusion starts up, springing out of errours with regard to it. We saw, from a brief glance at the history of the Church, how a lifeless conception of Faith led to torpour in the Church, and how the revival of the true idea of Faith was the forerunner and a main agent in its regeneration. The men of God in those days knew what Faith was. They lookt into their hearts, and found it there. They knew its lifegiving sustaining power. They knew how, when it walks abroad over the earth, it goes on conquering, and still to conquer. But when the struggle was over, when the victory was gained, doctrines after a time again became a matter of mere speculation: yea, even Christianity itself was often regarded and discust as a matter of mere speculation; as though the eternal Son of God had come down from heaven for no worthier purpose than that men should sharpen their wits by disputing about Him. In this manner it again grew to be held that Faith is little more than the assent of the Understanding to the truths proposed to it. And still, even in these days, two opposite errours with regard to the nature of Faith are widely spread, by both of which the souls of men are equally drawn away from the hallowing power of the Gospel. One of these is the Antinomian errour; which has ever gained ground in ages when men have been awakened to feel the living power of Faith, and to hunger after the righteousness of Faith. At such times the Father of Lies will try to bewilder and blind men with extravagant fantastical notions about the omnipotence of bare Faith, and will beguile them into severing Faith from that holiness of conduct, which is its necessary offspring and effect, and which if it produce not, its portion must be in the world of barrenness and of abortions. Most false and pernicious is this errour, which, forgetting that Faith is the root of the Christian life, would invert the order of that life, making it strike root upward, and bear fruit downward. *Its vine is of the vine of Sodom, and of the fields of Gomorrah: their grapes are grapes of gall; their clusters are bitter; their wine is the poison of dragons, and the cruel venom of asps.* This however is an errour against which it would be needless to warn any in this congregation. For it is an errour from which in this place we are guarded by manifold fences of custom and opinion, and by the respect our situation and station enforce upon us for the decencies and proprieties of life. Whatever may be the snares or incitements by which men are here drawn into sin, no one assuredly will run into it in order that grace may abound.

But there is another errour with regard to Faith,— even the errour which I have been combating through the whole of this Sermon,—the notion that Faith is mere belief, that it is nothing more than an operation and act of the Understanding: and to this errour I know not whether in a place like this we are not more peculiarly exposed. Let me not be thought presumptuous, brethren, if I address this warning more especially to you. I speak as one who has spent a large portion of his life, more than twenty of its best years, among you; as one who knows and feels what great reason he has for thankfulness on account of the many precious blessings he was here allowed to enjoy, in the tranquil seclusion from the cares and turmoil of the world, from its emulation and contention, its wear and tear, its ceaseless chase after honour and gain,—in the rich opportunities and aids here afforded for study and meditation,—in the daily intercourse with dear and honoured friends, able and ever ready to help, to encourage, to guide, to strengthen, drawing us forward by their advice, and still more by the light of their examples. O yes, my brethren! many and precious are the blessings, which are poured on you in this ancient seat of learning. The vision of them has returned with unwonted power upon me, now that, after an absence of years, I am come back to my former much-loved home, enabled by comparison more fully to appreciate your peculiar privileges and advantages. Much cause too have you for thankfulness on account of the many temptations from which you are preserved. But there is no earthly lot, which has not its accompanying temptations, no earthly blessing, which may not prove a snare, if we allow it to occupy us too exclusively, and to draw off our affections and energies from other fields of duty. It is a great privilege and happiness, that you should be permitted, nay, that it should be your special business and charge, to live in a world of thought, to go forth through time and space, seeking out and holding daily converse with all that is most beautiful and excellent in the works of man and of God. Great however as is the delight of such studies and speculations,—and great it is, and pure and noble, when contrasted with most other objects of human endeavour,—the more easily for this very reason may they beguile us into forgetting that such studies and speculations are not the highest aim of man's being,—into forgetting that there can be anything in practical life comparable in dignity and worth to the crown which rewards such as are swift and strenuous in running the race of knowledge. It is well known to what extremes the licentiousness of speculation on religious questions has been carried in a neighbouring country, in places like this devoted to the pursuit of knowledge. Through God's blessing, which has connected our Universities so closely with our Church, we have been saved from such extravagances. Nevertheless speculation, except it be duly balanced and kept in check by practical exertion, tends to absorb all our activity and power, and to weaken our other faculties, which must needs rust and dwindle from inaction: and in this respect too, where our treasure is, will our heart be also. Now we have few direct personal calls here to the practical labours of Faith,—few at least which may not easily be evaded by such as are loth to be disturbed in their literary luxury. Thus we can hardly fail to attach an undue importance to whatever proceeds from or acts upon the Understanding, to the truths which it draws forth into the light of day, and to the processes whereby it elicits them. Here therefore above all do we need to be reminded, that the true wisdom of the wise is to lay their choicest offerings, their gold, their frankincense, and their myrrh, at the feet of the Saviour.

This is your duty also, my young friends. It is your duty now: it will continue to be so as long as you live. Be diligent in fulfilling it; and it will become your joy, and your exceeding great reward. To you the world of knowledge is opening: you are looking abroad on its many fair prospects: you are launching out on one of its wide streams, or treading one of its winding valleys. You are sent hither on purpose that you may explore them, and that you may bear away as much as you can of the riches with which they are fraught. Do so, with all earnestness, with all assiduity, with a confident thirst after truth, with a glowing imagination, and a sunny heart. Only, while you are exploring the beauties of the earth, let them not charm you into forgetfulness of the heaven that hangs over your heads, of the heaven which alone will enable you to see the beauties even of the earth. You have most of you brought hither a treasure of Faith, which you received from the lips of your mothers: for this, through God's gracious mercy, is still the blessed privilege of England, that among the first words, which her children are taught to utter, are the name of God and of His Son Jesus Christ. Prize and cherish this treasure bestowed on you by her whom you love best upon earth, as the most precious part of your inheritance. Let it not slip from your hearts: you will find great difficulty in replacing it. Be sure that nothing you can gather here will be comparable in value to that treasure, except what helps to increase it: and let this be your stedfast endeavour: let it be your daily aim to grow in Faith. You will be called, among other things, to examine the outward evidences by which the truth of the Gospel is establisht: for to you it especially belongs to give a reason for the Faith that is in you. But remember, my friends, that the being able to give a reason for your Faith is a totally different thing from having Faith; and that, unless the Faith be really in you, your being able to give a reason for it will only be a witness against you for having it not. Do not imagine that your knowledge will produce Faith: scarcely will knowledge strengthen it. Faith, as a practical power, can only be strengthened practically: and this of itself is a conclusive proof that Faith is mainly a practical power. A single act of Faith, a single prayer offered up from the bottom of the heart, a single exertion of self-denial, of self-controll, for Christ's sake, a single effort to walk in the footsteps of your Lord and Master, will do more to strengthen and establish your Faith, than all the learning of all the theologians. While Knowledge wanders to and fro on the face of the earth, and finds no rest for the sole of her foot, Faith will ever return to you with an olive-branch in her mouth: and you may regard this as an infallible sign that the waters of sin are abated: you may bless the herald that brings you a token of forgiveness from the Prince of Peace.

To you, and to all here present, may God in His infinite mercy grant, that we may strive day by day to grow in Faith, and that we may thereby attain to the righteousness of Christ, and receive the sanctification of the Spirit.

SERMON III.

OFFICE AND PROVINCE OF FAITH.

1 John v. 4.

"This is the victory that overcometh the world, even our Faith."

THE chief object of the former Sermons has been to establish, that Faith, in its scriptural sense, is not a bare intellectual assent to religious truth, but a practical lively apprehension of it, whereby that truth determines and shapes our conduct, and manifests itself therein; that this Faith is essentially a practical principle, a practical power; and that its seat, as was truly laid down by the Fathers of the Reformation, is not in the Understanding alone, but mainly in the Will,—or rather in that central primary principle of our personality, in which the Understanding, the Affections, and the Will coexist in their original unity. When we have attained to a full conviction on this point, so as to keep ever in mind that this is the true nature of Faith, most of the difficulties, which beset the common lifeless notion of it, pass away; a wide prospect opens before us, in which objects, hitherto wrapt in mist, come forth clearly and intelligibly; and we gain a cheering insight into the workings of Faith, and its power. Indeed this is the stirring gladdening reward, which ever waits upon the discovery of truth, that it not only solves the question directly at issue, but throws a bright harmonizing light over the whole region around. For light is by its very nature diffusive, impatient of all exclusiveness, of all bound and limit, of all check and restraint, and cannot fall on any one object, without spreading over those about it. They who seek in a right spirit, in a spirit of faith and diligence and self-devotion, will not merely find what they seek, but far more. They come ever and anon to one of those centres, whence the rays of truth branch off, and where what may otherwise seem a confused medley and knot of intricacies, settles at once into order and distinctness. If we adopt the common acceptation of Faith, as a mere work of the Understanding, we are entangled at every step in the most bewildering perplexities. At every step our hearts and our consciences lift up their voices in denial of what we are taught to receive as the word of God. We are told that Faith is to justify us; and we feel that such Faith does not justify us. We are told that it is to produce holiness of life; and we feel that it scarcely exercises the slightest influence on our conduct. We are told that it is to endow us with all power and might; and we feel that it leaves us just as feeble and helpless, just as much the slaves of passion, and the prey of temptation, as ever. We are told that it is the victory which overcomes the world; and we feel that this is the very triumph of the world, to overcome, not the blind, but the seeing; that the captives and victims on whom it prides itself the most, are those who have been taught, who know, whose understandings acknowledge, that the wages of sin is death, and shame, and abject endless misery,—those whose reason declares to them that no lasting peace or joy or comfort is to be found, except in the presence of God,—those who, being in torments, behold Lazarus afar off in Abraham's bosom, yet see at the same time that there is a great gulf between, over which they cannot pass. We are bid to examine the evidences of Christianity, that so our belief may be rendered more certain. In such a state of mind a treatise on evidences is likelier to produce doubt than conviction. For however valid a title may be, hardly will titledeeds be found, in which captious ingenuity may not spy out a flaw: and then, if the validity of the title is to rest upon the deeds, it falls to the ground. At all events such enquiries draw us away from the sacred building which Christ reared, and from the duties which we have to discharge in it, to the quarries whence its materials are taken. In those quarries the idea of the building is nowhere to be found; we never see it as a whole; we learn nothing of the relation and harmony of its parts, nothing of its purpose, of the shelter it affords: instead of this we waste our time in a number of heterogeneous and comparatively petty researches. Or let our conviction become as strong as it is possible for any conviction built upon evidence to be, as strong as our conviction of the Norman conquest, or of the existence of the Roman empire; still we feel that, in the matters in which we want help, and in which we are promist that Faith shall strengthen us, such a conviction avails us nothing. We feel that, though such light may shine on the darkness of our nature, yet the darkness comprehendeth it not; that it does not transfigure the darkness into light, but only serves to discover forms of woe, prowling about or cowering beneath it. In fact Faith is not primarily a light of the soul. Though its gaze ought ever to be fixt on the Source of all light, it looks to that Source rather in the first instance as being at the same time the Source of all warmth and of all life. It is the living principle by which the soul drinks in life from the heavenly Fountain of life: and only as the recipient of the light from above, does it become the light of every one in whom it shines.

When a person is in the state of mind just described, a wise spiritual counsellor will hardly say to him, *The Bible declares that Faith does possess all the virtues, which you pretend you cannot find in it: therefore you must receive the declaration of the Bible as absolute truth, without hesitation or questioning, however your own feelings, however your own consciousness may revolt against it.* This is not the way in which St. Paul put down errour,—by a peremptory exertion of authority. He ever tried to win over the Understanding and the Heart, by showing how the truths he was commissioned to proclaim, inhere in the very first principles of the Christian life, and how the errours he had to reprove were at war with those principles. Nor will any rightminded teacher of the Gospel be content to prolong the discord between the word of God, and that voice which rises from the depths of man's soul. As St. Paul at Athens took occasion from the altar dedicated to the Unknown God, to declare that God to the Athenians, whom they were already worshiping without knowing Him, so will every teacher, who has the spirit of St. Paul, examine and interrogate the voice in man's heart, until he makes it bear witness to the truth of God's word. He will tune the strings, before he begins to play on them. Indeed this is one among the proofs of the antichristian spirit, which has borne such sway in the Romish Church, that it so often issued its dogmas with little else to support them than its anathemas. Yet they who build upon anathemas are as though they built upon barrels of gunpowder, and sooner or later are themselves consumed in the explosion. Whenever a doctrine of the Gospel is promulgated in such a manner, as to appear plainly at variance with the calmly exercised Reason and Consciousness of mankind, we may feel sure that either there must be something erroneous in its exposition,—from a misunderstanding and misuse of terms,—from the neglect, it may be, of coordinate truths,—from making that absolute, which was meant relatively;—or else that it is brought before a wrong tribunal, and tried by principles and categories which do not apply to it. Not seldom both these things will happen at once; for errours propagate each other; and one false step is mostly followed by a second, often in an opposite direction. In the present instance, as we have seen, the errour lies in the false conception substituted for the Christian idea of Faith. According to this false and lifeless conception, the mighty workings ascribed to Faith become utterly incomprehensible, repugnant to all experience, and would seem as though they could only be wrought by some kind of magical charm. Yet this is a notion by which numbers beguile themselves, —namely, that on intellectual assent to the articles of the Creed, especially if it be accompanied by an easy placidity of temper, and by decency of outward behaviour, entitles them to the privileges of the Gospel, and will prove a valid passport into the Kingdom of Heaven. In many minds, among those who sometimes venture knee-deep into reasoning, this nominal profession of Faith will be undermined by a tacit, half-unconscious unbelief; and then, alarmed by its tottering, they abandon all reflexion on a subject, the difficulties of which seem to become more intricate and obscure, the more they are examined and investigated. Thus, as the extension of a power beyond its proper sphere ever tends to weaken it even within that sphere, the usurpation of the whole realm of Faith by the Understanding has often led to a suspension of the rightful exercise of the Understanding in all matters relating to Faith; and Thought, when it would fain have been everything, became nothing. On the other hand bolder and more thoroughgoing thinkers, feeling the total inadequateness of an intellectual belief to effect a moral renovation, have too hastily taken offense at what they did not know to be a perversion of the truth, and in their recoil from a fallacious Faith have rashly sought shelter in the hollow lightless and shelterless caverns of infidelity. Every way it is awful to think of the multitude of souls that have been thwarted and checkt in the pursuit of a living Faith, from having the cold phantom of an intellectual Faith thrown across their path in its stead.

Nor will it suffice to reply, that, as these mighty workings are in the New Testament ascribed to Faith, we must therefore believe them implicitly; that we must receive them as a mystery, and not presume that we are to fathom all mysteries with the short reach of our Understandings. Most true indeed it is, that this and every other peculiar doctrine of the Gospel is a mystery, yea, a mystery which was hidden from ages and generations; although in this instance also there were many anticipations of the truth which was to be revealed, much yearning toward it, much groping about for it amid the darkness. Ever since the Fall it had been a mystery, how, by the brooding of what spirit, the invisible world could be enabled to burst through the shell of the visible,—how it could be clothed with such a glory as should not fade away before the garish light of the Senses. But through God's infinite lovingkindness the mysteries, into which so many prophets and sages had vainly desired to look, have now been made manifest to His saints; and we may still rely with confidence on our Lord's gracious declaration, that to His disciples, to those who believe in Him, it is given to know the mysteries of the Kingdom of Heaven. Or has this assurance been revoked? Has the gift of the Spirit been withdrawn from the Church? Are we no longer to walk beneath the light, but darkly, as though the night had overspread us again? Nay, but it is still given to Christ's disciples to know the mysteries of the Kingdom of Heaven. To those who believe in Him, it is given; but to those who do not believe in Him, it is not given. It is given to Faith; but to unbelief it is not given. Just such, however, we shall find in the course of our argument, is the case with all other mysteries, even with those of natural science. They too are revealed to Faith only: and the Faith in a manner forms the measure of the revelation. They who believe in nothing higher than mere generalizations, will discover nothing higher than mere generalizations. They who believe in laws, will discover laws. They who believe in principles, will have principles revealed to them. And a like reward will be vouchsafed to those who go forth on their enquiries into spiritual mysteries with a dauntless assurance that every word is true which comes from the mouth of the Alltrue, that all truth proceeds from Him alone, that to Him all truth must lead, and that whatever draws us away from Him is a lie, and springs from the Father of lies. We are to seek and search, not with our eyes half closed, as though we were fearful lest we should see too much of truth,—lest we should look beyond God, into a region where God is not. In this respect also, seeing that we have such a Highpriest, who Himself is past into the heavens, we may approach boldly to the temple of wisdom. For He who has delivered our hearts and souls, has also delivered our minds from the bondage of earth. Therefore let no man say to the waves of Thought, *Thus far shall ye go, and no further*. Let Faith propell them; and they shall roll onward, and ever onward, until they fall down at the foot of the Eternal Throne.

That this is the office and province of Faith,—that it is something far livelier, more powerful, more pervading, than any merely intellectual acknowledgement of truth,—that it is the faculty in man through which the spiritual world exercises its sway over him, and thereby enables him to overcome the world of sin and death,—appears from the wellknown definition or description of Faith in the Epistle to the Hebrews. The passage is somewhat obscure, owing to the difficulty of expressing the fulness of Hebrew thought in the dialectic language of the Greeks; and our translation merely renders the words of the original, without bringing out the meaning more distinctly. That meaning doubtless must be, that Faith is that power or faculty in man, which gives substance and reality to such things as are not objects of sight, and which fills him with a lively assurance of the things he hopes for. He who believes, in the Scriptural sense, must believe, not merely with his mind, but with his heart, and with his soul, and with his strength. This is the only Faith by which we can live and stand.

It has been urged indeed, in objection to the doctrine concerning the paramount importance of Faith, as proclaimed by the Reformers, that it was a new doctrine, at variance with that system of doctrines which had for ages been held in the Church. Now this, in a certain sense, we know and acknowledge: and therefore do we give God thanks that He was pleased to raise up Luther, to proclaim this great fundamental doctrine, and to gather the soldiers of Christ under the all-conquering banner of Faith. But must not every truth, when it is first drawn out into distinct vision, be new? although, if it be a great and living truth, it will have struck root long before in the heart of ages. Was not the Gospel itself new, when it first came down from heaven? and yet it had been the desire of all nations. Was it not an objection urged against the Copernican system of the universe, that it was new? And may we not discern an interesting analogy between the truths which the two great contemporary Reformers were commissioned to reveal? Man, when following the promptings of his own self-magnifying heart, will make himself the centre of the universe; yet only when he finds a centre out of himself, can he be led to truth. Nay, although both these truths had been hidden for ages and generations, had they not both been written long before, the one on the face of the heavens, the other in the pages of St. Paul.

Many of the struggles and conflicts in the history of

the Church have arisen from this,—that, while the mind of man in its progressive evolution was necessarily passing through new modes and phases of thought, attempts were made to perpetuate forms of doctrine, which belonged to antecedent epochs, and were at variance with the new one. It was attempted to uphold, not the pure spiritual doctrine of the New Testament, which is everywhere set forth in its essential universality, by being set forth in its living reality, and is thus capable of assimilating with every metempsychosis of human thought, but certain definite forms of words, in which that doctrine had been promulgated at some particular epoch, and which had not the same expansive assimilative power. It was attempted to force the man into the clothes of the boy, which cramp and fetter him, and which at every motion he rends and bursts. In Christianity, as in everything else that enters into the region of time, there is one side which is variable and progressive, as well as one which is permanent and unchanging. Christ, as God, is the same yesterday, today, and for ever: as Man, He grew in wisdom and in stature, and in favour with God and man. So too in a certain sense has it been with Christianity, even from the very first. Therefore was it of such importance, that the Church should combine the wisdom of the serpent with the harmlessness of the dove; that it should become all things to all men, so that every variety of character, which the diversity of climes or of ages might call forth among mankind, should be hallowed by Faith, that every thought and feeling might stand exalted and glorified in the spiritual firmament of Faith. Thus, when the Gentiles were admitted at the Council of Jerusalem, the Church of Christ grew, not only in stature, but in wisdom. It was made manifest that the partywall of ordinances had been cast down, and that He who was the Hope of Israel, was also the Saviour of all the ends of the earth. Again, when the Council of Nicea declared the consubstantiality of the Son with the Father, and when the great Athanasius was called up to proclaim and uphold the true idea of the Trinity, that which had thitherto been the implicit faith of the Church, was brought out into more distinct enunciation. Thus by age after age new constellations have been markt out; and names have been given to stars, which had till then been nameless. Time after time, fresh irruptions of heresy compelled the Church to define her doctrine more precisely, and to develope certain portions of it more fully. For this is the service which, in the Church, as well as out of it, errour has been made to render to truth. This too is the only way in which a heresy can be beneficially supprest,— by its refutation,—by a thorough satisfying exposition of that portion of the truth, the previous indistinctness of which gave occasion to the heresy, and which its advocates, with the narrowness of view often found in the acute and ingenious, brought forward too prominently and exclusively. Every attempt to stifle heresy in any other way,—be it by persecution, or be it by an authoritative dogma,—betrays a want of Faith,—a want of Faith in truth,—a want of Faith in the harmony by which all truths are bound together,—a want of Faith in that power of the Spirit, by which we are to be led to all the truth,—a want of Faith in God's revealed word,—a fear lest that revelation should not be able to demonstrate its accordance with perfect Reason,—a fear lest Wisdom should not be justified by her children. Thus all who insist upon a blind Faith, only shew the feebleness and timidity of their Faith. Nay, at the very moment when they are calling upon mankind to cast down their Understandings before what they assert to be an incomprehensible mystery, there is no little self-exaltation in assuming that their own Understandings are the measure of human capacity, and that what to them is obscure and perplexing, must needs be so for ever to all mankind. To complete the string of contradictions, they who begin with laying down that Faith is a work of the Understanding, proceed to declare that its dealings are with that which is incomprehensible and indemonstrable.

In this sense the doctrine, which became the watchword of the Reformation, concerning the justifying character of Faith, may to a certain extent be termed a new doctrine. It was not the shooting forward of a new star; but a star, which for ages had been standing overhead, and toward which the eyes of many generations had been turned, was more carefully observed; and its polarity was more distinctly recognized. Here too it was out of the darkness that the light was struck. The immediate reason, which led Luther and his brother Reformers to assert this truth with such zeal, and to make it the foremost article in their Confessions, was the prevalence of the opposite errour, the deadly heresy of good works, by which the Church was then overrun. From the very first indeed the truth with regard to this fundamental principle, as it had been declared with such power and clearness by St. Paul, had been acknowledged more or less explicitly by the Church. From the very first the Church had felt and known, that, as the grace and truth made manifest in Christ Jesus was the rock on which it was to stand, so by Faith alone could it stand thereon, by Faith alone could it withstand the assaults of the world. It had felt and known that, if it had built on any other foundation, if it had built on the sandy foundation of human works, that foundation would have slipt away from beneath it, and its fall would have been great and terrible as that of the Son of the Morning. From the very first those who embraced Christianity had perceived that its peculiar essence lies, not in the works which it enjoins, but in the truths, the eternal facts and living relations, which it reveals, and still more in the graces which it bestows; that, as a revelation, it could only be made to Faith, and only apprehended by Faith; and that its heavenly graces were only granted to Faith, and by Faith alone could be received and appropriated. The general scheme of moral observances prescribed by it was on the whole nearly the same which the Reason and Understanding of man, refined and ripened by the course of ages, had already laid down. That it was so, is proved by the remarkable fact, that the only ethical treatises which have maintained their authority through all ages and nations of Christendom, and which even at this day we know not how to supersede or dispense with, are those by the master of Greek philosophy, and by the master of Roman eloquence. But Christianity breathed the breath of life into that, which before was a body made of the dust of the ground, and which thus became a living soul. The code of duties might be nearly the same; but a spirit from heaven entered into it; and a light from heaven fell upon it. Now so long as Christianity was the antagonist of heathenism, so long as the warfare lasted, that which was especially distinctive of Christianity would naturally be set in the front of all theological argument; nor could there be a doubt whether Faith was a practical power, when they who bore witness to it rejoiced to do so by martyrdom. Hereby it overcame the world; and this was the crown which the victors strove to gain. On the other hand, after the Church had been set up on the high places of the earth, her attention was drawn more to details of regulation and administration,—to the fruits of Faith, rather than to the powers by which those fruits are to be produced. In course of time too she forgot that she was militant, because she had ceast to be so outwardly; and fancying that she was at peace with the world, she almost forgot that it was still her task to overcome the world. Thus she allowed the weapon, wherewith she should have overcome the world, to lie in its sheath, brandishing a foil in its stead. From the savage ignorance of the nations that came into her pale, she thought she must deal with them as with children, by the rudiments of ordinances; and hereby herself at length fell under the bondage of those rudiments. Good works became the main argument of her preaching. But good works have no life in themselves: they can only spring livingly from Faith. Hence when works are inculcated for their own sake, they will soon degenerate into dead works. The more formal they are, the more easily will they admit of being so inculcated: and then they become a mask, which evil is willing enough to wear. Such were the works with which the Pharisees covered over the sepulcral rottenness of their lives. Such were the works from the soul-crushing yoke of which St. Paul delivered the Galatians. Such were the works against which Luther roused the slumbering spirit of Christendom, by reproclaiming the selfsame doctrine, that *man is justified by Faith, without the deeds of the Law*. This doctrine had been acknowledged, at least implicitly, by the greatest teachers of Christianity in the interval between St. Paul and Luther: only they were not equally alive to the necessity of regenerating the Church by it. They did not see so plainly that, unless the waters are kept ever flowing in freshness and might from the heavenly spring, a crust of weeds is sure to form over them. This

Luther saw, with a clearness which nothing could dim, with a certainty which nothing could shake. In this conviction he said to the mystery of iniquity, *Be thou removed, and be thou cast into the sea;* and it was done. God was pleased again to shew forth how Faith has the power of delivering, as well as of overcoming the world.

Thus the deplorable condition of the Church in Luther's days was the main immediate cause which induced him to give such prominence to the doctrine he was called up to reproclaim, of Justification by Faith. But changes and revolutions in the Church, if they are wide-spreading and lasting, are ever coincident with analogous revolutions in the general history of the human mind. In them we see, as in a clock, the progress of Time's great circle; in them we as it were hear the striking of one of its epochal hours. Indeed, as the former revolutions are the most vivid and distinct types of the latter, so are they commonly the primary agents in bringing them to pass. Both light and clouds gather about the hills, before they descend into the valley, and overspread the plain. Now, if we consider the peculiar character which has markt the European mind for the last three centuries, especially in Protestant countries, we may discern how the doctrine of Justification by Faith could not but be the religious expression of that mind. To describe that character by a single word: it has often been observed that what peculiarly distinguishes the modern European mind is its predominant *subjective-*

ness, as contrasted with the greater *objectiveness* of former ages. This pervades all the forms of life, all the regions of thought. There has been a far deeper selfconsciousness, which has often approacht to a self-devouring disease: there has been a more minute self-analysis, a more piercing self-anatomy. Speculation has turned its eyes inward, has become more and more reflective. If we cast a look on the two main provinces of intellect in the great age which followed the Reformation, we find that in Philosophy the grand achievement of that age was the purifying the method of investigation, the gaining a deeper insight into the laws of thought. Whereafter in another generation Consciousness was asserted to be the ground of all existence; and an attempt was made to expand the proposition, that Thought involves Being, into a complete system of philosophy. Hence by various steps men mounted to the denial of all reality; until at the apex of the pyramid Self took its stand, as its own self-existent world, its own creative god. Meanwhile, as the natural counterpart of this exhausted idealism, the materialist equally denied all moral realities, and made out that the apparitions of all such things are nothing else than a fantasmagoria played off by the magic-lantern of self-interest. Thus each way the absolute necessity of Faith has been enforced; without which the Intellect either worships itself, or dashes to atoms on the rocks of the Senses. On the other hand, what distinguishes the great poet of the age subsequent to the Reformation, is, as has been repeated thousands of times, his knowledge of human nature. That is to say, he is not contented, like earlier poets, to represent men as acting and suffering, at critical seasons, under the sway of passion: he leads us into their hearts, and shews us the warfare raging there; not merely the calmness or the ruffling of the surface, the rolling and rushing of the waves; he plunges down into the depths, and enables us to discern what is bubbling up and boiling in the abyss. Herein too, as he is the master, so is he the representative of modern poetry, of which the general character has in like manner been reflective, instead of instinctive. Now the effect of such reflexion on religious minds must needs be a deeper consciousness of sin: and this is just what we find in the great Protestant, as compared with the Romanist divines. In the latter, as has often been remarkt, there is mostly somewhat of a Pelagian tendency; while to the Reformers this was an utter abomination: whence he, among the Fathers of the Church, who was the leading antagonist of Pelagianism, became their chief, almost their only favourite. For the more our inward eye is sharpened, the more exceeding sinful does sin become: the more we analyse our motives, the more impurity do we detect in them. When we merely look at the surface of man's heart, it may often seem to be tranquil, and to glitter in the sunshine: but when we dive into its recesses, we pass away from the region of light, and only find deep below deep, cavern beyond cavern, quicksand beneath quicksand. This must ever be the effect of a thorough conviction of sin. Then it is that *the channels of waters are seen: at thy rebuke, O Lord, are they seen, at the blast of the breath of Thy nostrils.* And we cry with the Psalmist, *Save me, O God! for the waters are come in unto my soul: I sink in deep mire, where there is no standing: I am come into deep waters, where the floods overflow me.* Nay, we burst forth into the still more piteous and awful exclamation, *Who will deliver me from the body of this death?* For we feel that the death is all around us, yea, that it is within us, that our souls are imprisoned helplessly in it, that it has coiled round every nerve, and crept into every vein. In an earlier more superficial state we may deem that there is a value in our services, in our fasts and penances, in our mortification and selfdenial, in retirement from the world and almsgiving. But such things brought no satisfaction to St. Paul. They brought no satisfaction to Luther. Hence he pined and wasted away, until the aged monk reminded him of the consolation which he had daily on his lips, though he had never yet tasted its sweetness, the consolation afforded by that article of the creed, *I believe in the Forgiveness of Sins.* From that moment the assurance of Justification by Faith dawned upon him. He had hitherto been seeking for it, but had been drawn away by selfreliance, by trusting in outward means, in what he himself was to do or suffer. Now he found it as the free gift of Grace: and thus, from that time forth, it became the animating soul of his whole life, inward and outward.

Hence too has the doctrine of Justification by Faith been the cardinal principle of what is sometimes tauntingly termed Modern Theology. If it was not brought forward so prominently in the theology of earlier ages, this was because men thought rather of the outward act, and of its occasional motive, than of its primary ground in a corrupt Will; wherefore they had not the same thorough all-pervading consciousness of sin. Thus they might still cling to the dream of their own merits, and hug it to their hearts. They could maintain that the actions and services of the regenerate might be meritorious: and the delusion reacht such a pitch, that the Church at length admitted the possibility of works of supererogation. Where such an errour could prevail, it is plain that the true doctrine of Justification by Faith must have been lost sight of; though even in the darkest ages of the Church the more spiritualminded, at least in the moments of their highest spiritual life, bore witness to the truth. In fact wherever the true idea of Faith is extinct, and it is regarded as a mere operation of the intellect, there must needs be a struggle in men's minds, which will either terminate in indifference, and tacit or open unbelief; or else something else will be superadded to Faith, in order to endow it with a portion of that life, of which it has been stript.

The lifeless notion of Faith, we saw above, will almost infallibly weaken the influence of Faith on the heart and conduct of him who entertains that notion; at least if he brings it distinctly before his own mind. For only so far as his Faith exceeds his own conception of it, can it have any living power: and that conception itself will withhold him from taking the only course whereby his Faith might be enlivened and invigorated. He will not cry to God from the bottom of a yearning heart, *Lord, I believe! help Thou my unbelief.* Instead of this, such a person would think over the evidence on which his belief is grounded, and would remind himself again and again how thoroughly convincing it is,—a process just as likely to accomplish his object, as laying bare the roots of a tree would be to promote its growth. Indeed it is a general law of our nature, that, while every power, the legitimate exercise of which is followed by a corresponding action, is strengthened thereby, on the other hand every power which is checkt in this its appropriate manifestation, is weakened, and gradually deadened. A tree that has been blighted spring after spring, ceases even to bud. A conviction that has failed of producing acts conformable to it, becomes less convincing every time it is appealed to: experience establishes its nullity. And as this must be the effect of such a notion on individuals, so, as was again proved in the last century, will it spread a chill and numbness through the body of the Church. They who believe only with the Understanding, soon cease almost to believe at all. Even the knowledge, which is only the knowledge of the Understanding, dwindles and sickens and shrivels.

This was evinced in the shallowness and feebleness of our theology, which was prone to turn aside from the peculiar truths of the Gospel to general propositions about the divine nature and attributes, such as belong to what is not very accurately termed Natural Religion. For these propositions, being inferences arrived at by reasoning, might thus be matters of a merely speculative Faith: nor does this Natural Religion call for more, inasmuch as it does not place man in any immediate personal relation to God. Whereas to Christ, the Incarnate God, our relations are wholly personal. He is not a notional abstraction, not an idea of the mind, enthroned in a logical vacuum. We are bound to Him by all our deepest, strongest, most personal feelings,—by our personal consciousness of sin, by our personal need of redemption, by gratitude for personal forgiveness, by love on account of love shown directly, personally to ourselves. Thus, while the God of this Natural Religion is an object of mere belief, Christ is an object of Faith: and where Faith shrinks up into belief, Christ will almost be lost sight of. To mere speculation, when disjoined from a living, personal, practical Faith, He is still, as He ever has been, *foolishness*.

Another result from the same lifeless notion of Faith was the irreligious spirit which pervaded the worldly, or, as it may truly be called, the profane literature of the last century, as compared with that of earlier ages; its total alienation from Christianity, its forgetfulness of God, its habit of looking at the world solely in reference to man, without discerning any traces of a divine order and government. For a notional belief may be put aside, when we please. Indeed it passes away of itself, when we turn our thoughts in another direction: nor does it come forward, unless we fix our mind specifically upon it. Whereas a living Faith cannot but manifest itself. It cannot lie still in the heart, but circulates through our being, animating, elevating, hallowing, all that we say and do.

In the outward condition of our Church, the inevitable consequence of this notional theology was, that it lost its hold upon the poor; whose intellects are seldom sharpsighted enough to perceive the evidence of demonstration; and who, not finding even the semblance of satisfaction elsewhere, feel a more pressing need of something that will touch the heart and stir the conscience. We in this place may dream we are fed, when we get nothing but the husks of knowledge: the poor must have the living Gospel; else they starve. Hence the rapid growth of Dissent in all parts of the land: for to the famishing the very coarsest food is more acceptable than a picture of the choicest dainties, or than empty dishes, albeit of silver and gold. And when it pleased God to call up men of a living Faith within the bosom of the Church, and to send them forth for the edifying of His people, the holders of a notional belief regarded them as enthusiasts and fanatics, and pointed the finger of scorn at them, and almost cast them out from the communion of Christian fellowship. At times indeed there may doubtless have been extravagances of doctrine,—there may often have been extravagances of manner and conduct,—whereby some of these men gave needless offense: for Zeal does not always measure and count her steps, or walk hand in hand with Prudence. But often, it is to be feared, what was most offensive in them, was the witness they bore in behalf of a living, as opposed to a notional Faith. Else their extravagances might easily have been excused, and, if mildly dealt with, would have been lessened and checkt. In fact no small part of these very extravagances was owing to the opposition they encountered. For this is the curse of all hostility, that it is almost sure to put both parties in the wrong. Even those who previously occupied an impregnable position of right, quit it for the sake of snatching a temporary advantage, or of inflicting a blow on the enemy. Of late years, through God's blessing, there has been a considerable approximation between the opposite parties in our Church. We have learnt to feel that we have a common cause, that we are all servants of the same Master. In some degree this may be owing to our having a common enemy to contend against, and to the restless tenacity with which we have been attackt. But in part it is assuredly owing to the growth and diffusion of a stronger living Faith. For a living Faith seeks unity, which implies diversity, and manifests itself therein: whereas a notional Faith imposes and exacts uniformity, without which it has no ground to stand on. God grant that this principle of union may still continue increasing in strength amongst us, and that it may go on producing its perfect work, the Unity of the Body of Christ; wherein all the gifts of all its members shall find their appropriate office! And if we want a common enemy to combat, we have one, a mighty one, a terrible one, meeting us at every step, lying in wait for us at every moment, besieging our houses, prowling about our chambers, riding in triumph through our streets, thickening like a pestilence where multitudes swarm together, and yet rising like the malaria out of lonely and desolate places, and finding its way into the student's solitary cell,— even Sin, in all its deadly manifestations both within and without us. To fight against this enemy will require all our united forces: and the only victory whereby he can be overcome, is the victory of Faith.

Thus wide and calamitous experience has shewn, time after time, how feeble a thing a notional Faith is, and how by it the great works, which in the Scriptures are ascribed to Faith, could never have been wrought. On the other hand, when we have gained hold of the conviction that Faith is a practical principle, and that its chief seat is in the Will, we begin to perceive how it may well be fitted for exercising such power, both inwardly, on a man's own nature and conduct, and outwardly, on the world he has to act upon; how through Faith he may overcome himself, and may thus be enabled to overcome the world. For the Will is the sovereign, to whom it belongs to rule and sway our actions. It takes counsel of the Understanding,—as a master however, not as a servant,—as a king seeking counsel from his ministers, but alone able to give that counsel the force of law. And this is the act of Faith,—the royal assent of the Will to the truths laid before it by the Understanding. The Will too is the seat at once of our weakness and of our strength. When the Will is weak, the whole character is weak: when the Will is strong, so is the whole character. Even within the range of our own observation, we must have found that the persons who by a tacitly acknowledged right exercise influence and authority, are those who have a strong determinate Will: and whithersoever we look in history, we shall see this conclusion confirmed; at least if we bear in mind that calmness is not weakness, nor violence strength. Now the strength of the Will lies in Faith, in a resolute persevering adherence to a purpose, which, being something to be done, something that as yet lies far off, must be an object of Faith: whereas the weakness of the Will, its fickleness, its proneness to be diverted and to turn aside from its course, spring from the want of Faith, from the incapacity of cleaving stedfastly to an object, which affords no gratification to our lower faculties and appetites. It is true, the strength of the Will in a character is far from a test of its moral purity and worth. Herein the children of darkness are too often wiser than the children of light. Although the full power and dignity of the Will can never be manifested, except when it is animated by Faith, and when that Faith is directed toward a right object, the lower part of our nature has so entirely supplanted the higher, that we are far readier to believe in the reality of worldly objects, even of such as are remote in time and space, and to act under the steady sway of that belief. For this is the deadly disease, the great crack and chasm in our being, the rupture by which the Will has been severed from the Understanding. Hence it is that we do that which we allow not: hence that which we would, according to the law of our Reason, according to the voice of our Conscience, we do not. For though our Reason and Conscience delight after a measure in the law of God, our Will is brought into captivity to the law of sin which is in our members. Our intellectual faculties, however they may have degenerated, through the servile taskwork in which they have been employed,—however they may have become gross and sluggish from the atmosphere they have been wont to breathe,—are still able, when we employ them diligently and with singleness of aim, to discern many glorious glimpses of truth. Our Affections, when objects worthy of love are presented to them, are still capable of admiring and loving the beauty of goodness; except when, by a long drudgery in the toils of sin, their native delicacy and freshness has been worn away: and then it will sometimes happen, that their appetites can no longer be stimulated, their cravings no longer glutted, save by crime. So that the origin of all that is weakest and worst, both in our Affections and in our Understanding, is the frailty and corruption of the Will. When the Intellect is directed toward lofty truths, it rushes to them with a magnetic sympathy. When the Affections are fixt upon that which is really and purely beautiful, then alone is there healthiness, freshness, tranquillity, contentment in their delight. Or is it not so, my friends? Surely you must often have felt this. And yet,—this too you must have felt,—so perverse is our Will, we degrade our Understanding, we debase and poison our Affections, by employing them in the service of sin. Instead of sending out the mind into the regions of heavenly truth, where it would come forth like a bridegroom from his chamber, and rejoice as a giant to run its course, we make it the purveyor of our vanity, or of our covetousness, or of our ambition: and this arises from our want of Faith,—because we will not believe our Understandings, because we will not believe our Hearts, when they tell us what are the noblest, most precious objects of human endeavour. Thus the Will, through its want of Faith, becomes wholly corrupt, wholly estranged from God, wholly given up to wilfulness and self-idolatry, stedfast in nothing except in walking in the ways of the children of disobedience. Even in our fallen state we may still reason out many things concerning God: we cannot but feel some glow of admiration and thankfulness, when we meditate on the infinite glories of His wisdom and goodness: but to serve Him, to obey Him, to bow our Wills to His, to follow His Will instead of our own,—this no child of man ever did, ever could do except through that aid of the Holy Spirit, which is vouchsafed to such as believe. This therefore is the disease in our nature, which especially needs to be healed; and for this disease Faith is the appropriate remedy;—Faith, whereby we give ear to the calmest voice of our Reason, and follow the purest promptings of our Affections, thus strengthening both the former and the latter; Faith, whereby our hearts and minds are lifted up from earthly things to heavenly, and are fixt thereon,— whereby we receive God into our hearts,—whereby we trust in Him, instead of trusting in ourselves,— whereby, when sinking under the consciousness of our own blindness and helplessness, the effect of our habitual sins, we take God's word for our guide, God's law for our rule, God's strength for our trust, God's mercy and grace for the sole ground of peace and comfort and hope. Thus, whereas at the Fall we were driven out from the presence of God in consequence of our unbelief, by Faith we are restored to His presence, and live continually in His sight, beholding His eye watching over us and guiding us, and His hand ever stretcht out to support us.

The common definition of Faith, which was cited at the opening of this discussion, and which describes it as the assent of the mind to certain truths, beyond the reach of Reason, delivered by testimony supported by the evidence of miracles, is erroneous, we have seen, so far as relates to the act which it represents as the constituent of Faith. For Faith, in its Scriptural sense, is not merely the assent of the Mind or Understanding to divine truth, but that of the Heart and of the Will, their assent, and their corresponding energy: and much perplexity might be avoided, many mischievous delusions might be checkt, if we were careful, in all the uses of the word *Faith*, to keep its moral element in sight; appropriating the word *Belief* to the merely intellectual act. Nor is that definition less mistaken with regard to the objects which it assigns to Faith. There is no such distinction, as that implied, between the provinces of Faith and Reason, no such contrast or opposition between the two principles. They may both have the selfsame objects, may both rule side by side over the same domain. The difference lies, not in the truths which are their objects, but in the manner in which those truths are received and apprehended. This is sufficiently proved by the description of Faith already cited from the Epistle to the Hebrews. We there see that the true antithesis is not between Faith and Reason, but between Faith and Sight, or more generally between Faith and Sense. The objects of Faith are not the things which lie beyond the reach of Reason, but the things which lie beyond the reach of Sight, the things which are unseen, the things which as yet are objects of Hope, and which therefore must be remote from the Senses. Nor is it the office of Faith to deliver man from the bondage of Reason, but from the bondage of the Senses, by which his Reason has been deposed and enthralled, and hereby to enable him to become Reason's willing, dutiful, active servant. In fact the truths which are the objects of Faith, are in the main the very same which are the objects of Reason: only, while Reason is content to look at them from afar, or, it may be, handles them and turns them about, or analyses and recompounds them, but after all leaves them lying in a powerless notional abstraction, Faith on the other hand lays hold on them, and brings them home to the heart, endowing them with a living reality, and nurtures itself by feeding on them, and leans on them as on a staff to walk with, yea, fastens them on to the soul as wings wherewith it may fly. Thus Faith surpasses Reason in power and vitality: it also anticipates Reason by centuries, sometimes by millenniums. It darts at once with the speed of sight to those truths, which Reason can only attain to slowly, step by step, often faltering, often slumbering, often wandering by the way. Nay, all the truths which are rightly the objects of Faith, have always, we may be sure, been true in the eye of perfect Reason. Else how could they be true at all? or what is Truth, except the very heaven of heavens, in which God dwells, which has girt Him round from the beginning, ever flowing in eternal purity from the breath of His Word? And what are the truths which human Reason discerns, except so many islands of this everlasting firmament, gleaming in upon us through the clouds with which our sinful nature has encompast us? Man's carnal Understanding indeed will assert that the clouds are the real firmament, and that the patches of blue are merely cracks in the clouds, through which we look into nonentity. But Faith knows that the firmament spreads over all, above and behind the clouds, and that every truth is a part of it: and Reason also, under the guidance of Faith, will learn to perceive this. Many truths, which at first appeared to be inscrutable mysteries, and which were even declared to be contrary to Reason by such as knew not that Reason has any higher office than that of systematizing the generalizations from the objects of the senses, have in course of time been discerned to be in perfect harmony with the laws of the spiritual universe, in proportion as Reason has been enlightened to behold those laws by the revelations and inspirations of Faith. And it would almost imply a cowardly distrust, to doubt that such discoveries will hereafter be carried further and further,—that more and more of the mighty firmament will be unveiled, according as the purificatory power of the Sun of Righteousness draws away the vapours whereby we are prevented from beholding it,—and that a deeper and deeper insight will gradually be gained into the infinite wisdom of God, as manifested not only in the works of Creation but above all in the work of Redemption; until all our faculties of heart and mind unite in perceiving and confessing that all the works of the Lord are verity and judgment, and that all His commandments are true. Not however that even then Reason will in the slightest degree supersede Faith, or interfere with it, or lessen its power or its importance. Rather will it enlarge the empire of Faith, adding new provinces to its dominion, enriching it with new grounds of hope and trust, with new causes and objects of adoration; as it ever has done, in the advances of Science, when Wisdom has gone hand in hand with Knowledge. Faith will still be no less indispensable than ever, to give life and substance to the truths discerned by Reason. In far the largest part of mankind, Faith, it would seem, must ever be, as it always has been, the only faculty whereby divine truth can at all be apprehended: and even the knowledge of the most learned, the speculations of the most subtile and profound, unless there be a living principle of Faith in the heart, will only shine as on a corpse, hastening its decay and dissolution.

This has often been manifested in the history of the world. When Faith dies away, the heart of a nation rots; and then, though its intellect may be acute and brilliant, it is the sharpness of a weapon of death, and the brightness of a devouring fire. Philosophy degenerates into Sophistry, Ethics into Casuistry; the Understanding toils in the service of Mammon and Belial; the Imagination, instead of purifying and elevating, stimulates and pampers the Senses. All the faculties with which man was endowed in order that he might turn this world into the temple and garden of God, busy themselves in building and decking out an earthly Pandemonium. Your own memories will remind you of divers instances of this: above all will your thoughts naturally recur to the state of literature and society in France during the last century; when a cry, great and grievous as that from the cities of the plain, went up before God; and when again it was shewn forth that the sins of nations, as well as of individuals, are their own scourge, of all ministers of vengeance the most terrible. Now *these things* also, as the Apostle says, *happened to them for example, and are written for our admonition.* They admonish us that the ground of this desolation, the origin of all these abominations, was the turning away of the heart and mind of the nation from God. Whereupon the restless intellect bred a herd of false gods, drawing forth idol after idol from the bowels of sin, and setting up Gluttony, and Lust, and Covetousness, and Ambition, and Vanity, on every hearth, and in every heart, as the deities it behoved man to bow down to and serve. To cater for these gods, ships sailed round the globe; armies marcht into the field at their beck: and this was the least criminal of the blood that was shed at their altar. Among the rites of this worship many had a far deeper taint of hell. Poverty was trampled upon; innocence was crusht; hearts were broken, or more fatally blasted; every virtue was denied and derided. It is so difficult for any one to form a right judgement on his own age and country,—a difficulty springing from many of the causes which render selfknowledge so impossible, with others superadded to them,—that I will not presume to pronounce how far any like symptoms may be discernible in the condition of England. Thus much however is plain, that, if one man through an evil-boding fancy, and from want of a right sympathy with the present order of things, may imagine dangers where they do not exist, motives, at least equally strong, may blind others to them where they do exist. And it should be borne in mind, that nations also, when they have begun to sink, have scarcely any power to check their descent; and that, unless some happy shock drives them upward, they commonly continue to fall with an ever increasing velocity. Most needful therefore is it that we should hold fast to that Faith, which alone can keep us from falling, inasmuch as through it we hold fast to Him who alone is able to do so. Yea, this is the more needful, in proportion as we have the greater weight to support, as there are mightier powers dragging us downward, powers only to be overcome by that which overcometh all things. And what a ghastly crash would it be, sounding to the uttermost shore of the universe, if England, with her thousand crowns of glory, and with the Church of God in her heart, were to fall down into hell! Let us not boast that our morality is purer than that of other nations, and that therefore we are safe. There is no stability for morality, except in Faith. The stern severity of the old Romans did not withhold their degenerate descendants, when the ancient Faith had been supplanted by Epicurean materialism and utilitarianism, from plunging into the lowest abyss of debauchery.

A right understanding on the distinction between

Faith and Reason, with the accompanying conviction that the separation and opposition usually establisht between them are utterly groundless, is not merely of importance as a speculative truth, but also because no errour on any great question bearing upon the moral nature of man has ever become dominant in the schools, without spreading abroad and producing much practical mischief. This twofold errour,—that Faith is an operation of the Understanding, and that its sole dealings are with matters which transcend the range of the Understanding,—has been a main cause in propagating that disastrous notion, which has been so prevalent during the last century and a half, that Religion has no concern with the affairs of ordinary life,—that it is a garb of mind which a good man will wear on a Sunday, but which every man of the world, every man of sense,—how the very names on which they pride themselves condemn them!—will cast aside during the rest of the week,—that it is the peculiar province of the clergy, into which the laity have no business to intrude,—that its rightful seat is in church, but that it would be out of place in the market or the senate. In the Romish Church, one might have thought, these worldly tendencies, so natural to man, would have been kept in check by those ordinances of ancient wisdom, which had carefully provided that every important act of our human life should be consecrated by the express sanction of religion. But this beneficent purpose was counteracted by that narrowminded and most uncatholic jealousy, which made the clergy desirous to maintain a monopoly of religious knowledge: whereby, according to a righteous judgment, the monopolizers themselves were the sufferers, and, instead of Christianizing the world, became themselves secularized. With us, on the other hand, whatever tends to render us the children of this world has an ally of formidable power in our intense commercial and manufacturing energy; which not only furnishes the Prince of this world with endless stores of baits and snares to catch souls with; but which fosters and stimulates our lower intellectual faculties, —faculties conversant with objects below man, and thus reminding us of our superiority,—while it rather checks and stunts the higher faculties, designed to soar towards objects above man, and thereby awakening a consciousness of our inferiority; which withdraws us from that immediate intercourse with nature, where at each step we see marks of a power independent of man, and immeasurably surpassing his loftiest conceptions; and which places us where everything is stampt with the impress of man's intellect, and attests his triumphs. In this manner the Prince of this world contrives, even in a Christian country, to engross all but the whole of men's time and thoughts; being aided and abetted in so doing by that philosophy which excludes Faith from his domain. He is willing to allow, if you insist upon it, that there is a God far away, in some undiscovered corner of the universe. But he will not allow that God can be present amongst us: he will not allow that the Kingdom of Heaven can have begun already.

No! he says: *possibly it may come by and by, nobody knows when: but Here and Now is the kingdom of earth: of that I am the sovereign: therefore fall down and worship me.*

Thus the separation of Faith from Reason undermines the power of Faith, casts it out from its boundless empire, shuts it up in a remote island, and leaves it to perish there; as it needs must, when it is not fed by the daily offerings of the heart. Whereas the rightful sphere of Faith is the whole invisible universe, as the ground and life and substance of the visible. In all the works of the creation, in the whole order and course of the world, it sees and feels and acknowledges the invisible things of God, even His eternal power and Godhead. It feels that God compasseth its path, and its lying down, and spieth out all its ways. Hereby it gives substance to the things that are unseen. It beholds them and gazes upon them as the true living realities; while the things that are seen become the perishable garment in which God is pleased to clothe His laws, the signs and tokens of His creative will. And when Faith performs its still higher office, of piercing through the dark vapours of sin and death, until it discerns the Cross rising out of them in heavenly peace,—when falling down at the foot of that Cross it lays hold on God's salvation and redemption,—it becomes the assurance and conviction of the things that we hope for.

May such Faith be granted to us! May we ever acknowledge with our minds, and feel in our hearts, that God is the only Eternal Reality, and that all things else are only real, so far as they are in Him! Then, when the pulse of Time has ceast to beat, we shall see Him in whom we have believed: we shall see that Sin is swallowed up in Death, and that whatever is of God liveth for ever.

SERMON IV.

POWER OF FAITH IN MAN'S NATURAL LIFE.

1 JOHN v. 4.

"This is the victory that overcometh the world, even our Faith."

AFTER the discussion concerning the nature of Faith into which we have entered in the former Sermons, there will be little difficulty in answering the second question proposed at the outset of our argument,— namely, whether Faith is a totally new principle, peculiar to Christianity, altogether alien from every principle by which mankind had previously been actuated; or whether, like love and obedience, and most of the virtues enjoined in the Gospel, it be not rather the perfection and consummation of what had already existed, the conversion of it to its right object, and the consequent enlargement of its power and range. At first thought, indeed, it would seem as if there could hardly be a doubt upon this point. As Christianity appeals to our Faith, it would seem that there must needs be something in man, whereto that appeal is addrest; that there must be something in him like Faith, imperfectly developt, it may be, latent or dormant, waiting for the manifestation of Him in whom we are to believe. As *he who believeth and is baptized shall be saved*, and *he who believeth not shall be condemned*, it would seem as if there must be a certain power of believing, for the exercise whereof man, even in his natural unbaptized state, is responsible; for the misuse of which he may righteously be condemned. It would seem as if Faith also must be a gift given to him who hath; while from him who hath not, it is taken away. And may we not draw a like conclusion from the analogy of the miracles which our Saviour wrought to heal men's bodily infirmities? Whithersoever He came, the blind saw, the lame walkt, the lepers were cleansed, the deaf heard; that is, each organ and member were restored to its appropriate use, was so strengthened that it was enabled to perform the task it was originally designed for. He did not give the lame a crutch to walk with: He did not give them a wooden leg. That would have been a sorry miracle, would have proved His own weakness, and not remedied theirs. Nor did He give them wings to fly with. That would have been the work of a magician, not of a Saviour. The magician displays his own power and craftiness in making that which is not. The Saviour manifests incomparably higher power and wisdom in the far more glorious and godlike work of saving and perfecting that which is. Such has been the counsel of God's providence from the beginning. When man fell, God did not sweep him away at once into the abyss of death, and create a new race of beings in his stead. He vouchsafed to shew forth His patience and longsuffering by bearing with man, by striving with him for his own good, in order to save him, if so be he would let himself be saved. The whole course of the destinies of the world has been ordained for this very end, to draw forth and foster and train up all the germs of good, which were originally planted in man's nature, and to deliver him from the curse of sin, whereby those germs had been blasted and stifled. Above all was this the purpose for which the Son of God became incarnate, coming, as has been observed already, not to destroy man's nature, but to fulfill it. As He came not to destroy or overthrow anything that God had said, whether in the Law, or by the mouth of the prophets, but to fulfill it;—as He fulfilled the moral Law, in His own person, by every deed and word of His holy life;—as He fulfilled the ceremonial law, by *offering one sacrifice for sins*, whereby *He hath for ever perfected them that are sanctified* (Hebr. x. 12, 14);—as He fulfilled the Law moreover, by stripping off, or rather unfolding, the husk of the letter, and manifesting it in its fulness and glory as the spiritual Law of Love;—as He fulfilled the Law, by shewing mankind, at once by His word and by his example, how it was to be and might be fulfilled, and by sending His Spirit from heaven to enable them to fulfill it;—as in like manner He fulfilled all that the prophets had spoken, being Himself the beginning and the end of all prophecy, fulfilling it in Himself, and laying the foundation for its fulfillment in His Church;—so too He came not to destroy anything that God had made, but to fulfill it, to fulfill God's purpose in everything. Therefore did He become man, perfect man, man in everything, sin alone excepted, the second Adam, in whom the idea of humanity was fulfilled. He fulfilled man's nature in Himself, being Himself everything that man ought to have been, according to God's primordial idea and purpose: and all His precepts, all His exhortations, all His gifts, all the graces that He bestows by His Spirit, lead and draw and carry on mankind to the same fulfillment of God's idea and purpose. Their end is to transfigure human nature from within, not to transform it from without. There is ever something in human nature that corresponds to them, however faintly and imperfectly, an echo that answers to them, a shadow or likeness, which we can discern, when we see what it resembles and shadows forth. A blasted tree is still a tree: a cankered flower is still a flower: the body of a man, however maimed or crippled or withered by disease, is still the body of a man: and if it is to be healed, the cure can only be wrought by a strengthening of the living principle within it, and by a weakening of the disease; so that the healthy power becomes the stronger of the two, and subdues the other. Accordingly our Saviour, in the execution of His gracious purpose to deliver man from the thraldom and disease of the world, did not call upon us to exercise a faculty which was not in us already. Had

He done so, His call must have been utterly vain: we should have had no ear to listen to it, no voice to reply to it. He appealed to that principle, which, weak as it was in its higher manifestations, and kept under, and almost crusht by the pressure of the world, was still, under one form or other, the ground of whatever is great and good in man, even when regarded merely as a creature of this world,—to that which is the nourishing atmosphere of his intellectual, his moral, and his social, as well as of his spiritual life. He appealed to our Faith.

If Christian Faith has often been represented as a totally new quality, a gift of the Spirit, to which there is nothing analogous in the unregenerate man, this has arisen in great measure from the notion that Faith is mere belief. For such Faith being notoriously powerless, as every conscience must often have avoucht, they who felt the inadequateness of such Faith for the office assigned to it in the Christian scheme of salvation, might naturally infer that the Faith, which is to be the living root of the Christian life, must be something wholly and essentially different from any form of belief discoverable in the natural man. And so in truth it is. Whereas, if the business of Faith be, in all men equally, to lift up the Heart and the Will, as well as the Understanding, from things seen to things unseen, and to draw us away from the impulses of the present moment to the objects of hope held out by the future,—to supply us with higher principles and motives and aims of action, than those with which the senses pamper and drug us,—then assuredly may the whole of man's life, so far as he is man, so far as he is a being raised above the beasts of the field, be called a school and exercise and discipline of Faith.

It is true, that, with reference to the affairs of this world, as has been remarkt already, we are not wont to hear much of Faith, to attach much importance to it as a principle of our own conduct, or to find much importance attacht to it by others. And this is one of the reasons why in common opinion such a broad line of separation is drawn between religion and the goings on of our everyday life; as though the only claim of religion were to cut off and set apart a certain portion of our time for its own special ends, instead of pervading and hallowing the whole. Hence we forget that the purpose of offering the firstfruits was that the whole lump might also be holy: we think that, if we offer the firstfruits, we have done enough: and then, when the firstfruits have no longer anything more than a formal value, our cupidity, finding an ally in that sound feeling which revolts from whatever is unreal and hollow, substitutes the refuse in their stead; as has often been exemplified in divers ways on the decay of religious feeling in every country, and not least in our own. This however is only another instance of acts which from their perpetual ceaseless iteration escape our notice. When we read the Bible, we are taught that *the just live by Faith*. But when we think about our condition in this world, about our manifold ties and dealings with each other, we seldom call to mind that, as members of a state, as members of a family, as neighbours living in social intercourse and mutual interdependence,—nay, that as men, as beings framed with thoughts and wishes which pierce beyond the outward shell of the objects set before us by the senses, which dive and soar beyond the little drop of time wherein we are immerst,—as creatures who do not feed, like the beasts of the field, and the birds of the air, and the fishes of the sea, on what the earth and waters cast up, but who have to prepare and provide our food long beforehand,—we do not call to mind that, as beings who "look before and after," who look above and within, as beings who think and read and know and love, as beings who dwell in houses and eat bread, it is only through Faith that we can do all these things,—it is only through Faith that we can live at all. Everything that we do from any motive whatsoever, beyond the blind impulses of the senses, and the brutish lusts of the moment,—everything that we do in any way for the sake of others, or with a view to the future, though it be no further than the morrow, must needs be in some measure an act of Faith. It could not be done, unless there were a living principle within us, whereby the invisible world is enabled to struggle and heave against the superincumbent weight of the visible, and for moments at least to shake it off and overpower it; unless there were a secret sympathy between our spirits and the spiritual essences of all things that live and move and are, by the strength of which they burst through the party-walls between them, and meet. Thus our whole lives, —thus the life of every being who lives any higher life than that of the beasts of the field,—of every being who projects his thoughts, consciously, and by the act of his own will, beyond the present moment,—is made up, whether we are aware of it or no, of numberless ever-recurring petty acts of Faith. This, which in one respect is the infirmity, in another is the chief dignity, and, so long as the invisible things are better than the visible, the noblest privilege of our nature, that, as the great Apostle says, *we walk by Faith, not by sight.*

To take one of the simplest daily examples: when we lie down on our beds at night, we lie down in Faith. We believe and trust that the dew of sleep will fall on our heavy eyes, and will bathe our weary limbs, and will refresh them and brace them anew. We believe and trust that we shall sleep in safety. We believe and trust that after a while the light will come forth again, and dispel the darkness, and will draw up the curtains of our eyelids, and will rouse us out of our forgetfulness, and will restore us to consciousness, and to the mastery over ourselves. It may be objected indeed, that brute animals also lie down to sleep, that birds fly home to their nests, and that they do this without Faith. I have purposely referred you in the first instance to an act, which, viewed outwardly, is common to us with brute animals; because this very act illustrates the difference between human beings,— who are made to live by Faith, and who therefore, even when complying with the irresistible impulses of their animal nature, exercise more or less of foresight and preparation, more or less of a conscious purpose,—and brute animals, that in this as in other respects obey a blind unconscious instinct. If there be any creatures below man, which provide for the future, with a conscious purpose of doing so, as at first sight one might be inclined to suppose of certain insects, they would exhibit the first germs at once of intelligence and of Faith. But it is more probable that what we see in them is here, as in so many other cases among the works of Nature, the type and foreshadowing of that which was to be fulfilled and perfected in man.

Again, when we rise in the morning, and betake ourselves to our daily task, we rise and set to our task in Faith. We believe and trust that the light will abide its wonted time in the sky, and that we may, each according to his station, *go forth to our work and to our labour until the evening.* And whatsoever that work may be, every step we take in it must rest on the ground of Faith. We must believe that the end we have in view must be something desirable, something worth striving after, and that will reward us for the toil it may cost. We must believe too that the road we take will lead to it, that the means we make use of are fitted for promoting it: and this involves a Faith in the constant never-failing succession of cause and effect,—a Faith that what has been will still be,—that all the changeful appearances of outward things are governed by certain laws, and that these laws, in spite of the changeableness of their manifestations, are fixt and lasting. Without such a Faith man could never act at all. For all action implies a purpose in the agent, an end to be effected, and means whereby it is to be effected: and whatever we may do, we do with the conviction that such and such means will bring about such and such ends. Indeed this Faith is so inwrought into our minds, as to be an inseparable part of them. It has been termed a primary elemental part of our intellectual constitution, by philosophers who wanted to raise a mound against the assaults of a pulverizing scepticism; and who perhaps might have gained wider views of truth, had they paid more regard to the importance of Faith, as a pervading essential principle of our whole humanity, and to its indispensableness as the only stable groundwork of whatever is right and true in feeling and knowledge and conduct.

Here we may see, what a vast interval there is between that knowledge of the laws of Nature, of their principles, connexion, and operation, toward which Science is gradually ascending, and that simple confident unquestioning Faith in the laws of Nature, which is necessary to the very subsistence of man as man. Think for a moment how much Faith is implied in the labours of the husbandman. How many causes must work together, in order that his desire may be accomplisht! He must have an undoubting assurance that, according to the covenant made with Noah, *seedtime and harvest, cold and heat, summer and winter, day and night shall not cease.* In this assurance he plies his daily task, "plodding on cheerfully" through many difficulties and discouragements, confident that, after moons have waxt and waned, the seed he sows will spring up, and will fill the golden ear, and be reapt in the joyful harvest, and be stowed in the foodful garner, and that men and women and children will receive the sustenance of their life from it. Such power has a living practical Faith in the laws of Nature. Its effect, even in this one mode of its manifestation, has been that the chief part of the earth has been constrained to bring forth food for the use of man, and that millions upon millions of human beings have been fed for hundreds of generations. And surely our Faith in the certainty and stability of the laws of the spiritual world ought to be no less strong,—nay, far stronger. For while Nature and her laws may be changed as a vesture,—being nothing more than the vesture wherein God, in this nook of time and space, is pleased to array His Will,—the laws of the spiritual world can never change or fail. Heaven and earth shall pass away; but not one jot or tittle of them. On them therefore we should rely, never doubting that, when we go forth to sow our seed of whatsoever kind in God's spiritual field, He will bless our labours with His increase, and in His own good time will make the seed spring up, and will ripen it for His heavenly harvest.

If we follow out the foregoing train of thought, applying it to the various pursuits and employments of mankind, we shall perceive, even looking at ourselves merely as creatures of this world, that, so far as we are indeed men, and live as men, like beings endowed with foresight and forethought, God has so framed our nature, and ordered our condition, that, whereas all our spiritual strength must grow from the root of Faith, and all our everlasting hopes must rest on the foundation of Faith, Faith, under one form or other, has likewise been made the groundwork of all that is distinctively human in man, of all his activity, of all his wellbeing and happiness even in this life. As far as we are acquainted with the various orders of the animated creation, there are two ways of living,—by Sense, and by Faith. The brute animals, that live altogether in the present, and for the present, live almost solely by Sense, under the sway of a blind irresistible instinct. Man, whose present fleeting state is designed to be a first step, as it were, and a preparation for a higher enduring future, is meant to live by Faith. In proportion as he fulfills his nature and purpose as man, in the same proportion must he live by Faith. When he lives by Sense, he forfeits and strips himself of his humanity, and degrades himself to the level of the beasts of the field. As we read of Nebuchadnezzar, that, because he did not acknowledge *that the Most High ruleth in the kingdom of men,* he was therefore *driven out from men, and did eat grass as oxen, and his body was wet with the dew of heaven, till his hairs were grown like eagles feathers, and his nails like birds claws;* in like manner we also, if we were not endowed with a Faith in the order and laws according to which God governs all things upon earth, should wander forth from the fertile fields of civil life into the waste wilderness of howling wants and ravening lusts, and should have to eat grass like oxen; and our bodies too would be wet with the dews of heaven, until our hairs grew like eagles feathers, and our nails like birds claws. Knowledge, thought, speech, all the bonds and ties of social life, would drop off from us. The bright and rich fabric of cultivation, which man has raised over the earth, would be swept away, or rather would never have existed. Our birthplace would be in the loose sand of the desert, our grave in the wild beast's den.

For this, if we compare the outward condition of mankind with that of other animals, must needs strike us at once as the pervading difference between them,—that, while other creatures in the main take the gifts of nature as she gives them, man new-moulds and shapes and mixes up and alters and modifies all things. He does not feed, like other animals, on that which the earth brings forth of its own accord. He does not lie down under the open sky, or take shelter in the natural cavern. He changes the face of the earth by plowing and sowing, by building houses and gathering into cities. He invents arts and manufactures. He works in iron and stone, in cotton and silk. He devises remedies against sickness, and crosses the great deep in ships. Employments of this sort engage nearly the whole activity of far the largest part of mankind: and none of them can be carried on without more or less of Faith. So is it with every other work whereby man proves that he has not been gifted in vain with eyes set in the front of his head, in order that he may look before him. Whoever looks forward, instead of chaining his eyes down to the ground,—whoever casts his thoughts onward beyond the present moment,—whoever does what he does, not for its own sake, but for the sake of some end to accrue from it by and by,—must do so by virtue of his Faith,—believing and trusting that the means he makes use of will lead to that end, and that the end itself is worth seeking, though at the cost of labour and trouble.

Hence we perceive that, even in the concerns of this life, in the matters which pertain to our earthly wellbeing, although this is not the peculiar province of Faith, its power has been great and wonderful; nay, has been such that it may be said in a manner to have *overcome the world.* When God sent man forth *to subdue the earth, and to have dominion over every living thing that moveth upon it,* Faith was the sword which He put into man's hand, wherewith that conquest was to be achieved: and so far as it has been achieved, it has only been achieved through Faith. Whatever difference there is between the face of England at this day, when the land from North to South, and from East to West, is the garden of plenty, and is strewn over with peopled cities and towns and villages and hamlets, where neighbours dwell together in peace and prosperity, in the bosom of their families, surrounded by the innumerable conveniences and comforts which have sprung from the marriage of Nature with Art,—whatever difference there may be between this and the face of England two thousand years ago, when vast forests and swamps and morasses spread from sea to sea, inhabited by wild beasts, and by men scarcely less wild,—this difference is altogether owing to the power and workings of Faith, in one or other of its manifold forms. Without a lively practical Faith in the permanence of the laws of Nature, and a strong reliance on their active aid, none of the labours of husbandry would ever have been undertaken. Without much of Faith in each other, much of mutual confidence and trust, there could be no social union, no cooperation among men. Without the assurance of a demand for the produce of his industry, no artisan would engage in his calling. Even money itself, the unbeliever's chief idol, like everything else that is symbolical, like everything the worth of which arises, not from what it is, but from what it represents, is a creature of Faith: and all commercial prosperity rests upon *Credit* and *Trust*, and is in proportion to their strength. So that Faith is not only the sword wherewith man is to subdue the earth, but also the sceptre wherewith he is to rule over it.

Thus Faith is absolutely indispensable to man, even when he is dealing with outward things, in order to make them minister to his sustenance and outward wellbeing. It is indispensable as the ground of all agricultural and commercial activity. The visible world however is not properly the region of Faith : nor are things pertaining to the body the proper ends for which its power is to be put forth. They have only become so, because, even as the member of a visible world, man is still a spiritual being, and because all true power is spiritual in its origin, and abides with that which is spiritual, with the Mind, with the Heart, with the Will. Still this is one of the lowest among the provinces of Faith, one of the lowest services it renders to humanity. Of deeper interest and importance is it, to look at Faith in its connexion with the higher parts of our nature : where in like manner we shall find that it is the root and foundation of whatever is noble and excellent in man, of all that is mighty and admirable in his intellect, of all that is amiable and praiseworthy in his affections, of all that is sound and stable in his moral being.

Here let me remind you how the state and condition in which we enter into life, have been so ordered and appointed, that infancy and childhood must needs be to all a perpetual exercise of Faith. During the first years of life we cannot do anything, we cannot know anything, we cannot learn anything, not even to speak, except through Faith. A child's soul lies in Faith as in a nest. He is so fashioned, is brought into the world in such utter helplessness and dependence, that he cannot do otherwise than put Faith in the wisdom and the love of all around him, especially of his parents, who in this respect chiefly stand in the stead of God to him. He must believe in them entirely, with a living practical Faith, nurturing his soul with what he receives from them. He must believe that they know what is for his good, and that they wish it. If he did not, if he doubted them, if he were to resolve that he would not rely on them, but on himself, he would not live a day. If he distrusted his parents love for him, he would starve. If he distrusted their wisdom, his mind would never learn to stand and walk: it would continue to crawl about on the earth. Indeed this is the effect of distrust, of unbelief, not merely in childhood, but at all ages. Only by Faith can we stand. The mind of the unbeliever never lifts itself up from the ground, so as to gain a firm footing, but sprawls and crawls about on the surface, startled and checkt by every ridge and every molehill upon it.

What has just been said may help us to understand why it has been ordained that in man infancy and childhood should last so long, and occupy so large a part of the term of his earthly existence,—why he continues so long in a state of helplessness and dependency, so long under restraint and tuition. The time taken up by his nonage would be altogether disproportionate, were we to look merely at the exercise of his bodily functions as the end of his being, and to compare his organic structure with that of other animals. If the lot of man were merely to live through his appointed span upon earth, it would be wasteful that so much painful toil and anxious care should be necessary to prepare him for doing so. But every child that comes into the world, is to be trained up, not merely as an heir of time, but as an heir of eternity. He is to be trained to live a life of Faith. Therefore was it expedient that he should continue so long under the discipline of Faith. This is the noble and awful office of all those who are set to train up the young, of all parents and teachers: and they should ever bear distinctly in mind that it is so. Above all should this thought be the animating and regulative principle of those who exercise any of the momentous functions assigned to our body by God, and by the wisdom of our ancestors,—that every student committed to their charge is an heir, not of time, but of eternity.

Moreover, as the helplessness in which we come into the world is a sign and witness to us of our spiritual helplessness, of our utter inability to help ourselves, and of our absolute need of some Being more powerful than ourselves to help us,—as it should give us a lively sense of this our need, should destroy all selfreliance, and should lead us, our lives through, to place our whole reliance on our Almighty Helper, without whom we could not but perish,—in like manner do we come into the world in utter ignorance, to the end that we may be constrained to feel how we know not, nor can know anything, without the aid of a teacher. For the same essential law extends over both parts of our nature, the intellectual, no less than the moral. As we can have no true Holiness or Righteousness, except it descend upon us from above, and be received by our souls with a submissive, selfsacrificing Faith, so by Faith alone can we become partakers of true Wisdom, of that Wisdom which dwelt with God *from everlasting, from the beginning, or ever the earth was.* Wherefore childhood is not to be regarded as a preparation for an afterlife to be spent in a different element: nor is the Faith, whereby the souls of children are nourisht and expanded, one of those *childish things* which are to be *put away,* as though it were a cramping restraint on our spiritual freedom, when we attain to manhood. It is not the husk, which is to drop off when the soul is fullgrown. The same heavenly fountain of light, which opens the blossom, is also to ripen the seed : nor do we need its light to work with merely, but just as much to see with. Indeed, even when we do not acknowledge or perceive it, we walk in great measure by its light: for without it we should be in utter darkness. This therefore is the living bond by which our days should be " bound each to each,"—this should be the principle of unity identifying the man with the child, and ever making our hearts "leap up," when we behold any mark of the covenant and agreement between human things and divine—our Faith. Instead of being weakened and cast aside by the development of our intellectual powers, rather should it be confirmed and daily strengthened thereby; inasmuch as all our faculties, if rightly exerted, would supply us daily with new evidences and certainties for the assurance of our Faith.

When we have thus learnt to look at childhood in its true light, as a discipline and exercise of Faith,—when we have recognized the beneficence of the ordinance, that, during our first years, our souls should grow up wholly by breathing the air, and as it were sucking the milk of Faith,—we shall perceive that the aim of a wise, farsighted education will not be merely to make use of Faith as an instrument for the cultivation of our other faculties, but to cultivate Faith itself as of all our powers the one which has the widest grasp, which stretches the furthest, and is the most universal in its application, being equally indispensable to the highest of mankind as to the lowest, and in the least things as in the greatest. Hence we shall easily discern the hollowness of divers paradoxes concerning education, which have been cast up during the last century by the restless eddies of popular opinion: paradoxes I call them, although they have gained credence far and wide; because they are entirely at variance with the practice and doctrine of earlier simpleminded generations. For example, hence we see how rightly, in ages before men were dazzled by the glare of their own ingenuity, it was deemed the fundamental principle of a wholesome education to bring up children in full, strict, unquestioning obedience. For every act of obedience, if willing and ready, not the result of fear or of constraint, is an act of Faith; and that too in one of its higher manifestations, as Faith in a person, and shewing its power of overcoming the world in that very point in which the struggle is the toughest,—by overcoming the spirit of selfwill born and bred in all such as are made in the image of him who first set up his own will against the commandment of God. Therefore is obedience rightly esteemed so precious an element of character, betokening, not, as presumption conceits, weakness, but strength, true, mature, selfsubduing strength,—not the want of a resolute will, capable of determining for itself, but a will truly resolute, a will which has disentangled itself from the many-knotted snares of our carnal nature, even from those so subtile and unfelt, wherein we fancy ourselves to be most free, of our vanity and pride. Whereas the practice, now far too prevalent, of refraining from requiring obedience of children, without at the same time explaining the reasons for requiring it, by depriving the obedience of its personal Faith and confiding submission, deprives it in great measure of its worth as an habitual element of the character; while, by appealing to the child's own understanding as the supreme and qualified judge of what he ought to do, it fosters that spirit of self-reliance, which springs up too readily in every heart, and which the world in these days does so much to pamper. In fact, so far have we lost the true Christian knowledge of human nature, and relapst into a heathenish anthropolatry, that to encourage a spirit of selfdependence is become an avowed aim in the modern theories and practice of education: and it seems to be an axiom assumed in these, as well as in modern theories of government, that no man, woman, or child ought to lower his dignity so far, as to believe and trust in any wisdom higher than his own. Yet, while we thus exalt and worship the very dregs of human nature, we have by a judicial forfeiture lost the Faith in its true dignity. Governments have cast away the Faith in their own rightful authority; fathers and mothers have let slip the Faith in theirs: through a mock humility they have shrunk from asserting it: and so, not having that Faith themselves, they have been unable to implant it in their subjects and children; whence the convulsions, by which all ancient Faith and every ancient institution have been shaken, have ensued by a natural consequence. For they who sow the wind, are sure to reap the whirlwind.

Another manifestation of the selfsame errour is the ill-judged pleasure which so many parents take in the precocious development of the reasoning faculty in their children,—in hearing them ask for the reason of everything that they are told, or that they are desired to do,—in hearing them utter that mysterious word *Why*,—a word which a wise man will not hear without something of awe from the lips of a little child, bearing witness, as it does, of a mind and will no longer at one with truth, but doomed to seek it by striving to pierce through the inward and outward darkness, whereby they are separated from it. The time for reasoning will arrive soon enough, the time when we must say *Why*. Often and often have we to say it, as we journey on in search of Wisdom, whether speculative or practical,—happy if we get any distincter answer than an echo,—but most unhappy if we waste and starve our reason in repeating and prolonging that echo. When the time for saying *Why* comes, let us say it, with a stout heart of Faith: let us wrestle with Truth, as Jacob wrestled with the angel, and refuse to part from it, until it gives us its blessing. But to precipitate this time in children is unwise and unkind; and produces minds, all sail and no ballast, which are driven along before every puff of wind, in momentary danger of upsetting, —minds which catch fire from their own restless revolutions.

Perverse too and enervating is the practice of coaxing or fondling a child into obedience, of winning obedience from love, in its more superficial external workings, rather than as a duty, from Faith. Let Faith be the primary principle; and love will follow, and be dutiful and stedfast. All other love is wavering and capricious. Indeed I cannot but think that this very habit of a weak, fondling, unbelieving affection on the part of parents is among the causes of that want of due honour for the parental name and authority, so lamentably common in these days, especially among young men; from whose language one might often suppose that they scarcely look on their father in any other light than as a restraint and curb on the indulgence of their own will. Not having been bred up to submission on a reverential principle of Faith, their selfwill disdains submission on any other principle, and rears against all controll. Let me refer to one indication of this,—a trifling one it may be deemed; but assuredly it is not an unmeaning one: I allude to the habit which sons have, in speaking of their father, to disguise and disclaim the bond of natural affection, and to call him *governor*, as the vulgar phrase is; a phrase which must needs be painfully offensive to every person of right and reverent feelings, and seeming to imply a shrinking from that sacred name, which God has hallowed by taking it to himself.

Still more noxious is another habit, which also is deplorably common, of bribing children into obedience. Forgetting that the end they ought ever to keep in view is to infuse and cultivate Faith, many parents are content if they get the dead works of obedience performed any how, and will promise their children some plaything or dainty, if they will only do as they are bid. Hereby, through a self-indulgent weakness, to spare themselves a little pain and trouble, they encourage stubbornness, and reward disobedience: for the reward, which would not have been bestowed on a prompt compliance, is in fact earned by the previous resistance. Moreover they do what in them lies to strengthen the child's carnal, sensual propensities, which are far too strong already, while they weaken his Faith. They appeal to his senses, as allowedly the most effective principle whereby he can be wrought upon: and they teach him that, even in doing his duty, he is not to do it for its own sake, but for the sake of some paltry outward gratification to be gained by it. They teach him that God's judgments are less to be desired than gold, and far less sweet than honey; and that in keeping them there is no reward comparable to an apple or a toy.

Above all, hence may we perceive the heinous folly

of that unholy and degrading doctrine, that the truths of religion are not to be instilled into the minds of children, that the names of God and Christ are never to be mentioned to them; because forsooth their Understandings cannot frame an accurate conception of God. And what Understanding can? Must we not still confess with Elihu, that, *touching the Almighty, we cannot find Him out?* Nay, what Understanding can make any advances towards such a conception, save by degrees, receiving it first by Faith, implicitly, dimly, with humble awe, and then endeavouring to search out more and more of the infinite meaning of the truth it has received? When the Understanding goes forth, in its own strength, on a voyage of discovery, thinking to take possession of an unknown God, it ever finds that *He makes darkness His secret place,* and that *His pavilion is dark waters, and thick clouds of the skies.* Yet still, as of old, *the secret of the Lord is with them that fear Him.* And surely this thought must be a consolation to the intellect,—prone as it is to forget and weary of the things that are behind, and only to rejoice when pressing onward to what is before,—that it shall always have something before it,—that it shall never *find out God to perfection,*—that in Him there is a treasure of Truth, which countless ages of ever-increasing wisdom will not exhaust. Besides, what is there that a child can fully comprehend, either in itself, or in the outward world? Poor and scanty will be the stock of our knowledge, if we are never to learn anything, except what we can master from the first. What right too can any one have to rob a child of the most precious part of its inheritance, of its inheritance in the kingdom of heaven? In the children of religious parents it may often be seen,— and sometimes, by a wonderful and inexplicable dispensation, even in the children of parents who have lived without God in the world,—that a truly deep and strong feeling of God's mercy and love may spring up in the heart of a very young child, and that He still *ordaineth strength out of the mouths of babes and sucklings*, that He may put His enemies to silence. We may see in them that our Lord was not merely speaking figuratively, when He said that *of such is the kingdom of heaven*. Indeed we who bring young children to Christ from their very birth, may feel assured that the Holy Spirit will ever be ready to work in their infant hearts, fostering and ripening every seed of godliness which their parents may sow in them.

These hints may serve to shew how momentous the work of Faith is in the intellectual and moral education of man. It is so from the very first unfolding of the infant heart and mind; and so it continues as we grow in years. A child cannot learn his alphabet, cannot learn the name of anything, cannot learn the meaning of any word, except through Faith. He must believe, before he can know. This, which is the law of our intellectual being, at all stages of our progress in knowledge, is most evidently so at the first stages.

If the child did not believe his teachers, if he distrusted or doubted them, he could never learn anything. In like manner the whole edifice of our knowledge must stand on the rock of Faith; or it may be swallowed up at any moment, as has been seen in the history of philosophy, by the quicksands of scepticism. Faith too must be the cement whereby all its parts are bound together, each to each; or a blast of wind will scatter them. Every fresh accession of knowledge requires fresh exercises of Faith,— Faith in evidence,—Faith in the criterions, and in the faculties, by which that evidence is to be tried. Faith too is indispensable as the motive principle whereby alone we can be impelled to seek after knowledge. Only by Faith can a man be inspired to desire knowledge, as a thing excellent in itself, and worthy to be ensued through years of laborious study. For it is not a thing that we can feel or see. The mind alone can give substance to it, and cherish an assurance of its worth. Often it lies far away, out of all ken; and he who longs and strives after it, knows not what he is longing or striving after: he merely wishes to know truth, without foreseeing what manner of thing the truth he wishes for may be. But he feels assured that, if he does seek earnestly and diligently, he shall find; and that the discovery will be an overpayment for all the trouble it may cost him. At every step too, few or many as they may be, toward the attainment of this knowledge, which is never laid hold of at once,—more especially at the first steps,—do we need to be supported by Faith, lest we be disheartened by the difficulties we must have to encounter. For in every undertaking the first steps are hard and irksome: only by degrees do we get used to the new motion, and cease to feel it as constraint. Nor can we at all clearly make out how these first steps will lead to the knowledge we are seeking. It is long before we get so much as a Pisgah view of the Promist Land: and there is ever more or less of a wilderness to traverse ere we reach it. We have to begin in the dark, trusting to our teachers, trusting to the experience of others, believing, and acting upon the belief, that after a time, if we persevere, light will dawn upon our path, and that we shall behold and enjoy that knowledge, which we have diligently and faithfully pursued. We must have seen in the visions of Faith that our Rachel is *beautiful and wellfavoured:* thus alone shall we be willing to serve seven years for her; which years will then *seem but a few days for the love we bear to her.* Then too, even though we may be deceived the first time with a Leah, we shall gladly go through another seven years of service, if so be we may thereby at length gain the true Rachel.

They more especially, who are to attain to any eminence in knowledge, must have a strong Faith in the desirableness of knowledge for its own sake, not for any end of personal distinction, or for any advantage, save that which lies in the actual possession of the knowledge, simply and solely because the mind of man is made to gaze upon Truth, and because this contemplation is its own reward. And here let me be allowed to express a doubt, whether, in the changes enacted of late years in the system of this University, sufficient regard has been paid to the cultivation of Faith, to the upholding of this great principle, that Truth, of whatsoever kind, is to be desired and aimed at for its own sake. The branches of learning here selected as the objects of instruction may indeed in one sense be regarded as means; so far as they are selected on account of their fitness to develope and strengthen the character, especially the intellect, to prepare it for ulterior studies, or to qualify it for the able performance of the duties of practical life. Thus we may justly prize knowledge to a certain extent as the means of personal improvement. On the other hand whatever tends to make knowledge valued as the means of personal distinction, debases it; while at the same time it debases the character which is stimulated by such a motive; thus counteracting that very effect whereat we ought chiefly to aim. Those alterations have indeed been made with the best intentions, but perhaps in no slight measure under the influence of that delusion, by which our age has been so infatuated,—the idolatry of means, of mechanism, of the Understanding, and of all it gives birth to. Nay, there seems to be something like a want of Faith, in distrusting the power of Truth to win the youthful heart, unless she can bribe it with honours, and make it drunk with emulation. Yet surely we in this place have strong arguments to uphold our Faith, surrounded as we are by the memory and the memorials of the power she has exerted over the hearts of men for so many centuries. *Walk about our Zion; go round about her; tell the towers thereof; mark ye well her bulwarks; consider her palaces; that ye may tell it to the generation following,*—yea, that ye may tell it aloud in the ears of this generation, all these buildings were raised by the faithful love of Truth, in order that there might never be wanting those who should wait at her altars; and thousands upon thousands of her servants have been nurtured here age after age, and have been strengthened and confirmed in their devotion to her. We are often taunted with lagging behind the age: let us at least do so in this. Let us *stand in the old paths, where is the good way, and walk therein.* However the races of the swift, and the shouts of the crowd, may sound in our ears, let this be a sanctuary uninvaded by the tumult of Competition, unsullied by the dust of Emulation. Even if the promotion of knowledge were the sole purpose we ought to have in view, that purpose is rather thwarted than furthered by such means. For surely the knowledge we desire to promote, must be a permanent increasing possession, not a mere instrument to be thrown aside when the momentary object is attained. And I would further crave leave to express a doubt whether the dearth of deep, extensive, and accurate learning in these days, the rarity of a zealous enduring activity in any special department of knowledge, the rapid abandonment of the studies followed in this place by many of those who no longer have the same stimulants to spur them on, be not in great measure owing to the faithless practice of trusting to emulation and competition as the main motives of exertion; whether the golden apples which Knowledge drops by the way, do not rather check than draw on her pursuer; and whether, while our system is thus hurtful even to the successful few, it does not altogether damp the efforts of many more, who soon find themselves distanced and thrown out of the course. In this matter also, I would fain believe, the most powerful ally we can call to our aid, is Faith. Only through Faith, and by that patience and perseverance which a firm Faith alone can give, has knowledge ever been increast and exalted. Here again has it often been seen how Faith, in all its forms, is the victory which overcomes the world. In almost all ages there have been not a few, who, from the love of knowledge,—that is, from a desire for the knowledge of things as yet unknown, from a love therefore, of which the ground and principle was Faith,—have turned away from the world, and have closed their hearts against its temptations, and have been careless of its honours, and have cast away its bribes, and have disregarded its jeers and scoffs, deeming all other things loss in comparison with the unseen object of their hopes. Yet, as we read that, when Solomon besought God to give him an understanding heart, God said that He would also give him that which he had not askt, both riches and honour, so that none among the kings of the earth should be like him,—thus has it often happened to those who have sought after wisdom and knowledge with a self-denying, self-sacrificing Faith. They too have gained more than they sought. They have gained honour and power, if not during their own lives, yet for hundreds, or even thousands of years after their deaths. The names of kings and princes and of mighty warriors have turned pale by the side of theirs. Nay, in the course of ages they too have so far overcome the world, as to lift mankind out of savage ignorance into the light of comparative knowledge and civility.

Indeed the very faculty of wishing is an indication of our being formed to live by Faith. For what are the things we wish for? Not what we have already. Not, at least in most cases, what we see before us. The wishes of a being endowed with Reason and Understanding and Imagination stretch beyond the range of his senses. To wish for sensual things is covetousness, which therefore is idolatry, the transfer of those feelings and those attributes to the idol, which of right belong to the idea. It is a perversion of the power of wishing, turning it away from the unseen and invisible to the outward and carnal and visible. When thus abused, our wishes make us still more the slaves of the world, and embitter that slavery with wearing anxieties, insatiable cravings, and gnawing repinings. Their true meaning and purpose is to shew that we are not at home where we are, that we are not at one either with ourselves or with the world, that neither are we what we ought to be, nor is the world. Hence the great Apostle exhorts us to *desire spiritual gifts, earnestly to covet the best gifts*, which are altogether objects of Faith, which Faith alone can obtain, or pursue, or even wish for. In like manner, whatsoever among the gifts of this world is deemed a worthy object of desire by the better part of mankind, —knowledge, honour, power,—is also an object of Faith; and not only while they are striving after it, but even when they have attained to it. They set their hearts on something afar off, on something invisible, on something that they can only call up by fixing the eye of thought steadily on the mists of the future. In proportion to the energy of Faith manifested by any one in framing such a conception, and then in pursuing it earnestly and perseveringly, and in overcoming or pushing aside the temptations and other hindrances that may cross his path, is he esteemed, even by the children of this world, to rise above his fellows. One man will seek after honour. But what honour? Not that which lies and dies in the flattering tongues of the people around him, or in the shouts of crowds dinning within reach of his own ears; but that alone,—at least if there be anything estimable and admirable in him,—which lives in the opinions of the wise and good, and is to float on the breath of after-ages. Or what do men seek, when they seek power? It is true, they seldom seek the only pure and deathless power, the power of overcoming the world by the manifold victories of Faith. They are oftener allured by the halo which surrounds and bedims that true power, than by the naked glory of that power itself. But still the power which a magnanimous man aims at, is not a power that he is to wield with his own hands, or to see the operation of with his own eyes. It is the power of sending forth his thoughts through a land, and of embodying them durably in laws, and of writing them on the will of a people. It is the power of working where he cannot see or be seen, of working by Faith, and upon Faith. Nay, even the desire of money, of all human desires the meanest, is not the desire of that which we see before us. We prize money, not for what it is, but for what it represents. A brute animal would not care for it.

So again,—to turn for a few moments to another side of our nature,—is Faith the animating principle, and the only sound root, of all our human affections. What an important element it is in the dutiful reverential love, which children should bear to their parents, we have seen already. It is implied in the very words *dutiful* and *reverential*: for there can be no duty, but what rests on Faith, no reverence, but what springs from Faith. Nor is Faith of less moment in the love which parents ought to bear to their children. Indeed it constitutes the main difference between that love and the parental instincts of brute animals. So much longer and more laborious a training being needful in the human race,—a training, the difficulty and delicacy of which increases with the increase of civilization,—the children of men were not left to a blind instinct, which civilization ever tends to weaken and which finds place only in the mother's breast: they were committed to the keeping of a principle strong enough to make all those long years appear short, and to turn all those anxious toils into pleasures, to a principle which does not wear out, but grows stronger the more it is exercised. The peculiar characteristic of parental love is that it is forward-looking, that it sees in the child not only what he is, but what he is to be. Hereby alone is it enabled to make light of the difficulties and cares which it has daily to encounter. Hereby alone can it overcome the weaknesses of that fondness which looks only to the present. Hereby alone can it recognize that, in this world of masks and contradictions, true love must often wear the aspect of severity, and the moral nature of the child is to be trained and cultivated, however his carnal nature may repine and revolt against it.

May we not add, that, without Faith there would be no such feeling as love? For what is it that we love. Not that merely which we see with our eyes. Such love would not be love, but lust. Love in all its forms—every feeling that deserves the name of love —looks beyond what it sees, as it were, to the hidden sun that is still lying below the horizon. The whole world of sight cannot satisfy it. Were there not something more, something better, something nearer akin to the soul, it would starve. Beautiful as the dawn may be, we still feel that the beauty of the dawn is the work of the unseen sun, and that the dawn perishes and fades quickly away, but that the unseen sun is everlasting. The true object of love is altogether an object of Faith, an object that we cannot know or perceive, except by Faith, the heart and the soul. In fact the very idea of man is an object of Faith. That which constitutes a man is not what we see and handle, not the hair and the flesh, the arms and the legs, the mouth and the eyes, but the unseen spirit whereby all these members are united and animated and actuated. And this unseen spirit or soul is the only object that we can truly love; as the love of this unseen immortal soul, which likewise can only be apprehended by Faith, is the one thing that true love can desire and hope for. They who lust after such things as are objects of sight are like brute beasts that have no understanding, no Faith, no power of conceiving or imagining or believing in anything beyond what they see. To such men all the beauty and loveliness and brightness and glory of this world are in very sooth so many pearls cast before swine: they know not their worth, trample upon them, and defile them. But love, unless it be falsely so called, is not the creature of the eye, or of any other of the senses. It does not rest upon that which it can see and grasp: nor does it fall to the ground, when that support is taken away. Being rooted in Faith, in a Faith in the moral nature of its object, it manifests itself by acts of Faith,—by reverence for the sacred purity of that moral nature, by ready selfsacrifice, by joyful selfdenial. It lives and flourishes in the absence, as well as in the presence of its object after its death, no less than during its life. Having recognized that the beauty of the dawn is the work of the unseen sun, it still feels, when evening darkens into night, that the sun is not lost, not extinguisht,—that, though hidden, it is lying below the horizon, and that in the fulness of time it will rise out of its hiding place again. As it is only by Faith that we can love those who are with us in the body, so by Faith may we still love those who are laid in the grave. This is another of the victories whereby Faith overcomes the world. It conquers Death, and wrests his victims from him. This however it cannot do, unless there be a power from above to strengthen it; unless we have learnt to believe that Death has already been conquered, and that He who conquered it conquered it for us: in other words, unless we believe that Jesus is the Son of God. This therefore belongs to a subsequent part of our argument. But, even on this side of the grave, in no portion of our nature is there a deeper need of Faith. For fierce and obstinate and deadly is the war which the senses wage against it: nor is there any other warfare in which they have gained so many desolating victories. Through their blasting contamination those feelings, which were designed to be the first of our earthly blessings, have been the most dreadful of our curses, and have caught more souls in their toils than any other angel of hell. Much do we need the assurance of Faith that there can be no true joy in love, unless it be pure and holy. We need it to quell our insurgent senses: we need it to crush our tumultuous passions: we need it to silence our deceiving understanding, which is ever ready with a host of sentimental sophistries to snare the heart into sin. In many respects, one may trust, the intellect of mankind has on the whole wrought good: but in this, I am afraid, if we look through the literatures of all nations, we shall find that it has done immeasurably more for the corruption than for the purification of the soul, far more to inflame the Senses, and to delude the Judgement, than to confirm Faith.

And as Faith, whereby we recognize the moral nature of our brethren, is the ground of all our social affections, so for the happiness of life is it indispensable that we should put Faith in our brethren, that we should trust them and trust in them; not wholly indeed, —not so as to make them our sole, or our main stay,— but so that we may work together cheerfully and confidingly in the various tasks of duty. Our attention has already been drawn to the importance of Faith as the condition of all commercial enterprise. In fact it constitutes the chief difference between savage and civilized life. Among savages every man's hand is against his brother; and they know it: hence they dwell aloof from each other. But we, who dwell together beneath the sheltering roof of law, feel that every man's hand is to a certain extent with his brother. Notwithstanding all that selfishness does to insulate us, notwithstanding the faithless-ness which we behold in our own hearts, and which we therefore ascribe to our neighbours, we feel that we can put some trust in each other, that in certain emergencies of difficulty we may rely on our neighbours to help us. Thus, in order that men should live together in the bonds of social union, it is necessary that they should live by Faith. No such bond would ever have been formed, except through a Faith in its power; and only by the same Faith can it be maintained. The more too men live in Faith one with another, the more they live in mutual trust and confidence, the more they open their hearts to each other, the happier, the nobler, the better will their life be. Still, as at the beginning, it is not good for man to be alone. It is not good for his earthly happiness: it not good for his moral wellbeing. If he does not see the image of God in his brother, he will worship it, shattered as it is and disfigured, in himself. But he who is without Faith in his brethren is alone. His companions only make him feel how utterly alone he is. He is as much alone, as if he were lying in his grave; and sees nothing about him but rotten hearts, and mouldering wormeaten souls. Righteously too have jealousy and suspicion been ever regarded as among the meanest and most hateful features of the human character, as features which cannot coexist with any gentle or generous feeling. And as they poison the heart in which they lurk, so do they not only blight the happiness, but degrade the character of those who come under their shadow. For in this respect also is Faith of marvellous power. To think and believe ill of our brethren is the very way to make them what we believe them to be: to think and believe well of them encourages them and makes them better. Your despair of them drives them also to despondence: your hope of them fills them with hope. The one dismays them, almost as if they saw the spectre of their sins stalking abroad in the sight of the world: the other is like the angel of their better nature cheering them and beckoning them forward. The most conspicuous examples of this are those of such frequent occurrence in war; where there is the most immediate occasion for combined energy; and where the noblest and perhaps the most valuable quality in the character of a general is confidence in his soldiers. Your hearts must have glowed, when you heard of that heroic and sublime battlecry, *England expects every man to do his duty*. What then must have been its power on those who heard it, with the enemy full in sight! The spirit that gave it could not but conquer; well might he feel that in giving it he had done the utmost he could do: and the shout that replied to it from the whole fleet was an instantaneous assurance of victory, This too was one of the victories of Faith. So will it ever be. Unless we trust in our brethren, unless we hope well of them, we ourselves shall have no heart to labour for them; nor shall we be able to stir and rouse their heart. But if we do trust in them, and in this trust lead them on boldly, our Faith will draw them after us; and they will oftener surpass our expectation, than fall short of it.

Great as the power of Faith is in all the lower provinces and offices of our being, it is no less,—rather is it still greater,—in the highest, in our moral nature, of which it is the indispensable groundwork. This is a topic at which we can only take a glance: any attempt to do more would entangle us in investigations too prolix and abstruse. The controversies which have arisen about the first principles of ethics, and the degrading sophistry which has maintained that all the springs and principles of human conduct lie originally in the region of the senses, shew the absolute necesssity of Faith to direct and steady us even in moral speculation. Indeed all the primary principles and ideas of morality belong wholly to Faith, never come within the ken of the senses; nor can they be elicited from the senses, or their objects, by any abstractions of the Understanding. Unless we feel them in ourselves, unless we have a full Faith in our inward consciousness, unless we rest, heart and soul and mind, on the truths it declares to us, we have no foundation to build on The first principles inhere in our spiritual nature: we cannot pick them up without us: and in this as in other departments of knowledge the business of reasoning is to evolve the truths involved in those first principles, and to shew their consistency and harmony. If a man will not believe that he has a Conscience, you cannot convince him of it, as you might convince him that he has a spleen, by an anatomical process: you cannot cut open his soul, and lay it bare to the bodily eye. Nor can you compell him to acknowledge the ideas of Duty and of Right by any arithmetical or geometrical operation. You can only try to awaken his Conscience, which must be its own evidence: you must try to shew him that his own heart and soul bear involuntary witness to the truth which he denies. Else, so long as we follow the windings of our reasoning, without some positive reality to guide and controll us, we are for ever stumbling upon suicidal doubts. "To be, or not to be?" this is the question, which we argue at every step, with regard to every truth. Yet such a question can hardly be put, except on the brink of self-destruction; unless it be with a full assurance of the answer, for the sake of taking up the truth of Faith among the truths of Reason. The history of philosophy has shewn again and again, that, when men will not believe in spiritual realities, they cannot stop short here. They are borne on in their negative course, and with a far greater right deny the reality of the objects of sense: so that the senses themselves require the sanction of Faith. The truth alone can make us free, even intellectually.

But it is in practical morality that Faith, being so essentially a practical principle, the spring and life of all action, is all in all. Our Reason, when rightly employed, may discern many speculative truths. Until they are substantiated however and vivified by Faith, they exercise no practical influence on our lives. It is not written, that we stand by Reason, but that we *stand by Faith*. It is not written, that the just live by Reason, but that *the just live by Faith*. By Reason no man ever lived, no man ever stood. For we cannot stand upon ourselves: we cannot breathe in a vacuum. We must have something to stand on, something to breathe: and this we receive from Faith. And surely there can be no one amongst us, who can be such an idolater of Reason, that he will refuse to give thanks to our Heavenly Father, for that these things are so. Surely it is a great comfort, a great blessing to man, that he has something to stand by, something to live by, beside Reason; which, even when strongest, is so feeble practically, and which in the great majority of mankind never half opens its eyes. Else it would have been a happy event for man, that he ate of the Tree of Knowledge, had that tree been also the tree of life; had the mere knowledge of good and evil been enough to make him choose the good and refuse the evil. But it is not so. The whole story of the world declares that it is not so. The story of every heart declares that it is not so. Although good and evil are not set before us nakedly, but along with blessing and cursing,—although the experience of all mankind, and that of our own hearts, declares that this fellowship is indissoluble,—we refuse the good, which is blessed, and choose the evil, which is accursed. For, though we have the knowledge, it is dead knowledge. We have no Faith in it; and it has no power over us. Thus the origin of the weakness and frailty and corruption of our Nature lies in our want of Faith; in this, that we will not and cannot believe what our Reason and Conscience proclaim to us.

Every moral idea, we have seen, is an object of Faith. Whatsoever power it may have exercised over mankind from the beginning of time down to this day, it can only have exercised through Faith. And thus that grandest and mightiest idea, which this world, viewed solely by itself, suggests to us,—that idea which concentrates all our human affections, and gives a living reality to all our moral speculations,—the idea of Country is also an object of Faith, and can only act through Faith. It is a cheering spectacle, in the midst of so much that excites deep sorrow and shame, to behold the sanctity and the power of this idea in the two great heathen nations of antiquity, to see with what devotion their noblest children worshipt this their earthly deity, with what ready zeal they brought their choicest sacrifices to it, how gladly they laid their lives upon its altar. Most touching too is it to read the outpourings of the love which the children of Israel bore to their Zion, to the holy city of Jerusalem. This sacred idea of patriotism, this love of country which animated our fathers and by which their language, every national institution, and the very ground beneath their feet were endeared to them, has, I am afraid, been greatly bedimmed and enfeebled of late years. Instead of revering ancestral institutions, we idolize modern abstractions, and lose our individuality in a cosmopolitical indifference. Yet this our England, the noble mother of so many illustrious children, of so many whose names shine among the brightest in the annals of earthly fame, of so many whose names are written in the Book of Life,—this our England, that feeds and trains our spirits with the wise and glowing words of so many poets and philosophers, the glory of the earth,—whose sacred buildings, yea, whose very air has been hallowed by the prayers of Saints and Martyrs for thirty generations,—surely this our England, with so rich a dower of earthly and heavenly treasures, well deserves to be the queen of all our earthly affections. Or is her claim to them, which the heathens would have acknowledged with triumphant exultation, lessened and forfeited, because all that is excellent in this world is linkt in inseparable union with the Church of God? Surely, brethren, she has still the highest earthly right to all our love, to our fullest devotion. It should be our joy and pride to serve her, yea, to offer ourselves up for her service.

Let me conclude by suggesting to you, my brethren, that there is also another object in which it behoves you to have Faith,—even in your own selves. Marvel not at what I say. Many of you, yea, doubtless every one of you, already feels too much confidence in himself. One of you trusts in his strength or nimbleness of limb, another in his comeliness, another in the refinement of his manners, another in his ready memory or quickness of apprehension, another in the play and spring of his fancy, another in his logical acuteness or penetration, another in his learning or knowledge.

Many may deem they have several of these grounds for confidence in themselves; some perhaps deem they have all. One and all we trust far too much in the tinsel and trappings in which our souls are arrayed, in the particular gifts we may have received, in the faculties we may have acquired, in that which belongs to us, in that which lies on this side of our consciousness, and keeps us from looking beyond. But in our souls, in our real selves, in our immortal spirits, few have much Faith, most none. These our souls can only be discerned by Faith; and by Faith alone can we estimate their value. My young friends, have you ever been wont to consider what precious things your souls are? They are precious even in the eyes of those who love you among men. They are precious in the eyes of your parents, whose hopes are bound up in you. They are precious in the eyes of your brothers and sisters, of your friends, to whom your good name will be a blessing, your shame the deepest of woes. They are precious in the eyes of your Country. She calls you forth to serve her in posts of honour and power. Some of you will be called hereafter to serve her in the administration of her laws. Some of you will take part in her legislature. Some of you will have to distribute the wealth you inherit from your ancestors. Some may be employed in increasing her wealth in the various departments of commerce. The province of some will be to exercise your gifts in healing the diseases of the body. Some, a consecrated band, are purposing to devote yourselves to the office of waiting around the altar of God, and dispensing the Bread and the Word of Life. All these are noble and glorious callings, noble and glorious because they are girt with duties: and greatly favoured are you, whom God has chosen to serve Him in the high places of His kingdom, you, whom he raises above others, in order that you may minister more largely, more assiduously, and more beneficially to others. You will go forth into all parts of the land: and on the manner in which you fulfill your appointed task, the weal and prosperity of England for the next, nay, for many generations, will in no slight measure depend. To each and all of you I may say, *England expects every man to do his duty.* If you serve her faithfully and strenuously, with zealous hearts and holy lives, the calamities, which at times appear to be threatening her, may through God's blessing be averted. If you are faithless, if you betray and forsake the service of your country, to serve your own lusts, to gain pleasure for yourselves, or riches for yourselves, or power or honour for yourselves,— then . . . O may God vouchsafe to raise up others, who will serve her better than you! In her eyes, in the eyes of England, my young friends, your souls are very precious. But still more. They are precious in the sight of the angels that stand before the throne of God. They are precious in the sight of God Himself, who gave His Son to die for you. They are precious in the sight of His Eternal Son, who shed His blood upon the Cross to save you. They are precious in the sight of

T

the Holy Spirit, who came down upon you at your baptism, and is ever watching over you to sanctify you. My dear friends, let your souls, which are thus precious in the sight of your parents, of your brothers, of your companions, of your country, which are thus precious in the sight of the holy angels, which are thus precious in the sight of the Triune God,—let them be precious in your own sight. Cast them not away on vanity and frivolity; starve not, nor wither them in the toils of interest or ambition; yield them not up to be defiled and rotted by the lusts of the flesh: watch carefully lest such precious jewels be injured or polluted by any manner of impurity: and pray continually to God, that, as He has called you to His salvation, so He will vouchsafe to fulfill His good work in you and to render you faithful and zealous to serve Him in whatsoever path He may ordain for you.

SERMON V.

POWER OF FAITH AMONG THE HEATHENS, AND AMONG THE JEWS.

1 JOHN v. 4.

"This is the victory that overcometh the world, even our Faith."

THE first part of these Sermons was employed in considering the nature and character, the seat, and the province of Faith. Owing to the difficulties in which this question has been involved, and to the many delusive errours which have prevailed with regard to it, we were compelled to discuss it at considerable length: and I endeavoured to establish that Faith is not merely a speculative, but mainly a practical principle,—that its seat is not solely in the Understanding, but still more in the Will,—and that its province is not confined to those truths which are above the reach of Reason, but that, agreeably to the description given in the Epistle to the Hebrews, it embraces the whole invisible world, and must be exerted more or less in all man's dealings with whatsoever lies beyond the immediate span of the senses, and the cravings of the present moment. So that the provinces of Faith and Reason, instead of being distinct, may rather be said to be coextensive,—not indeed actually, with reference to the intellectual and spiritual condition of man at any given point of time, but ideally. Every truth of Reason, if it is to exercise any practical influence, must also become a truth of Faith, must be recognized and substantiated by the Will, must be cut off from the Tree of Knowledge, and grafted into the Tree of Life. Every truth of Faith, too, if it be a truth at all, must also be a truth of Reason; although the Reason of man, in its present imperfect development, may not yet have apprehended it as such. For Faith, being the faculty whereby we are to live, cannot wait for the tardy advances of Reason. It runs before, and spies out the land, which Reason will afterward explore slowly and gradually and in detail: and when Faith is borne aloft in heavenly vision, it may anticipate Reason by hundreds, or even by thousands of years. Moreover, although every truth of Faith is also a truth of Reason,—as, we shall feel sure, if our Faith is strong, it will hereafter be ascertained to be, seeing that the chief hindrance to the progress of man's Reason has ever been the feebleness of his Faith, —yet their ways of apprehending their truths are very different. Reason looks at them, and about them, and searches them through and through, and makes out their bearings and relations. Faith on the other hand lays hold on them as they are, in their totality, and from the very first takes possession of them, even as

Abraham through Faith took possession of Canaan: and when the objects of Faith are religious truths, it takes possession of them in the same manner, by building an altar to the Lord, by offering up its worship and thanksgiving for the revelation it has received. Nay, as it was by means of the field of Machpelah that Abraham first gained an acknowledged property in the land of Canaan, so is it by the burial of what we were wont to hold dear, of our former carnal, sensual nature, that we are to gain an assured inheritance in the land of Faith.

Having thus been brought to the conclusion, that whenever an unseen object,—whether it be an object of the outward world, lying beyond the immediate sphere of sight, or shining upon us and beckoning to us out of the mists of the future, or whether it be an idea or principle of the intellectual, or the moral, or the spiritual world,—that, whenever any such object, of whatsoever kind, exerts a practical power on the will and conduct of man, it must needs be an object of Faith, and must act upon him through Faith, we proceeded to enquire how far Faith manifests itself as an active principle in the life of man, when viewed solely as a member of this world, and to take a brief, hasty survey of the chief regions of its operation. As every act, the motives of which spring from anything beyond the range of those senses, wherein our souls are "cabined and cribbed," beyond that "narrow pinfold" of space and time where we are "confined and pestered," must needs be an act of Faith, Faith, it is plain, must be the proper element of all human action; and only when man acts by Faith, can he shew forth any portion of his humanity. Thus we saw that Faith is the power whereby the earth has been cultivated and brought into subjection by mankind. It is the foundation on which all wealth and trade and commerce must rest. It is the bond by which alone society can be held together. We then traced some of the workings of Faith in man, as an intellectual and moral being. We saw how children lie cradled in Faith, as in a mother's arms; how their understandings, their affections, their moral nature can only be shaped and unfolded by Faith. Finally a few hints were given, pointing to the great and momentous truth, that Faith is the root and pervading life of all knowledge, of all love, of all duty. The earlier parts of this review having been carried into somewhat fuller detail, we were enabled to pass more rapidly over the latter part; for the same line of argument bears upon both. Sundry questions indeed might have been started, which it would have been interesting to pursue: but the investigation could hardly have been followed out, without involving us in metaphysical subtilties. At all events they would have carried us too far. The limits assigned to these Sermons warn me that it is time to wind up the argument. They warn me that I must not linger too long amid earthly thoughts, but must endeavour to lead you to the contemplation of Faith in its highest office and relation, as the eye with which the earth looks up and beholds heaven, as the bond of union between man and God.

For the sake of continuity however, to bring out the connexion between what has been said and the higher parts of the subject, it will be expedient in the first place to take up a few threads of the foregoing argument. I have tried to shew, how in every way in which man has to exercise his humanity,—whether by acting upon inanimate nature, or in his own manifold relations with the beings of his own kind,—Faith is the victory that overcomes the world; how every victory over the world ever gained by man, whatever may have been its object and effect, has been gained by Faith, and by Faith only. Now in the lower regions of human action, we have seen, the victories of Faith have been great and glorious. It is true, they are nothing like what they ought to have been, nothing like what they would have been, unless the power of Faith had been perpetually crippled and shackled and counteracted by man's corrupt will and selfish, disorderly passions and appetites. They are poor and mean in comparison with what Faith would have accomplisht, if she could have walkt abroad freely, without these hindrances and obstacles. Three fourths of the earth would not then be still lying waste at the end of her sixth millenary. Nine tenths of mankind would not be still cowering in gross darkness scarcely broken except by the flashes of their passions. Nevertheless such is the power of Faith, whenever it has room to act at all, that in spite of all that has checkt and retarded its progress, its achievements in these lower regions have been great and splendid. It has woven a fine network of cultivation and civilization, which is spread over the fairest parts of the earth; and it has reared a lofty tower of knowledge, the top of which holds converse with the stars. This was man's mission, when he was sent forth to subdue the earth, and to have dominion over everything upon it. He was to make everything bear the stamp and impress of his ruling mind; and he was to subdue everything, not merely for the purposes of his outward bodily, but also for those of his intellectual life by bringing the confused mass of perception, which the objects of his senses present to him under the dominion of order and law; so that, while his body was fed by the fruits of the earth, his mind should be nurtured by its spirit, and should be trained and unfolded by tracing the workings of the Divine Mind, as set before him in the universe. In this mission man has gone on labouring from the first, with more or less of diligence and success, never wholly abandoning it, though never fulfilling it to perfection. For, although even in these labours he has been grievously crampt and fettered by the evil propensities of his nature, cumbering his activity, diverting it from its proper objects, and thwarting union and consort, yet the intellectual and bodily faculties employed in such works are not the immediate seat of those evil propensities: they are the parts of his being which have suffered the least from the taint of sin. In the results of these labours therefore, imperfect and inadequate as they are, we may perceive how great is the power of a living, animating, active Faith: and they may serve as tokens and assurances of the wonderful effects which it would produce, if the whole man, body and heart and mind, were to flow along with the unity of a mighty river under its unresisted, continuous sway. At the same time, while man in these lower provinces of his activity has done much through Faith toward overcoming the world, his victory over the world even in these respects, if viewed as the victory of Faith, has been anything but complete and clear. The conflict has not been one in which Faith has gone forth in its naked spiritual might, severing itself from everything carnal, and refusing all alliance therewith, in order to assert and establish the absolute lordship of spirit over matter. It has rather been a warfare of outposts, with an alternation of gain and loss. The world has lifted up its head again; and man, through the weakness of his Faith, has been overcome. Nay, the world has, so to say, turned his batteries against him, and armed herself with the trophies which he had erected upon her. Every victory he gained over her supplied her with new and more powerful and deadlier weapons to wield against him. She has assailed him with the luxuries of civilization, with the lust of possession, with the pride and craft of knowledge: and the self-idolater has ever been especially ready to bow down and worship the work of his own hands. The harlot charmed him the more for the silk and jewels in which he had deckt her out: and he had been bound, as though Delilah had bound Samson with the hair which she cut from his head.

Still, notwithstanding all these drawbacks, the power and works of Faith in these lower regions have been great, at least in comparison with her feebleness in those higher regions, which more peculiarly belong to her. She made men till the ground, and unite into communities, and build cities, and ransack every country, and every order of created things, to discover materials for wealth. In so doing she had little resistance to surmount. For, though even in such matters man cannot act except through Faith, the Faith requisite is not fixt on purely spiritual objects, but on earthly objects more or less remote from the reach of the Senses. Nor is man here called upon to exert his spiritual Will, in subduing his carnal Will, and making his faculties minister to spiritual aims: rather are his higher faculties employed as the servants of his carnal Will, and taskt for its purposes and ends. When this is the case, whenever man brings the forces of his being to bear on a single purpose, even though that purpose be evil, we see proofs of the power of Faith: nor has there been any lack of those who were ready in full confidence to set about removing mountains, if riches or honour were to be pickt up beneath them. So too has Faith been able to inspire men with an ardent, unquenchable thirst after knowledge. For knowledge likewise is of an ambiguous nature, has no determinate, invariable moral value, may be rendered subservient to worldly ends of gain or fame, and may thus be desired and possest by the evil as well as the good. The serpent was the subtilest among all the beasts of the field; and his wisdom may too easily be found apart from the harmlessness of the dove. When it is so however, his doom is still to crawl along the ground, never to rise above it, and to eat dust all the days of his life.

But though Faith was strong enough to effect much in these ways for mankind, and was thus a weapon of great efficacy in their hands for the purposes of their earthly life, her power lessened in proportion as her objects became more spiritual; and just when her aid was the most needed, that power almost entirely past away. In vain did Faith try to lift the affections from visible things to invisible, and to fix them steadily thereon. Vain were her efforts to give a substantial living reality to the shadowy ideas of virtue. Her office, we have seen, is to be the copula between the Heart and the Mind, between the Understanding and the Will, the atoning principle in man's disjointed nature, investing the Affections with the sanctity of Duty, and rendering Duty a living power and presence in the soul. Now so long as Instinct enforced the commands of Duty, and a sacred horrour kept the passions at bay, Faith did indeed enable even the natural man in some measure to fulfill the obligations of parental, filial, and fraternal love. Herein we may perceive an indication that the true spiritual objects of Faith, the spiritual objects which will lead it to put forth its might, must be divine; as was recognized more or less distinctly by the wisdom of those lawgivers, who were so anxious to strengthen their laws by binding them to the throne of heaven, according to the conceptions of divine things which bore sway in their own minds, and in the minds of their countrymen. But when Faith had to pass beyond the region, where these sanctities added authority to its voice, it became powerless, and shrank from the struggle with the fierce passions which encountered it. The idea of Chastity could not make man curb his lusts: the idea of Temperance could not calm his appetites: the idea of Justice could not repress his cupidity: the idea of Modesty could not bend his pride: the idea of Integrity could not animate him to withstand the bribes of power and favour: the idea of Truth could not withhold him from following the seductive strains of falsehood. These might stand like stars overhead, bright and pure, and far off: they might be gazed at in the hours of contemplative abstraction: but they exercised no power over the business of workday life, and were lost sight of amidst it. Man may admire an idea: he may hymn its praise: he may discern its truth, its beauty, its fitness, its majesty: but it has no power to constrain. Love alone can do this: and when that love has so hard a task, as that of overcoming all outward temptations, and all the evil tendencies of our nature, it must be the love of Christ, love springing from the Faith in Jesus the Son of God.

Besides, in dealing with the outward world, man had ever-recurring palpable proofs demonstrating the validity of those laws of Nature, on which he relied. In the pursuit of knowledge he was encouraged by a rich mass of evidence, shewing that it is indeed power, power both over nature and over man. Thus in neither of these instances was Faith mere Faith: it did not stand alone: it was not a pure, longsighted, spiritual conviction of that which is invisible. It had outward proofs to lean on, outward confirmation to support it, as well as outward motives of a mixed character, evil as well as good, to animate it. But when it set itself to controll and quell man's evil appetites and passions by enforcing the laws of Reason and Conscience, the whole might of the visible world fought against it: the senses confederated to deny its authority; the web, which from our earliest infancy they are daily spinning around our heart and mind, and which we find so soft and easy, so congenial to our spiritual sloth, held it down. Then it became plain, that, though men have eyes, yet they cannot see,—that, though they have ears, yet they cannot hear,—anything beyond the roar of the wheel of Time, and the spray that flashes off from it. Then was it seen how the light of earthly day sweeps all the stars out of heaven. In vain did Faith cry to the Will, to arouse itself, and shake off the bondage of the Senses. The Will would not shake it off; nay, was their voluntary servant; nay, by its own act and deed pulled down their yoke upon its neck, and riveted their chains still faster. In vain did Faith preach to the Will, that it ought to shake off its bondage. The Will said, *ay*, and fell back into its lethargy again. Faith lookt round for something to support it: but there was nothing: no creature would uphold it. The visible things, instead of being regarded as the signs and witnesses of the invisible, became their masks, and hid them from the view. To no purpose did Faith proclaim eternal laws, and appeal to eternal ideas. Laws upheld by outward sanctions, and enforced by temporal power, might indeed stand and bear authority. But laws, of which the only sanction was inward, laws resting on nothing but timeless power, were left to be gazed at in the void in which the intellect enthroned them. The idea of Duty had no sword in its hand, no hand to wield a sword. The ideas of Chastity and Temperance grew dim before the glaring lamps of the revel. Who could look at the naked idea of Justice, when Injustice stood by arrayed in gold and purple? At the very best, these ideas were the exclusive property of the learned and thoughtful. The poor, the ignorant, the bulk of mankind, ninety-nine hundredths of the whole human race, were totally shut out from them, and saw no more of them than they see of those stars which can only be descried through a telescope. And when the idea of the Dignity of Human Nature was set up, to guide and win men to virtue, it was an idea which all experience, which every one's consciousness belied. Hence it was as ineffectual to quench men's passions, as a burnt out cinder thrown into the midst of a blazing furnace. In a word, whatever power Faith may exercise toward overcoming the world in the lower regions of human activity,—where it has so many outward motives to help it on, and where it has no ceaseless struggle to maintain against man's corrupt Will,—in its higher office, where that corrupt Will is the very enemy it has to contend against, to subdue, to elevate, it is utterly impotent, so long as man is left to himself: and this impotence arises in great measure from the want of a worthy, satisfying, living Object, whereto it might cling, and whereby it might raise itself up.

This worthy, satisfying, living Object is to be found, not in anything that the outward world can supply or imply,—not in man, either as he exists in reality, or according to the fictitious idea of his dignity,—but solely in God. God alone is the worthy Object of Faith. He alone can fill all its boundless capacities, can fulfill all its wants. He alone can endow it with that strength, which will indeed overcome the world, wholly and for ever. God will do this; none else can. Not however the naked idea of God, as a being of infinite power, above all the conditions of time and space, and exempt from all the limitations of personality. Faith being a living knowledge,—a knowledge differing from other knowledge, not so much in the grounds and evidence on which it rests, as in its commanding power over the Will,—He who is the worthy, satisfying Object of Faith, must be a living personal Being, a Being to whom we stand in a living personal relation, who acts upon us, and will continue so to do. Nay, in its higher manifestation, as trust in

Him in whom we believe, Faith requires, not merely a living personal God, but a God on whose love we can rely. Now the God of what has erroneously been called Natural Religion,—the God of what might with more propriety be termed contranatural Religion, if indeed a mere creation of the Understanding can deserve the name of Religion at all,—is not such a God, as has been observed already. He is a bare notional abstraction, devised to supply a ground and consistency for the truths of Reason,—to supply a first link for the otherwise never-ending chain of causes and effects, a bond of unity for the multitudinous phenomena of the universe,—but standing in no direct personal relation to man. He is necessary indeed originally to our existence; but, so far as regards our afterlife, it is the same thing whether there be such a God or no. Hence he is not an object of Faith, but solely of belief. The Reason may be brought to acknowledge him: but he will exercise no more power over the Heart and Will, than any truth of geometry or ontology. If the Heart is to be stirred, if the Will is to be roused and renewed, Faith must have a God to believe in, who is not like the God of philosophy, a shadowy complex of negations to the conditions of time and space, shrouded in the abyss of eternity, but a God who cares for His creatures, and watches over them, and has given proof that he does so. *He who cometh to God must believe that He is a rewarder of them that diligently seek Him.*

Hence that idea of God which is implied in the

idolatrous worship of the heathens, defaced and distorted and fearfully corrupted as it is therein, is so far forth juster and truer than that idea which Philosophy tries to set up in the centre of its exausted receiver; inasmuch as the heathens believed that their gods would take thought about them, and would vouchsafe to hold intercourse with them, and would give ear to their prayers, and help them. Nay, they even believed that the gods could be moved with pity toward men, and could love their devout worshipers. In such a conception of God Faith has a worthy Object; and could she have clung thereto, without relaxing her hold to grasp the bloated phantoms of the senses, man would have been greatly strengthened in his warfare with the world. How marvellous the power of such Faith is, even when most grossly debased, how it quells the strongest passions, and crushes the most ineradicable instincts, may be seen at this day in the thousand-yeared superstitions of India. In the better ages of the great nations of antiquity, when the hearts of the people bowed with a willing obedience to the laws, it was in great measure on account of the religious sanction whereby they were hallowed. Here the masters of poetry and art sought and found their inspiration. Even the domestic hearth became dearer, and men fought more bravely for it, when it was associated with the altar of the gods. Through this Faith the greatest religious teacher of the heathen world, when his hour came, calmly and cheerfully drank the fatal hemlock.

But instances like this were very rare. There is no more humiliating and dismal example of the miserable weakness of human nature, when left to itself,—of the manner in which Faith, when it has no arm from on high to uphold it, is overcome by the world,—than when we see how those heavenly truths, which at times glimmer through the darkness of Paganism, were blotted out from sight for the most part by the vapours sent up from the pollutions and corruptions of men's hearts; or, if they were not wholly lost, served merely to illumine the mists with a fierce and bloody glare. Although the heathens had been taught to know something of God, they glorified Him not as God. Sight overpowered Faith; so that they lived not by Faith, but by Sight. They gave the glory of the invisible God to the visible creature; and, as in the dream of the patriarch, the powers of heaven did obeisance to the earth. Nay, they gave that glory to the putrid exhalations of their own hearts, and set up their own foul passions, their lust, their ferocity, their cunning, their cupidity, on the throne of the heavens. Thus was the victory of the world over Faith made manifest. Such was the disruption of man's being,— into such chaotic confusion had the perversion of his Will plunged his Understanding,—that he forgot the eternal, indissoluble union of holiness with wisdom and power, that of evil with weakness and folly. So long indeed as those whose intellects were more penetrating, held fast to the traditionary Faith of their Fathers, merely endeavouring to purge it from the impurities which human errour and frailty had attacht to it, many bright rays of truth dawned upon them; as we see in the greatest poets and philosophers of the ancient world. But too often the Intellect only displayed its own weakness and blindness; either corrupting the olden Faith still more, by peopling it with the monstrous brood of the Imagination; or else exercising its merely negative power in destroying that Faith altogether, and calling upon the simpler-minded to come and sit in the seat of the scorner. The result of which process was to give mankind up to the dominion of the senses; while the few who recoiled from this debasement, could find no way of conquering the impulses of their nature, except by extinguishing them.

God however had not left Himself without a witness on earth. He would not so forsake mankind, as that there should not be a single eye of Faith to look up to Him among all the nations, that there should not be a single altar, a single heart, from which prayer and thanksgiving and praise should mount to heaven. When the whole world was turning away from Him, to enwrap itself in its own nether darkness, He called Abraham to be the father of them that believe, and promist that from him in the course of ages should spring One, through Faith in whom all the nations of the earth were to be blessed. Thus did God ordain that Faith should overcome the world. When man had given himself up to the worship of the creature, of the earth and its fruits, of the flesh and its lusts,

God said, *I will light up the light of Faith in the heart of Abraham; and that Faith shall pass from father to son, and from generation to generation, until in the fulness of ages it shall spread over the whole earth. By that light man shall again see Him who is invisible, and shall live in His presence, and shall glorify Him. And this shall be the victory of Faith. Whereas man has given himself up to all unrighteousness, through Faith he shall be clothed in the pure righteousness of My Only-begotten Son. Through Faith sin shall be cast from the earth. Through Faith all the nations of the earth, whose portion now is amid cursing and woe, shall be blessed.*

By Faith Enoch and Noah had already overcome the world. Enoch overcame the world so completely, that, in the midst of the world, *he walkt with God.* The veil of the world, which hides God from man, was withdrawn from before him: he entered within the veil, and was no more seen by those whose sight the veil bounds. Noah too overcame the world, so as to walk with God; and when all the children of the world were swept away by reason of their unbelief, Noah through Faith was preserved from the universal destruction. Then, when the waters abated, and Noah came forth from the ark, and built an altar to the Lord, was seen the victory by which Faith overcomes the world. Yet, notwithstanding this awful testimony to the vanity of the world, and to the power of Faith, mankind was anew swallowed up by the waters of unbelief. From that time forward, the first recorded victory gained by Faith, in its highest relation, over the world, is that of Abraham. God revealed Himself to Abraham; and Abraham believed. When God called him forth from his country, and from his kindred, and from the house of his fathers,—as He has ever called forth those in whom He has chosen to be more especially glorified, above all when He purposes to bless man with a more plenteous outpouring of His Spirit,—as He called forth Moses,—as He called forth the Apostles and the Reformers from their kindred and their fathers house,—as He still in our days calls forth those whom He vouchsafes to make His angels in declaring His grace to the heathens,—when thus called forth, Abraham did not doubt, or tarry, but through Faith burst the bonds of ancient habit and familiar affection, and followed whithersoever the word of God led him, knowing that the Lord of the whole earth must of all guides be the surest, of all protectors the mightiest. So again was the same power of Faith to overcome the world, to overcome the strongest yearnings of natural love, made manifest when Abraham went forth with his son, the child of so many promises, and of such long anxious expectation, to offer him up to the Lord. By these two victories Abraham shewed that he was worthy to lead that army of the faithful, who, overcoming the world each in his own person, were in the course of ages so to overcome it for mankind, that the Son of God shall take all the nations of the earth for His inheritance, and that all His enemies shall become His footstool.

It was by direct, special, personal revelations of Himself, that God awakened the life of Faith in Abraham, and in the family of Abraham, by revelations of Himself as of a personal Being, and addrest directly and personally to Abraham. The Lord of heaven and earth declared himself to Abraham, not merely, as He does to all percipient and intelligent beings, in the unity and order and wisdom and beneficence of the universe,—not merely by the voice of reason, as He does to every one who can hear and interpret that voice,—not merely in those yearnings and aspirations, which, wherever they are not quencht, point men's hearts and souls heavenward,— but in an especial and immediate manner, renewing a likeness of that intercourse which had originally been granted to man in Paradise. Abraham was taught, that the Creator and Governor of the world does not leave mankind to the general operation of the laws He has ordained, without regard to what men may be, or do, or suffer, but that he watches over them severally, and overrules the course of events according to that which he sees in them. He was taught, that the Judge of all the earth doeth right,— that the natural world is not a thing by itself, working mechanically and blindly, without respect to good or evil,—but that the visible sphere of the laws of Nature is encompast by a higher invisible sphere of moral law, whereby its movements are regulated and determined. He was taught, that God does not sit aloof from His human creatures, even though the imaginations of their hearts are evil from their youth, —but that He will hold communion with them,—and that, in proportion as man's Faith is strong, and works in him by an unhesitating obedience, in the same proportion will he receive plainer and more blessed assurances of that communion. By like revelations was the life of Faith preserved among the descendants of Abraham; until God saw that the people, whom he had been training in the house of bondage and of affliction, to the end that they might acquire such a strength of character as would hold fast the precious gift committed to their keeping, were grown ripe and fitted for the fulfilment of His purpose. Then, as His purpose was, that the light, which had hitherto been burning on the hearth of a single family, should be set up on high in the face of the world on the altar of a whole people,—that the truth, which had hitherto been the heirloom of one household, should be the inheritance of a nation,—such being God's purpose, He who had hitherto shewn Himself by private, personal revelations, as the God of the family of Abraham, now manifested Himself by mighty deeds, visible in the eyes of multitudes, as the God of the earth and all of its nations, as the King of kings and Lord of lords, as the Lord of hosts, the God of battle. At the same time He revealed His name, as the eternal, self-existing I AM. And as God manifested His power outwardly by a great national deliverance, by leading a herd of bondmen out of captivity, and turning them into a nation, and making them ride on the high places of the earth,—hereby bringing to pass a visible outward fulfilment of the promise He had made to Abraham,—so did He display that Righteousness, which also had been revealed to Abraham, declaring His Will under the form of national law and national institutions. Thus, by this second great manifestation of Himself, God raised up a nation who should believe in Him and who should preserve the knowledge of the living God, and the trust in Him, amid the mountains of Judea, while all the rest of the earth gave itself up to the abominations of idolatry. By these means was the knowledge of God, and the Faith in Him, to be kept alive among the Jewish people, as the principle of their national life and individuality, until the time when He Himself should appear in the form of man upon earth, and should be lifted up from the earth, that He might draw all nations to His feet, and should send forth His messengers to declare His salvation to all ends of the world.

Such accordingly were the manifestations of God wherein the Israelites believed. They believed in Him, as the Maker of heaven and earth, as the Lord of heaven and of all the kingdoms of the earth,—as the living I AM, and praised Him who rideth on the heavens by His name JAH. But they also felt that they had a nearer, closer, more special bond of union to Him. He was the God of their fathers, the God of Abraham and of Isaac and of Jacob, the God of Israel, the God who had chosen them out from all the nations of the earth to be His peculiar people,—the God who by a mighty hand and an outstrecht arm had delivered them from their bondage in Egypt, from the power of Pharaoh and of his host,—who had led them safe through the Red Sea, dividing its waters in twain, and making them pass through the midst of it,— who had wonderfully supported and preserved them through the perils of the Wilderness,—who had brought them in triumph to the land of Canaan, the land promist of old to their fathers, and had driven out the heathens before them, and had given them the land for an everlasting possession. This was the firm ground of the Faith and trust which the children of Israel placed in Jehovah. This was the record and testimony which God establisht in Jacob and appointed in Israel, commanding that the fathers should make all these things known to their children, so that the generation to come might know them, and might in turn declare them to their children; in order that generation after generation might set their hope in God, and not forget the works of God, but keep His commandments. The memory of these wonderful manifestations of God's uplifting power and guardian care lived in the minds of the Israelites, and gave them a lively hope and trust in Him, to whom they owed these marvellous deliverances, to whom they owed their existence as a nation,—in Him, who, after He had declared His purpose to Abraham,—though generation after generation past away without any sign of its accomplishment, though all appearance and likelihood of its accomplishment had vanisht, and the very recollection of it had almost become extinct,—yet did not suffer His purpose to sleep, but, at the very moment when it seemed on the point of being utterly defeated, when the craft and power and cruelty of man were conspiring to overthrow it, at that very moment brought forth His people, and exalted the shepherds of Goshen into a nation, and raised up the child who was cast among the bulrushes, to be the champion and deliverer of his brethren, nay, to be their ruler and lawgiver, nay, to be the declarer of God's holy name, the utterer of God's holy law, for all the ends of the earth, and for all the generations of mankind. In reading the book of Psalms, which, according to the nature of lyrical poetry, more than any other book expresses the peculiar national feelings of the Jews, we see what a vivid recollection of these ancestral events filled and animated their souls, down to the latest age of which any memorial is there preserved. Indeed that recollection seems almost to become still more vivid in those Psalms which appear to belong to the period subsequent to the Babylonish captivity. For a nation in its glory lives in the present, a fallen and reviving nation in the past; as we ourselves have witnest in the recent history of Europe. Their later deliverance had only freshened the memory of that former one, from which the nation dated its birth, and had confirmed and enlivened the trust, which the earlier one had been designed to awaken. In truth this should always be the effect of every new mercy that we receive from God. It should not merely excite us to thankfulness on its own account, but should recall our thoughts and stir our hearts to a still deeper thankfulness and a still firmer assurance of Faith, on account of that great primary, all-surpassing proof of God's mercy, which was manifested when we too were delivered out of the house of our captivity.

This appears to be the peculiar form and character of that Faith which animated the Jews, as a people; if we look at it apart from those special inspirations, which were at times vouchsafed, along with a gift of prophetic intuition, and which taught the persons illumined by them, that the past redemption out of Egypt was mainly precious as the type of a still greater, far more wonderful, and far more blessed redemption,— that the land of Canaan given to their fathers was as a dreary wilderness, compared with the heavenly inheritance designed for the faithful,—that their beloved Jerusalem, although beautiful and glorious and the joy of the whole earth, was a poor shadowy miniature of that eternal city in the heavens, whose builder and maker is God. The Faith, which was a living principle in the hearts of the Jews, and which manifested itself so often by heroic action and endurance,—nay, which became so inwrought in them, that seventeen centuries of dispersion and oppression have not been able to destroy it,—was a Faith in Jehovah, as the God of their fathers, and their own God, who in manifold wonderful ways had shown Himself to be the Protector of their fathers, and who had chosen them out from all the nations of the earth to be His peculiar people. In this Faith there is an element, which men may easily distort into an alliance with the evil tendencies of their nature, and which may gain a more readily acknowledged sway over them by that alliance; though it is hindered thereby in its rightful work of delivering them from the bondage of those evil tendencies. Man, in all ages, and of almost every shade of character and belief, has been too apt to regard himself as the special favourite of heaven. Herein is involved a very crude and faint and inadequate notion of that infinite mercy and love wherewith the Almighty Creator and Redeemer embraces all His creatures. But that crude and imperfect notion is the more willingly received, because in its perverted shape it is made at once to flatter our selfish and our malignant passions. Eager to appropriate and monopolize everything, man would even appropriate and monopolize God. Although the light of God's love, when it falls on us, should humble us, by leading us to feel how dark we were without it, and should make us reflect some rays of it on every object around, yet the notion of God's special favour has often been deemed by men to sanction their thinking proudly of themselves, as though there must be something in them whereby that favour has been earned; while on the other hand they have assumed that scorn and hatred must be the portion due to those whom the divine sentence had cast out. More especially has this been the case when they have fancied that the favour of heaven was bestowed on them by an arbitrary act of Will,—when they have not discerned, or have forgotten, that the God, whom they believe to regard them with peculiar grace, is a God of holiness and justice.

By the heathens this was never discerned: at least their popular religion was often at direct variance with any recognition of this truth. To the Jews it had been declared, and fully displayed, although they were perpetually blinding their hearts to it. Along with the historical groundwork of their Faith, they had a Law, by keeping which they were to shew forth their Faith; and every commandment in that Law was as it were a fresh step toward overcoming the world. The Righteousness of God, which had dawned on the mind of Abraham, was set before the eyes of the nation that sprang from him, on the stone tables of Sinai. But as the Faith of the Jews was founded on outward demonstration, on wonders wrought by a mighty hand in the sight of mankind,—as they were taught to believe in Him who overcomes the world, by visible signs that He does indeed overcome it,—so their Law likewise consisted mainly in outward observances, being, as St Paul terms it, the rudiments fitted for the childhood of Faith. Under the patriarchal dispensation there had been no law. Infants are not trained by rules, but by the ever-present, ever-watchful love of their parents. And so, in the infancy of mankind, it was by perpetual immediate revelations that God declared His Will. Children on the other hand, when they pass out of infancy, have rules laid on them,—*touch not, taste not, handle not;* which rules they are to keep, and the transgression of which is followed by sensible punishment. In like manner the Law given by the hand of Moses to the Israelites, if we look not beyond the letter, was mainly a Law of outward injunctions and prohibitions, prescribing and forbidding certain outward acts; even as, in the rules given to children, outward acts are what we enjoin and forbid: for their childly capacities would not comprehend the meaning and application of a more spiritual law. At the same time, as in the rules given to children, the inward principles, which are to govern their after lives, though not expressly enunciated, should always be involved and implied,—so that their obedience may pass by an easy progress through the stage of blind, implicit Faith to the higher stage of conscious, voluntary, intelligent Faith,—thus the inward spiritual principles are ever involved and implied in the Law of Moses. Nay, those very commandments, which our Lord declares to be the sum of the Law and of the Prophets, had already been proclaimed in the Wilderness.

Nevertheless, as outward things are always separate and stubborn and loth to coalesce, while all spiritual things by an eternal harmony and concord unite into one and blend into an image and likeness of the Father of Spirits, the Faith of the Jews, which was founded on outward demonstrations of God's power, and the obedience of the Jews, which was to be shewn by the observation of an outward Law, did not grow together into an inseparable union, after the manner in which a spiritual Faith must needs grow together inseparably with a spiritual obedience. In reading the Law, as the Apostle declares of them (2 Cor. iii. 15), there was a veil upon their hearts. Often too they turned the Law itself into a veil, the letter of which darkened and concealed its spirit. Hence we may understand why, as was observed at the beginning of these Sermons, there is so seldom mention of Faith, according to the fulness of the Christian idea, in the Old Testament, and why the form under which it appears is that of trust. The Jews could trust in God, and could act nobly and boldly in that trust: for a high degree of such trust may exist apart from that earnest endeavour after righteousness, which ought ever to go along with it. But few of them lived by Faith: only the just can so live: and they alone, who do live by Faith, can be just. To take up the foregoing parallel: in children, even in those who love their parents the most, we often see strong eruptions of selfwill, and an oblivion of their parents commands, when temptation is at hand, and their parents are out of sight. Answerable to this is what we find in the history of the Jews. Even those who were the strongest in their Faith or trust in God's upholding and protecting providence, and who by this Faith were enabled in outward act to overcome the world, to vanquish the most formidable outward enemies it could bring against them,—even those who were full of this lively animating trust, and who in this trust encountered and overthrew every obstacle,—even they,—as we perceive, above all, in the awful example of David, —could yet fall at times so wofully and appallingly, that earth might well have trembled from her entrails, and nature given another groan. Among the countless victories which the world has gained over Faith, I know none the contemplation of which so stuns and confounds us, as when he, who had gone forth a youth in undoubting Faith, and slain Goliath,—he whose life had been visited by so many mercies, and whose soul had been illumined by such bright inspirations,—the holy Psalmist of Israel,—became the murderer of Uriah.

Those who are blind to their own hearts, and whose conception of human nature is squared according to the abstractions of their understandings, account such inconsistencies proofs of hypocrisy. And crushing proofs indeed they are of the hypocrisy which is within us, and of which we ourselves are unconscious, crushing proofs of the sway which the Father of lies has gained over mankind. But the hypocrisy, the lie, spreads through the whole of our unregenerate nature, and merely strikes us with more horrour in these examples, from the bright gifts with which it is coupled. We are warned what man must be, when even the noblest of men have such a dark chasm in their souls,--when he who seems to stand with one foot on the threshold of heaven, is tottering with the other on the brink of hell. This dark chasm meets us at every step in the history of the Jews. Their Faith itself opens our eyes to behold their miserable want of Faith, and our own. As we see in them what a glorious thing Faith is, when it is strong and true, so in them too do we see what wretchedness and shame are man's portion, when, loosing his hold of Faith, he falls into the formless chaos of unbelief. Much had been revealed to the Jews. They alone among the nations knew with what never-slumbering care the Almighty Creator watches over His creatures, and preserves them. They alone knew His Righteousness, how His holy Will, which gives law to the universe, is a law likewise to Himself. But in proportion as their spiritual discernment became more piercing, in proportion as they gained a clearer and fuller insight into their own moral condition, in the same proportion did it become plain that the revelation was incomplete. They could not harmonize the parts of it together. If they turned their thoughts upward, to that which God had declared to them concerning Himself, they knew that He is a *jealous God*, and yet that He *shews mercy to thousands*: they knew that He *forgives iniquity and transgression and sin*, and yet that He *will by no means clear the guilty*: they knew that He is gracious and longsuffering, and yet that He is righteous and holy. On the other hand, when they lookt at themselves, they had the most certain assurances of God's favour and lovingkindness: yet they were bound to obey the Law, and, being all transgressors of the Law, had fallen under His wrath. They knew that God never forsaketh the righteous: but they were unrighteous: how then could they trust in Him? how could they look for anything but wrath? They did not keep the Law: they could not. Although God compast them around, as the mountains stood around Jerusalem, He had not yet come down to dwell in men's hearts, and to endow them with a strength above their own, so that they might serve and obey Him. He was near to them; but they were still far off from Him. He had chosen them to be His people; but they made themselves an abomination in His sight. The Law was the flaming sword of the Cherubim, turning every way, to keep the way of the Tree of Life, and repelling them from it.

For bridging over this chasm, which still separated man from God, two ways were set before the Jews, the same in their termination, but differing apparently at the outset: and both of them were ways of Faith; as indeed every way must be, whereby man draws nigh to God. One was the way of sacrifice, by which expiation and atonement were to be made, and which was to be a type and sign of the slaying and offering up of the carnal will, the carnal nature, to God. Thus, when performed in a right spirit, sacrifices were acts of Faith. They were acknowledgements that there is a Being greater than the world, its Lord and Ruler, —that all the gifts of the world are His gifts,—that they have a real worth only as coming from Him,— and that the firstfruits of them are ever due, as marks of gratitude, to the Giver. Moreover the Jewish sacrifices were confessions of sin, acknowledgements that man is not what he ought to be,—acknowledgements that there is an archetypal humanity to which man ought to attain, but does not,—acknowledgements that there is a rightful and righteous Judge, to whom he is accountable for his transgressions, whose wrath he has to deprecate, whose forgiveness to implore. But here again the world overcame Faith, even as it did also in the case of the Law. It overcame Faith, when it wrested the Law from Faith,—when it hid the spiritual meaning of the Law, and crusted it over with carnality,—when it choked and stifled the spirit with the letter,—when it persuaded men to keep the letter for selfish, carnal ends. And so, whenever the works of the Law are wrought otherwise than from a living principle of Faith,—whenever the works themselves are accounted good and held to have any value,— whenever they are made subservient to any earthly, selfish purpose, to man's glory or interest,—the weakness of Faith is laid bare, and the world triumphs over it. Indeed the very necessity for a law results from the weakness of our Faith. Were we strong in Faith, our hearts and minds would ever be fixt on the principles of right and duty; we should walk in their light, and see everything by that light, without being drawn astray by the temptations and delusions of the world. Only because we are so apt to lose sight of the heavenly

lodestars, do we need earthly guideposts: and one of
the saddest and most humiliating victories of the
world over Faith is to persuade us that the use of these
guideposts is to lead us, not to a heavenly, but to an
earthly city. In like manner the spiritual significance
and purpose of the sacrifices were forgotten. They
were regarded as having an efficacy in themselves to
propitiate God. Thus they were turned into engines
of superstition, that is, of Faith crouching and writhing
under the weight of the world. So utterly had men's
feelings and perceptions been perverted, they deemed
the one thing desirable to be, that they might escape
the punishment of sin: they lookt upon God with fear,
because He would draw them away from sin: they
besought Him to let them continue in sin; and they
fancied that the blood of bulls and of goats might
bribe Him to do so. As they themselves had been
deluded and blinded by the shows of the world,
they thought that God also might in like manner be
deluded and blinded. *Wherefore, when the Onlybegotten
Son cometh into the world, He saith, Sacrifice and
offering Thou wouldest not; in burnt offerings and
sacrifices for sin Thou hast had no pleasure. Then
said I, Lo, I come, to do Thy will, O God.* Whatsoever
does not spring freshly and livingly from Faith, cannot
be wellpleasing in the eyes of God. This carnalminded-
ness, which is fain to deck itself out with the shells of
dead works, was so common among the later Jews,
that it has been deemed the distinguishing feature of
the Judaizing spirit. Yet, alas! it has not been con-

fined to the Jews: it has shewn itself in all ages of the Christian Church: and its tokens have been of the same kind, an excessive attachment to outward forms, to ordinances, to ceremonies, a proneness to believe that these are the things of paramount importance, that these are the chief instruments of salvation, and that there can be no salvation without them. For in the Christian Church, as well as in the Jewish, we are taught by numberless examples, that Faith, when it is not pure, does not overcome, but is overcome by the world.

To the early Jewish Church God spoke by means of types. By types He foreshewed the atonement which was one day to be accomplisht. In this, as in all things, the plan of His providence has been adapted to the wants and capacities of man. During the youth of a nation, as during that of individuals, the sign and the thing signified are more readily regarded as one and the same. But with the progress of years the dividing, analysing Understanding becomes stronger. The notion gains ground, that the sign is a mere sign; as indeed it must be, when severed from the quickening power of Faith. Some still cling to it, though without believing it to be more: others reject it. In such a state of feeling it is requisite to speak more distinctly to the intellect by words, the great bond and only clear medium of intelligent intercourse and communion. This was the work for which the Prophets were sent. As the Law had foreshewn the atonement by types, the Prophets declared it by words. In them we find the consummation of the Jewish religion,—a consummation which was the close of the first, and the preparation of the second Dispensation,—the more distinct and definite announcement of Him who was to overcome the world, not for Himself merely, but for all such as will believe in Him;—of Him through whom the Faith, hitherto confined to Judea, was to be spread over the world, who was to have the heathen for His inheritance, and the utmost parts of the earth for His possession;—of Him, who was to sit down at God's right hand, until all mankind were brought to acknowledge Him, and all His enemies were made His footstool;—of Him, who came to do the will of God with His whole heart, and Faith in whom will give men a whole heart, will alone enable them to do the will of God;—of Him, in the day of whose power His people were to be willing, and to spring forth in the beauty of holiness, like dew from the womb of the morning. This was the Faith the Prophets were commissioned to proclaim to the Jews, a Faith which was to be an assurance of things hoped for: but this Faith also was overcome by the world. That which was spiritual in the prophecy, was corrupted by carnal interpretations. Instead of looking forward with yearning to the coming of a spiritual Deliverer, of a spiritual King, the hope and desire of the Jews was a temporal Deliverer, a temporal King. Instead of rejoicing that they were God's chosen instrument for freeing all nations from the bondage of ignorance and sin, they were content that the nations should remain in that bondage, if they might but themselves sit down at God's right hand, and make all their enemies their footstool. Thus they in great measure forestalled that carnal misconception of the nature of Christ's Kingdom, which in after ages became so prevalent in Christendom, and through which Rome claimed to be the spiritual, as she had been the temporal mistress of the world.

Hence we see that the revelation made to the Jews was incomplete; and so it was seldom adequate to produce anything like a Faith which will overcome the world. The victories gained beneath it were mostly outward and partial. Outward enemies might be conquered; but the far more formidable ones within the heart were still strong, and seemingly invincible. The revelation was incomplete, both in what it made known concerning God's relation to man, and concerning man's relation to God. It did not shew how a God of holiness could look with favour on a sinful world. It did not show how a frail creature could render a service acceptable to God. These were man's two great wants. He knew them not indeed: still less did he know how they were to be removed: but in proportion as he was taught to discern more of God, and of himself, the more did he become conscious of his bondage to the world; the more strongly did he feel that he had not that assurance of invisible things, which would overcome the world. The revelation which was completed on the day of Pentecost first taught us plainly what we wanted, at the same time that it fulfilled all our wants. We wanted the knowledge of a Saviour: we wanted His atonement, His intercession. We wanted the indwelling presence of the purifying, strengthening Spirit. We wanted Christ, both as Jesus and as Emmanuel. This is the mystery which was hidden from the beginning, the mystery which so many prophets and sages desired to see into, and could not. And this mystery was made manifest, when the Son of God took our nature upon Him, to shew us how we are to overcome the world, and to endow us with that Faith which will enable us to overcome it.

SERMON VI.

FAITH IN CHRIST, THE VICTORY THAT OVERCOMETH THE WORLD.

1 JOHN v. 6.

"Who is he that overcometh the world, but he who believeth that Jesus is the Son of God?"

HITHERTO we have been speaking of partial, imperfect forms of Faith, of forms under which it has seldom been able to accomplish anything like its great work of giving man the victory over the world. And this its weakness and imperfection has clearly been owing in great measure to the incompleteness and insufficiency of its Object, which had not such a constraining power as could set man at one with himself, or make him feel at one with God. The perfect supreme harmony, the inseparable, indivisible unity of Faith, working by love, and shewing itself by a life of obedience, is only to be found in Christianity. Wherefore the Apostle, after having declared that *Faith is the victory which overcometh the world*, adds, *Who is he that overcometh the world, but he who believeth that Jesus is the Son of God?* This is a glorious subject, a subject of the deepest interest and widest importance, and would furnish ample matter for a whole course of Sermons. For what does it embrace? the whole Object of Christian Faith, the whole substance of Christian Duty, in their union and unity. All however that it will be possible for me to do, is to call your attention to some of the peculiarities, whereby Faith in Christ is distinguisht from all other Faith, so that the very name of Faith has in a manner been specially appropriated to it, and whereby it is enabled to effect, what no other Faith can, its great work of overcoming the world.

Who is he that overcometh the world, but he who believeth that Jesus is the Son of God? That none else can, is plain and certain. All other Faith is overcome by the world. The office of Faith, we have seen, is to raise our hearts from visible things to invisible, from the objects of the present moment to the hopes held out by the future. Its great end is to deliver us from the bondage of sense and the senses, of self and selfishness, and to make us live spiritually, in the spirit and by the spirit, for spiritual objects, and with spiritual aims,—to enable us to discern the hand of God in all things, so that we may live with a wakeful consciousness that we are ever in the presence of God,—that we may live as children under the eye of a loving Father, reverencing Him with holy Fear, fearing to disobey Him, fearing to displease Him, fearing to do wrong in His sight, assured of His love, and therefore loving Him, and anxious to shew forth that love in all things, looking to Him for counsel, for aid, trusting Him undoubtingly in every time of need. This is the great work which Faith is designed to accomplish, to restore man to the presence of God, which he lost at the Fall. This is the true victory whereby it is to overcome the world,—whereby it is to overcome everything in the world that would lure or drive us away from God,—whereby it is to draw aside the bright gaudy curtain which the world stretches out before us, and to open our eyes to behold the living God sitting on His eternal throne above it. This is the great and glorious work of Faith: but this work in the natural man it is utterly unable to bring to pass. It is utterly unable to do anything of the kind, anything at all approaching to this. So long as its operation is bounded to the outward world,—so long as its sole aim is to make us prefer a remote worldly object to a near one,—so long therefore as, instead of battling against the world, and striving to overcome it, and to cast off its yoke altogether, it merely labours to raise the world out of its rude barbarian nakedness, and to invest it with the gorgeous clothing of thought, to stamp it with the image of its human lord,—so long Faith has great power. But when its purpose is to disenthrall the spiritual affections from the bondage of the carnal appetites, or to give reality to the ideas of the Reason, and authority to the voice of the Conscience, and to set up Duty in its rightful sovereinty over mankind, it is powerless,—as powerless as the vital spirit in a plant is to unfold a cankered blossom.

Nor is it less impotent to pierce through that thick dark veil, which the visible universe has spread before the face of God, ever since man gave himself up to the worship of the creature: sooner might it lift off the crust of the earth, and lay bare the seething throes of the elementary furnace beneath. Philosophy may indeed evolve a certain idea of God: but her God, so far as he is merely hers, has no power over the heart, none over the will. He is made up of negations. Therefore, as we cannot conceive any action, except where there is some cognateness between the agent and that which is acted upon, he may well be placed, as he was by the Epicureans, in absolute apathy and indifference. It is only for *the living God* that the soul can *thirst*, that *the heart and flesh cry out*. Even among the heathens, it was only when incarnate in the attributes of humanity, that the divine idea exercised any sway over their lives. At the same time it is plain that there can be no strong Faith in Polytheism. The light, which is to possess such a genial heat as to make the earth bring forth her fruits, must be concentrated in the sun, not split and scattered among the stars. Besides all Polytheism rests on a ground of Pantheism, which is the speculative consummation of the victory of the world over Faith. Nor can there be a strong Faith in a mythological religion, in a form of religion in which the objects of worship are manifestly indebted for the chief part of what is recorded concerning them, if not for their very existence, to an allegorizing and personifying fancy; as is proved by the slight practical influence which was exercised by the beautiful mythology of Greece. For Faith grows bloated and sickly, when it has to feed on fictions: it thrives solely on truth. Superstition will indeed swallow fictions voraciously: in fact, this is its essential character, that it substitutes fictions for the truth. But Superstition is slavish, the slave of the world and of the senses, and thus the antipode and antagonist of Faith; which is free from the bondage of the world, being made free by the truth. Being the atoning principle in the mind, it is shaken and marred when the faculties jar against each other: but when the Imagination is allowed free play, to adorn the objects of popular worship, it will infallibly invent much that the Reason and Conscience will reject. Here therefore that want of stability will betray itself, which is ever the characteristic of the doubleminded. On the other hand, when it pleased God to reveal Himself by outward manifestations of His power and guardian care, and to declare His Will outwardly by express positive ordinances on the stone tables of the Law, although this revelation produced admirable examples of a dauntless, unwavering trust in God, still Faith, as we saw in the last Sermon, even where it was strongest, seldom wrought its rightful effect of hallowing the life and conduct. The declarations of God's Will, which man received the most readily, were those which best admitted of being brought into alliance with his proud and loveless nature. And as the revelation itself had been outward, so there was ever a strong tendency under it to rest in the outward act, and to regard that as the only thing needful or important. Thus, while the carcase of Heathenism was rotting under the combined action of scepticism and voluptuousness, the glory of Judaism had departed, and the law was ossified into lifeless formalities.

Such was the miserable helplessness of Faith,—crawling like a worm along the ground, unable to lift itself up, and already bruised and maimed by the tread of Sin, which seemed on the point of extinguishing it,—when God vouchsafed to manifest all the riches of His grace to mankind in Christ Jesus. Down to that time Faith had seldom been successful except when employed in decorating and emblazoning the chariot of the Prince of this world, or when sent before him to prepare a way for his conquests. But as to stopping and driving back his chariot,—a child might as well stretch out its hand to drive back a rushing whirlwind. Moreover, as the departure of the spirit is ever rapidly followed by the dissolution of the body, Faith having wholly lost the power of raising man's soul to anything above him, was also losing its power as the uniting, organizing principle of human society. What then was the way which God took to strengthen Faith, so that it might indeed enable man to overcome the world? Did he come with some mighty outward manifestation of His omnipotence, riding upon the cherubim, and flying upon the wings of the wind? Did He lay bare the skeleton of Nature, to shew man the idol he trusted in, shaking the earth, and shivering its cities, and sweeping the sea over the heads of the mountains? Or did He set up some huge monument, some centuple pyramid, or tower in which Babel would have been a petty chamber, in order that pilgrims from all the ends of the earth should flock, generation after generation, to behold and be convinced by this demonstration of a power so greatly surpassing that of man; as we may imagine that the inhabitants of the remoter side of the moon must needs be perpetually travelling to gaze on the vast orb of the earth? Or did He establish a kingdom, which should cast the chains of its dominion around the globe, and by which all the empires of the world should be swallowed up, as the serpents that sprang from the rods of the magicians were swallowed up by the mightier serpent from the rod of Aaron? Yet this was the very disease of the world, that it would only perceive, that it would only believe in, that it would only trust in, that it would only worship the outward and visible. And was this disease to be cured by a revelation, the glory of which would itself have been outward and visible? He who has read history aright knows that terrific visitations and desolating calamities, though they may strengthen Faith in those in whom it is already strong, only foster superstition where Faith is weak, and render unbelief still more reckless. They who will not believe in God, ascribe His works to Beelzebub. *Let us eat and drink*, is the cry of those, who merely know that tomorrow they die. Or, if the wonders of the universe, those which are permanent and changeless, and those which are ever varying,—the wonders of light and motion and order and life,—did not sufficiently bespeak a living Maker and Governor, was this to be done by any dead mass? On the other hand, what the effect of a temporal kingdom would have been, we are taught by seeing how Faith grew faint and failed, when the Church forgot her spiritual destination, and attempted to erect a universal monarchy. Should one lesson be insufficient, another is afforded by the sensual debasement which has everywhere followed the sword of the false prophet of Arabia. Constant experience proves that no wonders can convince those whose hearts are proof against the higher spiritual evidences of truth,—that they who hear not Moses and the prophets, will not be persuaded though one should rise from the dead.

How then did the Lord of heaven and earth manifest Himself to a race so loth to believe in anything, except what appealed to their senses? How did He call mankind from the slavery of sense to the free obedience of Faith? Again the Lord came not in the strong wind. The Lord came not in the earthquake. The Lord came not in the fire. A babe was born in a stable at Bethlehem; and shepherds were called to look thereon. In this manner did the King of kings bow the heavens and come down, to overcome the world. This was the pomp of His coming, this His army, this His retinue. This was His first lesson to all such as were to believe in Him, admonishing them how they were to overcome the world. And as His birth was, such was His life. Poor, lowly, destitute, forsaken, reviled, persecuted, homeless, driven from place to place, an object of scorn and hatred, mockt, scourged, crucified, an outcast from the world, put to death by the world,—how did He overcome the world? By patience, by meekness, by longsuffering, by purity, by holiness, by perseverance in welldoing, notwithstanding all that the world could do to hinder and deter Him,—by unweariableness in all the offices of love toward His enemies, no less than His friends. Then did the powers of hell tremble on their seat, amid the rolling sea of everlasting darkness, when the Spirit of God, descending upon Him who had shewn His purpose to fulfill all righteousness, declared Him to be the beloved Son, in whom the Father was well pleased. Then were the gates of brass broken, and the bars of iron cut in sunder, to let out those whom the world held in the bondage of its lusts and passions, when the voice of Him who was hanging on the Cross was heard beseeching His Father to forgive His murderers; for that they knew not what they did.

Many, brethren, and mighty are the aids whereby the believer in Christ is assisted and encouraged to overcome the world. One main ground of the weakness of Faith, we have seen, had always been our inadequate knowledge of its great Object. Without Christ, we know little of God in His true relation to man; we have but an imperfect knowledge of man, especially in his relation to God; we can frame no conception of a possibility that God and man should be at one. For the heroes and demigods of the heathens always had their full share in the evil of man's nature; and their superiority was rather physical than moral. But Christ, as perfect God, shews us what God is; as perfect Man, shews us what man ought to be; as at once perfect God and perfect Man, shews us how God and man may be at one. Something indeed of God had been made manifest from the beginning, and was spread out before the eyes of mankind by a constant, ineffaceable revelation, which day told to day, and night uttered to night,—even His eternal power and divinity, His power, and the wisdom and goodness displayed in the order and harmony of the universe. But from these manifestations, which ought to have been plain and convincing to a being endowed with a reasonable understanding, man turned away, and ascribed the power and the beneficence to the created things themselves, and lookt upon them as their own lords and rulers, yea, and as his also, as the lords and rulers of his heart and soul: and so he said, *There are gods many, and lords many.* Even in the manifestation of Himself made on mount Sinai, in the

Law, God only permitted Moses to behold the back parts of His eternal Will. He still did not let His face be seen. The spirit was indeed latent in the Law; but the Law was outward, as every positive law must be. The perfect manifestation was reserved for the time when all the fulness of the Godhead was to dwell bodily on earth in the Man Christ Jesus; for the time when the Word, which was God from the beginning, was made flesh, and dwelt amongst us, and we beheld His glory, the glory of the Only-begotten of the Father, full of grace and truth. This then is one great victory, whereby he who believes that Jesus is the Son of God, overcomes the world, He sees God, whom the world would hide from him; and the phantoms and spectres of the world vanish before the light of the Eternal Father.

So again from Christ's allperfect example,—from His purity, from His holiness, from his patience, from His meekness, from His gentleness, from His unswerving resolution not to resist evil, but to overcome evil by good, from His unceasing diligence in doing His heavenly Father's will, from His unremitting activity in every ministration of love to the whole race whose nature He had taken upon Himself, even to the most unworthy, even to His bitterest enemies, —from this glorious pattern of that Love which suffereth long and is kind, which vaunteth not itself, seeketh not its own, is not easily provoked, thinketh no evil, rejoiceth in the truth, beareth all things, hopeth all things, endureth all things, and never faileth—from this great Exemplar of what man ought to be, we may learn through Faith, and through the aid of the Spirit shewing us the things of Christ, to gain a victory over the world, and over our own carnal hearts, the worst, and to us far the deadliest and most unconquerable part of the world. Fain would they beguile us into believing that we may be content to be, nay, that we ought to be, something very different from this. They would beguile us into believing that, as we have fleshly appetites, we may indulge those fleshly appetites: and here as ever the serpent understanding is ready with its sophistries, to persuade us that the only restraint we need impose on ourselves, is that markt out by nature, when it made excess injurious. They would beguile us into believing that our own gratification, our own exaltation, our own glory, the taking care of ourselves, the raising ourselves to eminence, are rightly the main business and purpose of our lives. They would beguile us into believing that we are to fall down and worship the image of honour and dignity which the world has set up; that if we are reviled, we are to revile again; that, if we are smitten, we are to smite again, blow for blow, and wound for wound, taking care that our retaliation be at least not lighter than the offense. They would lead us to interpret St Paul's exhortation, not according to the life-giving spirit, but according to the killing letter,—to heap coals of fire on our enemy's head, not for the sake of melting his wrath and kindling his love, but of consuming him. They would make us strive to overcome evil by evil, in doing which, as the Apostle's words warn us, we should ourselves be overcome by evil: whereas, whenever we strive to overcome evil with good, we are performing our part in that great work of Faith, which is to overcome all the evil in the world.

The features of this picture, when seen by the all-revealing light of Christianity, do indeed look hideous and revolting. Yet they are not taken from the worst side of human nature, from that which is acknowledgedly and wilfully sinful. They are representations of that which the natural man does not condemn, but rather approves,—of that which custom and the opinion of the world have generally sanctioned, —of that which persons usurping the name of philosophers have pronounced to be right and fitting. And though man, without the light of Christianity, may attain to a much purer and nobler conception of duty, he will hardly perceive, without that light, how the vulgar notions just mentioned are not merely at variance with, but in direct opposition to the truth, and how the fundamental principle, to which everything is referred, and by which everything is estimated in them, is in fact the one main principle and source of evil in the world. Now what must ensue from our beholding our nature, not merely its outward form and seemly countenance, but the inmost network of its nerves and muscles, its impulses and motives, as reflected to us in the spotless mirror of the perfect man Christ Jesus? what but a conviction of the utter corruption and depravity of our nature, of our total estrangement from all holiness and godliness,—of a corruption not confined to our outward actions, not to be eradicated or healed by any amendment of conduct, but spreading through every pore of the heart, and poisoning the very lifeblood of the will, of which self-pleasing, self-indulgence, self-exaltation, self-idolatry, under one form or other, are the main actuating spring and motive. In the perfect God, Christ Jesus, we see what God is. In the perfect Man, Christ Jesus, we see what man ought to be. In the perfect God and perfect Man, Christ Jesus, we see how the holiness of God may be in entire union and unity with the godliness of man. In Him we see how the world may indeed be overcome, how the Kingdom of Heaven may descend upon earth and how the throne of God may be establisht within it. But when we look at ourselves, what do we see? except how we have been overcome by the world, overcome by it in all manner of ways,—overcome by its charms, overcome by its bribes, overcome by its lusts, overcome by its darkness, overcome by its glare, overcome by its flattery, overcome by its scorn, overcome by its terrours,—how we have been fettered and manacled and bound to its car,—nay, how we have rusht forward of our own accord, and cast ourselves under its thundering wheels, and have bid them roll over our souls, and have even deemed we were rejoicing, when writhing beneath them. Thus on being taught to discern the true relation between man and the world, do we discover that we have been shamefully overcome by it. And how and why have we been thus overcome? Through our want of Faith: through our want of Faith in that which is invisible, and our giving up our hearts to visible things: through our want of Faith in the future, and our prostration before the present: through our want of Faith in reason, in conscience, in hope, in love, and our persuasion that material, palpable, sensual pleasures,—pleasures that we can see with our eyes, and grasp with our hands, and taste with our palates,—pleasures that pamper our carnal hearts, and flatter our selfwill, and magnify us in our own estimation,—are the only true realities. And as it is through our want of Faith, that we have been overcome by the world, so through Faith alone can we rise out of this disastrous defeat, and overcome that whereby we have hitherto been overcome; through Faith in Him who is invisible,—through Faith in that heavenly peace and joy which await all such as endeavour through Faith to attain to them,—through Faith in Reason and its laws,—through Faith in Conscience, as the voice of God,—through Faith in the beauty of holiness,—through Faith, as the ground of that Love, which, after the example of Christ, will also believe all things, and hope all things, and endure all things, and never fail. This Faith God has graciously vouchsafed to strengthen, by manifesting that grace, which before had been hidden, in the person of His Only-begotten Son, and by shewing us in Him how man ought to live, in order to feel the atoning power of Faith, in order to find peace in himself, and favour with God.

But here the world, as it had hitherto drawn us away from God by its deceitful lures, now tries to scare us from Him. It lifts up its voice within us, and cries, *In vain dost thou behold the holiness and lovingkindness of God. In vain dost thou perceive what a noble being thou thyself oughtest to be, thou whom God made a little lower than the angels, and whom He crowned with glory and worship. Hadst thou kept thy first estate, then indeed this sight would have been a pure joy to thee. I myself rejoiced and was glad, when God first sent me forth on my course through the heavens, when the morningstars sang the hymn of the creation, and all the sons of God shouted for joy. But when thou by thy sin madest me a partaker in thy curse, then was I turned away from God; then I hid, what before I manifested; and from that time forth I have made thee my slave, who wert placed upon me to be my master. I have worn thee out in beautifying and enriching my face. I have forced thee to give up thy heart and soul, and all thy heavenly hopes and aspirations, for such poor scantlings of wages as I might deign to dole out to thee. But though I treat thee thus, thou canst not escape from me. Thou art bound to me by thy weakness, through which thou canst not lift thyself above me. Thou art bound to me by thy passions and appetites, which have overrun thy soul, and which sprout up so thickly* within thee, that thou canst never root them out, and clear thyself from them. Above all, thou art bound to me by thy sins, which have made thee an outcast from God, which render thee an abomination in His sight, and not one of which thou canst ever wipe out. Vex not thyself therefore with thoughts about heavenly things, which can never profit thee, which can only deepen thy anguish by the vision of what thou hast lost, of the love thou hast outraged and forfeited. Abide contentedly with me, feeding on the husks of those pleasures wherewith I won thy soul, until I gather thee to thy fathers, and swallow thee up. Eat, drink; for tomorrow thou shalt die.

This struggle between the feeling of sinfulness, of helplessness, and of condemnation, on the one hand, and the desire awakened on the other hand to fulfill the demands of duty, and to realize the idea of humanity, in such a manner as to find favour in the sight of God,—the same struggle, of which St Paul gives so awful a representation in the seventh chapter of the Epistle to the Romans,—is what oppresses a man, and almost crushes him, when his eyes are opened to behold the glory of the Godhead, and of the perfect Manhood in Christ, and turn, with the light derived from thence, to look into the abyss of sin within him. The representation given by St Paul is indeed that of a man under the Law, whereby we have the knowledge of sin: but it implies the far deeper consciousness inspired by the Gospel, whereby sin has become yet more exceeding sinful. It represents the condition of a man who has the light of the Gospel, without any feeling of its comfort. Many are the forms which this struggle takes, many the sophisms wherewith the enemy would deceive us, according to the character of the heart on which his assault is to be made. But no one has ever attained to a deep, living, personal knowledge of Christ, to a deep, living, personal conviction of the blessing of being reconciled to God, without passing in one way or other through this fiery baptism, and being brought to acknowledge his natural estrangement from God; although to many this crisis may be greatly tempered by the effect of God's grace, working gradually, and without any violent check, on their souls. Many may never have departed so far from Christ, as to feel any strong revulsion when they give themselves up to Him altogether. Very many however are there, who, as in the Eastern tale,—if I may be allowed to take an apt image, which has been applied somewhat similarly by a German poet,—find all the nails and bars and holdfasts of the vessel, in which they have hitherto been sailing securely along, all the maxims and rules of their former experience, all their aims and purposes and desires, start suddenly out of their places, as they approach the magnetic mountain,— and who, though they reach it, do so only after battling nakedly against the waves, with peril of their lives. Now in this last dread conflict which we have to go through, before the world will loosen its hold on our souls, there is no help for us, there is no strength for us, except in Faith. The more we strive after purity, the more we become conscious of our impurity. The more earnest our efforts grow, the more hopeless must they be, unless they are supported by Faith,—by Faith in the perfect righteousness of Christ, and in His gracious purpose to bestow that righteousness on all such as believe in Him. This is the consolation which gleams upon St Paul, after his wandering through that dark labyrinth where the vision of Right and Duty seemed only to repell man. This is his comfort, after that exclamation of despairing anguish, sent up from the very heart of mankind,— *O wretched man that I am! who shall deliver me from the body of this death?* On earth there is no deliverance: in man there is no help. But there is a deliverance; and for this he thanks God through Jesus Christ our Lord. For there is no condemnation to those who are in Christ Jesus, walking not after the flesh, but, by Faith, after the spirit.

This is the great, decisive work of Faith, in our spiritual life. When our sense of our own utter helplessness is thoroughly awakened, when we are bowed down by fear and shame, by a feeling of reprobateness and condemnation, then Faith beholds the gracious love of God offering us forgiveness for the sake of the perfect righteousness of His Son,— offering to clothe us with that righteousness, that we too may be righteous as He was, if we will but strive to tear off that clinging robe of sin, which we have hitherto been girding fold after fold around our souls.

and will endeavour to put on the righteousness of Christ. Faith beholds this, and embraces the offer thankfully, joyfully, with prayer and praise, casting away all self-reliance, all trust in human works, trusting solely, living wholly, in the perfect righteousness of Christ. The soul feels that it has no longer any need of the sun or the moon to shine on it: for the glory of God lightens it; and the Lamb is its light. Thus, in this most terrible of all the struggles that man has to go through, Faith, and Faith alone, enables him to overcome the world.

After this critical victory has been gained, the rest of our warfare, though our life on earth must still ever be a warfare, is comparatively easy. We must still indeed live by Faith: we must stand by Faith: we must hold up the shield of Faith against the fiery darts of sin. Faith, which in man's earthly life we were led to regard as the sword wherewith he is to conquer, in his spiritual life, as the Apostle teaches us, is rather his shield. For in our spiritual life our main business is to stand on the defensive, to guard ourselves from evil by Faith, so that the Spirit of God may work freely in us, and that we may not be hindered in fulfilling God's purpose with the sword of the Spirit. They, however, who fight against evil after such a conflict, fight with the feeling that they have already been conquerors, with the feeling that God is for them, that Christ has justified them. *Who*, they are enabled to say, *shall separate us from the love of Christ? Shall tribulation, or distress, or persecu-*

tion, or famine, or nakedness, or peril, or the sword? Nay, in all these things we are more than conquerors through Him that loved us. Neither death, nor life, nor angels, nor principalities, nor powers, nor things present, nor things to come, nor highth, nor depth, nor any other creature, shall be able to separate us from the love of God, which is in Christ Jesus our Lord.

Who is he that overcometh the world? Even he who believeth that Jesus is the Son of God. In the first ages of the Church the very act of believing this implied a great victory over the world. It implied a victory over the carnal understanding, and over the carnal heart. It implied that he who so believed was not ashamed of that Cross, which was a stumblingblock to the Jew, and foolishness to the Greek. It implied that he had discerned the mystery of the Kingdom of Heaven, that he had lookt through the mask of the world, and seen the eternal realities behind it. And as the profession of such a belief was encompast by danger and scandal,—as it compelled men to burst the bonds of habit, and often those of family and friendship and companionship,—as it always required a sacrifice of inveterate prejudices and prepossessions, mostly of wordly advantages, and not seldom of the strongest affections,—the very profession, thus proving the sincerity of the belief, was so far a victory over the world. At present, on the other hand, such a profession, unless followed up by earnest consistency of conduct,—unless we really take up that Cross, which was stampt on our forehead in our infancy,—is attended by no danger or shame or difficulty, is in most cases the natural result of outward circumstances, and so of itself can afford no proof that the belief profest is truly rooted in the heart. A slight movement against the stream indicates some sort of energy: with the stream even things without life float along. But are there no difficulties in the way of a belief in Christ as the Son of God, which still render such a belief a victory over the world? Surely, if of old the fetters of Habit and Custom withheld men from believing in Christ, so do they now. For Custom does not merely resist what is opposed to it, but undermines what rests upon it. Great as is the power of Habit, its power is that of making us act mechanically, rather than with a lively consciousness of what we are doing. Thus it is the direct antagonist to Faith. Every one must have experienced how the strongest impressions lose their force after a while, unless they are met by some responsive activity, by means of which an inward principle may be substituted for the decay of the outward stimulant; unless the spiritual man be constantly alert to keep off the drowsiness which creeps over the natural man, no less when basking in the sun, than when chilled by the frost. This is a part of our slavery to the world. The soil is soon worn out by a repetition of the same crops; and hardly anything is more difficult than to reinfuse life into words and notions, which have long lain dead on the surface of our souls.

Still too, as of yore, the Incarnation of the Son of

God, the Manifestation of God in the flesh, the Reconciliation of man to God by the self-abasement of the Eternal Word, is foolishness to the Greek. These truths are foolishness to those who worship the formal laws of the Understanding, and who are held in bondage thereby, so as to deny the very possibility of that, which, standing above those laws, seems to trample upon them. They are foolishness to those who hold that there can be no truth, except what can be ground or spun out of the materials supplied by the senses. They are foolishness to those whose hearts and consciences do not in some measure bear witness to them, to those who, feeling no need of them, cannot recognise their necessity. As in all knowledge we must believe, before we can understand, so must it be most especially in that knowledge, the very first germs and rudiments of which lie altogether in Faith. And as it is solely by a diligent and faithful study of the revelations of the natural world that we can discover the Laws of Nature, so is a like diligent and believing study of the revelations of the spiritual world the only means whereby any truths pertaining to it can be discerned.

Moreover, the palaces and theatres erected by human knowledge have become so vast and gorgeous, that we in our days may perhaps have stronger temptations to abide contentedly therein, instead of going forth to build and to people the house of God. While the universe has been continually expanding before the advances of Science, men have been apt to fancy that it had outgrown God, because it had outgrown their conception of Him. When they have discovered some new province of His empire, as no place was markt out for it in their previous system of things, they have thought it must belong to some unknown God; whereupon some have anticipated in reckless indifference, others in faithless dismay, that this unknown God must dethrone the God they had hitherto worshipt. In wandering and wondering over the immensity of the circumference, we have often forgotten that it must have a centre: and the Creation has still concealed the Creator, all the more because man deemed that he saw an image of himself in it, the work of his own hands, the reflexion of his own mind, and did not recollect of what mind his was the image, did not perceive how this very spectacle, which so dazzled and delighted him, bore testimony to its being so. Yet it is most certain, that the immeasurable superiority of modern Europe in Science, as well as in other respects, to the rest of the world is owing to the influence of Christianity. Indeed physical science, as has been justly remarkt, has been almost confined to Christendom. For this there are many grounds. Christianity has given man an assurance of the unity and intelligent purpose pervading all the operations of Nature, an assurance which accompanies him as an unseen friend and guide in all his speculations. It delivers him from the bondage of Nature, from the thraldom both of the senses and of the fancy, and has thus elevated him above Materialism, into which he would soon fall headlong, were he to lose its sustaining power. It enables him likewise to feel something like a fraternal sympathy and communion with Nature, a reverence for the work of the Allwise and Benevolent Author of his own being, a reverence equally removed from voluptuous idolatry and from superstitious fear. We know that all the gifts of the Natural World are the gifts of God, that the beauty of the Natural World is the visible expression of His wisdom and goodness, that the laws of the Natural World are His laws, and, as proceeding from Him, universal and unchangeable, until He shall will to change them. We have a feeling too that the Natural World is in some measure a sharer in our Fall, and that it is waiting for the time when, along with its lord, it shall be delivered from the bondage of corruption. To the influence, often perhaps the latent influence, of these thoughts and feelings, do we owe that deeper, more spiritual love of Nature, which distinguishes Christian poetry and art. In Science likewise it is the Truth that has made us free; and the benefits of this freedom have been extended in some measure even to such as have rejected the truth whereby it had been obtained. For, like all God's gifts, this too has not always been rightly used and duly acknowledged. Though Christian Wisdom is the great parent of Natural Science, it by no means follows that all men of science must have been Christians. Here again the weakness of man's Faith, his proneness to idolatry has shewn itself. He has evermore given up his heart and soul to that to which he had devoted his mind. He has fallen down and worshipt the laws, which he himself had found out. Yet, as it is through the operation of Christianity that even they who reject it have been enabled to attain to whatever eminence they may have reacht in science, so does the unseen, unfelt influence of Christianity preserve them from gross Materialism. Indeed manifold symptoms have shewn themselves during the last hundred years, in the more intelligent nations of Europe, betokening how easily and inevitably, if we were to abandon our Faith in Christ, all that is good and wholesome and precious in the present condition of society would be swallowed up in the desolating licentiousness of a Pantheistic Atheism.

Thus even in the progress of Science we find evidence that Christian Faith is the victory which overcomes the world, and that without this Faith the mind as well as the heart of man would have been wholly overcome by the world. In like manner, if we cast our thoughts over that vast mass of events which is presented to us by the history of mankind, we may perceive that Christianity alone has brought anything like order and unity into that mass, that it gives a meaning and purpose to what would otherwise be a mere chaos, that through it alone can we understand even what the heathens were unconsciously and blindly striving after. In a former Sermon, when considering the power of Faith as exemplified in man's natural life, we found that Faith is the main spring of everything done by man according to his humanity,—that it is the ground of all social union,—that by it his affections are elevated into duties,—and that through it his duties acquire a living power over his soul. In that discussion it was assumed, with reference to our immediate purpose, that the objects of Faith are ideas or ideals; such being the highest objects of contemplation attainable by man, independently of Revelation. And we were lead to the conclusion, that the deplorable inefficacy of Faith was owing in no slight measure to the insufficiency of those ideas or ideals. They are too vague and indistinct. They require too arduous an exercise of thought in him who is to bring them clearly before his mind. Hence by the bulk of mankind they are indiscernible, except through a faint tradition: and the few whose minds are capable of such speculations, and who devote themselves thereto, are apt to forget that there is any necessary connexion between the world of thought and that of action. In a word, the great want is that of living objective reality. It is supposed that these ideas and ideals are mere fictions of the mind, that the only thing feasible, and therefore to be aimed at, is to approximate to them, and that at best no reality can resemble them more nearly than a globe resembles a star. But in Christianity all these ideas are realized, and are set before us, and brought home to our hearts, in forms far more glorious and perfect than it had ever entered into the mind of man to conceive. Thus here again we find that

Christianity does not destroy man's nature, but fulfill it.

For instance, the idea of a father has ever been one of the most sacred, one of the most powerful over the spirits of men. Among all nations has it been so. It is graven on our hearts in our infancy. Numberless acts of love, the daily support and nurture of our life, bodily and spiritual, habit, custom, authority, law, deepen and brighten the impression year after year. Yet how far is any living reality from answering to it! How often do the shows of the world jar against it, and almost seem to mock at it! That this has been deeply felt, we see in poetry, which gives utterance to the universal feelings of mankind, and in all forms of which the representation of children struggling against the will of their parents has been a favorite theme, the more so on account of the moral conflict which such a struggle involves. Nay, our Lord Himself declares that He was come to set the son against the father. With what new power therefore, and glory, and sanctity, was the name invested, when we were commanded to address God Himself as Our Father! when *He sent the Spirit of His Son into our hearts, whereby we cry, Abba, Father!* In like manner how was the filial relation hallowed, when we were taught to discern a mysterious analogy to it in God Himself! when in Him we beheld a Father, in Him an Eternal Son! And how are the duties of this relation enforced upon us, when we are told that the Eternal Son Himself learnt obedience by the things that He suffered,—yea, that, when He was fulfilling all righteousness upon earth, He was subject to His earthly parents! Again, what a swarm of passions, starting out of every foul corner of the heart, have in all ages disfigured and distorted and debased the conjugal relation! How, on the other hand, is that relation glorified and sanctified, when we are exhorted to regard it as an image and likeness of that between Christ and the Church! when we are thus taught to discern that the essence and consummation of love is self-sacrifice for the purification of its object; and thus likewise are enabled to see what true devotion is, in her who is nothing except in her union with her Lord, and whose highest aim is to receive His image into her heart. Great and noble too as is the feeling of Patriotism, great and noble as is the idea of Country, the taint of earth still cleaves to it. In whatever form of government that idea may be embodied, there is often a struggle between conflicting principles, between Law and Right. We have to do, and even to love, what we cannot approve. And as a strong light will be bordered by a dark shadow, so, where there is such a host of contending interests and passions, an ardent lover of his country is mostly a jealous enemy of her neighbours. But in that holy community which Christ establisht, all exclusive, invidious feeling was to pass away. In His Church there was to be neither Jew nor Greek, Barbarian nor Scythian; but all were to be gathered together in Him, as members of His body, and every one members one of another.

It will not be requisite for me to pursue this train of thought through the various branches of Duty, for the sake of shewing how every duty was exemplified by our Lord in its highest excellence. Such contemplations must be familiar to you all. They are for ever brought before you in one shape or other; it being one of the chief arguments of Christian preaching to shew how whatsoever things are true, whatsoever things are noble, whatsoever things are just, whatsoever things are pure, whatsoever things are lovely, whatsoever things are of good report, if there be any virtue, and if there be any praise,—all these things were realized in the life of Christ, for the building up of the creature into the perfect image of God. In Him alone we see how the manifold rays of Duty are one in the pure light of Love, their diversity arising from the difference of the objects on which that Love shines. In Him we see how Love is infinite Fulness, so that the world itself could not contain the record of its manifestations.

One exception indeed may be urged, with reference to that very virtue which we have been considering through the course of these Sermons. Our Lord, it may be said, has not set us an example of Faith. This however is only true, so far as a state of imperfection is the necessary condition of Faith, only so far as Faith is essentially incompatible with that divine intuition which belonged to Christ as God.

So far as Christ was a man, His whole life was a life of Faith. As the Son of Man, He alone lived, as every child of man ought to live, wholly by Faith, by Faith in God, shewing forth the inexhaustible riches of His Faith toward His human brethren, coming to them again and again with every demonstration of power and love, if so be He might awaken the better spirit which was slumbering in them opprest by the weight of sin, and might rouse them out of the sleep of death,—undeterred by the ghastly apparitions of evil, which met Him whithersoever He turned His eyes,—persevering unto the end for the joy set before Him of gathering His redeemed from all the quarters of the world. That which He did through divine intuition, we can only do through Faith. In Him, the Author and Finisher of our Faith, we have not only the ground for a full, lively, undoubting Faith in God, but also the strongest motive and encouragement for an active Faith in our brethren. As no aspect of evil could daunt Him or make Him despond, none should daunt or dismay His servants. As He brought life out of death, so should they persevere, trusting that in His strength they may even do likewise. And whereas he who looks on the doings of mankind with a worldly eye, if his eye be keen enough to pierce through the fair coating spread over the surface of life, is apt to feel bitter scorn and disgust at his fellowcreatures, he who looks at them with the higher wisdom of Faith in the Son of God, will not dare to entertain anything like scorn toward a soul for which Christ died, and which is precious in the sight of the living God.

In our Lord's last discourse with His disciples, on the eve of His crucifixion, after telling them that in the world they would have tribulation, He bids them be of good cheer; for that He had overcome the world. Wherein lay the consolation of this thought? and why did He, the Lord of the world, descend from His heavenly throne, to fight against the world, and to overcome it? The thought was to cheer their hearts, because He had overcome the world for their sake and in their behalf, to the end that He might glorify the Father, that He might give eternal life to as many as the Father had given to Him,—to the end that the Father might be glorified by their overcoming the world, through Faith in Him, the only true God, and in Jesus Christ whom He had sent. He overcame the world, to the end that through the glory of His victory all nations might be drawn to enroll themselves in the army of Faith, in that Church Militant, which by overcoming the world is to rise into the Church Triumphant. He overcame the world, in order to give us an example how we are to overcome it, going before us as the Captain of our Salvation, that we might follow in His victorious steps, and might walk in the light which His Cross sheds on our path. Yet even this does not exhaust the glory of His victory, the riches of the grace which He obtained for us thereby. He overcame the world, in order that He might mount up on high, and might lead captivity captive,—in order that, when

He was seated at the right hand of the Father, far above all principalities and powers, He might receive gifts for men, that the Lord God might dwell amongst us. And ever since He has been pouring down the manifold gifts of His Spirit upon His Church, and upon all who believe in Him. To one He has given the spirit of power, to another the spirit of knowledge, to another the spirit of prudence, to another the spirit of boldness, to another the spirit of fortitude, to another the spirit of perseverance, to another the spirit of patience, to another the spirit of longsuffering and forbearance, to another the spirit of meekness and gentleness, to another the spirit of temperance, to another the spirit of purity and holiness. All these and many other gifts have been given to the prayers of Faith: nor has there been any other limit to the gifts, than the strength of our Faith to ask for them. The more they who have believed that Jesus is the Son of God, have askt of the Father in that Faith, the more they have received. Of these gifts the Church has been built, upon the foundation of Faith: and they to whom these gifts have been granted, have gone abroad over the earth, preaching the grace and the glory of God to all nations, each, according to the gift he had received, shewing forth the power of Faith to overcome the world, calling upon his brethren to become partakers in the victory of Faith, and giving them a living assurance that the gates of hell shall never prevail against those who believe that Jesus is the Son of God.

But how can this be? it may be askt. Where is the

victory of Faith? Where is the sign of her power? Or how happens it, if she has all this power, that the World has not long since been overcome? How happens it that Sin has not long since been cast out? How happens it that, after eighteen centuries of Faith, when the World should long since have become the submissive footstool of Christ, it still lifts itself up against Him, and tempts men to cast themselves down from its pinnacles? How comes its sway over mankind to be still wellnigh as great as ever? To these questions the only answer is that of our Lord to His disciples: *Because of our unbelief.* Therefore have we been unable to cast the evil spirit out of the world: because we have not believed that Jesus is the Son of God; because, even when we have tried to fight against evil, whether inward or outward, we have fought against it in our own strength, which in such a contest is too surely proved to be weakness; because we have not believed that evil had been overcome for us, and that He who overcame it is sitting at the right hand of the Father, able and willing to strengthen all who believe in Him, so that they also shall overcome as He did. If we indeed believe that Jesus is the Son of God,—if we indeed believe that the Son of God was made man, and suffered all the weaknesses and pains that flesh is heir to, and died on the cross, for our sakes, that He might bring us to God,—then we shall feel assured that He who gave us His Son, will with Him also freely give us all things. We shall feel assured that the Son Himself desires to be satisfied by the travail of His soul. We shall feel assured that, as He is the Lord of all power and might, He will readily give power and might to those who seek it at His hands. Whenever we fight against the world in this Faith, we shall infallibly overcome the world: and when we are overcome by the world, through our want of Faith, do we not still bear testimony to the same truth, that he alone can overcome the world, who believes that Jesus is the Son of God? Finally, as it is by this faith alone that we can overcome evil in this life, so at the last day will it be solely through the righteousness of Faith in Jesus as the Son of God, that any shall overcome the world and the Prince of the world.

Who is he that overcometh the world? He who believeth that Jesus is the Son of God. In the Epistle to the Hebrews the Apostle recounts many of the great and heroic deeds wrought through Faith under the ancient Covenant of works, by those who had not yet received the promise. Now Faith, we have seen, has been mightily strengthened since. It has been strengthened by the full revelation of Him in whom we are to believe. It has been strengthened by the adoption we have received, which casts out the spirit of fear, and draws us heavenward by the cords of love. It has been strengthened by the clear light of Christ's example, which enables us, if we follow it, to walk without hesitation or wandering along the path of duty. It has been strengthened by the knowledge that the world has already been overcome, for us, and in our behalf,—by the knowledge that our warfare is not ours merely, but a warfare in which God Himself is fighting on our side, and that His omnipotence is the pledge of our victory. It has been strengthened by the gifts of the Spirit, which are ever granted to the prayer of Faith, every fresh gift forming a fresh ground for confidence, a fresh assurance that he who believes in Jesus as the Son of God shall indeed overcome the world. Surely then they who have received the promise, they who have beheld the blessed fulfilment of all that the fathers lookt for,— who have seen it all fulfilled with a largeness of grace and glory, such as the imagination of man had never conceived,—surely they who have had all these advantages, must also have been enabled to shew forth the power of Faith in overcoming the world. The fittest conclusion for these Sermons would be a like enumeration of those who have been raised up as the chief heroes of Faith in the Church of Christ,—of those who have shewn the most conspicuously that Faith in Jesus, the Son of God, is the true victory that overcomes the world. And a glorious cloud of witnesses might be called up from the history of the Church during the eighteen centuries of her existence, a cloud gathering from all lands, and rising like the morning at once from the East and from the West, from the North and from the South (Ps. cvii. 3). Only it would require the pen of an angel to set forth all the noble deeds which have been wrought during that period by Faith in Jesus as the Son of God. Nor will they be set forth, until the day when the Author and Object of this Faith collects the jewels for His everlasting crown; when in every jewel, of whatsoever shape or hue, it will be seen that Faith has been the shrine wherein the light embosomed in it has been held. And even if the conviction of my own feebleness did not withhold me from such an attempt, the time would not allow me to do more than choose out a very few of the most remarkable among the achievements of Faith.

By Faith the first believers sold their possessions and goods, and had all things common.

By Faith the Apostles rejoiced that they were counted worthy to suffer for the name of Christ.

By Faith Stephen saw the heavens opened, and the Son of Man standing on the right hand of God. By Faith, when stoned, he fell asleep, praying that God would not lay the sin of his death to the charge of his murderers.

By Faith Peter received the Gentiles into the Church.

By Faith Paul called the nations to the knowledge of Christ. By Faith he founded Church after Church, whithersoever he went. By Faith he stood before Felix, and Festus, and Agrippa. By Faith he was in labours more abundant, in stripes above measure, in prisons more frequent, in deaths oft. By Faith he gloried in the things which concerned his infirmities. By Faith, being carried in bonds to Rome, he turned his captivity into the means of enlarging and strength-ening the Empire of Christ. By Faith he forgot the things that were behind, and, reaching forward to the things that were before, ever prest toward the mark of the high calling of God in Christ Jesus. By Faith he desired to depart and to be with Christ. By Faith He was content to remain for the furtherance and joy of our Faith.

By Faith the glorious company of the Apostles sealed their testimony in behalf of their crucified Lord with their blood.

By Faith the Son of Thunder, who desired to call down fire on the Samaritan village, became the Apostle of love. By Faith he sought out the backsliding convert amid his band of robbers, and brought him back to the obedience of the Gospel. By Faith, when too feeble to walk, and scarcely able to speak, he still bad his friends carry him daily into the midst of the congregation, and said again and again, *Little children, love one another.*

By Faith Polycarp, when above ninety years old, being commanded to revile Christ, with the promise that he should be set free, replied, *Eighty and six years have I served Him; and he has done me no wrong. How can I blaspheme my King, who has saved me?* By Faith, as the executioners were about to nail him to the stake, he said, *Leave me as I am: for He who ordains that I should endure the fire, will enable me to stand unflinchingly at the pile, without your nails to hold me.* By Faith, while they were kindling the fire, he prayed: *O Father of Thy beloved and blessed Son Jesus Christ, through whom I have received the knowledge of Thee, O God of angels and powers, and of the whole creation, and of the whole family of the just who live before Thee, I bless Thee that Thou hast thought me worthy of this day and hour, to obtain a portion among the martyrs, in the cup of Christ, for the resurrection both of soul and body to eternal life, in the incorruptibleness of the Holy Spirit. Therefore, and for all things, I praise Thee,· I bless Thee, I glorify Thee, through the eternal Highpriest, Jesus Christ, Thy beloved Son; through whom be glory to Thee along with Him in the Holy Spirit both now and through all future ages: Amen.*

By Faith thousands of weak frail mortals, even women, felt their hearts glow with joy, when they heard the rabble in their bloodthirsty frenzy cry, *The Christians to the lions!* the exultation of their victims triumphing over that of the murderers.

By Faith the blood of the Martyrs became the seed of the Church.

By Faith the persecuted Christians, in a time of dismal pestilence and famine, alone tended and nurst their persecutors, buried them when they died, and calling the people together distributed bread amongst them; whereby the people were moved to glorify Him, whose servants shewed such love to their enemies.

By Faith the Syrian hermit, Telemachus, came from the far East to Rome, and, resolved to stop the gladiatorial contests, rusht into the middle of the amphitheatre, and threw himself between the combatants; whereupon, though he was slain by the fury of the populace, the horrour excited by that act, and the admiration of his selfdevotion, brought about the abolition of those games, which the Emperors had been unable to suppress.

By Faith Ambrose preserved the churches of Milan from the Arian Empress and her Gothic soldiers. By Faith, making use of rebukes and warnings and threats, he withheld Valentinian from sacrificing to idols. By Faith he forbad the bloodstained Theodosius to approach the altar, until, as he had followed David in his crime, he had also followed David in his penitence; whereby the emperor was moved to an earnest and lasting repentance.

By Faith Chrysostom, when deposed, an aged exile in a remote savage land, assailed by all manner of sufferings, still watcht over, exhorted, and comforted, his Church at Constantinople, still laboured for extending the Kingdom of Christ among the heathens, and died with the words he was ever repeating on his lips, *Glory be to God for all things*.

By Faith Athanasius, during forty years of persecution, in banishment time after time, upheld the true doctrine of the Holy Trinity against the power of the Emperors, and was the chief human means whereby that doctrine was received and acknowledged as the central truth of the Catholic Church.

By Faith Gregory, when he saw the captive Angles, exclaimed that, were it only for their beauty, they ought to be received into the brotherhood of the angels, and sent Augustin to preach the Gospel in this land.

By Faith Boniface, leaving his home, and refusing high ecclesiastical honours, went into the wilds of Germany to convert the heathen natives. By Faith he cut down the huge oak of Thor, while the people were raging tumultuously around, expecting that the vengeance of the god would burst upon his head. By Faith he built a church to the true God, out of the oak he had cut down, and persuaded the people to worship there. By Faith he baptized above a hundred thousand souls in the name of the Holy Trinity, and built many churches and convents in dreary savage lands. By Faith, when placed at the head of the German Church, he still in his seventy-fifth year persevered in enlarging the Kingdom of Christ, went forth to convert fresh heathen tribes, and met his martyrdom with patient joy.

By Faith the Hermit Peter and Bernard stirred up the nations of Europe to march as one man, kings and princes and lords, with their assembled vassals, to deliver the birthplace and tomb of the Saviour from the Unbeliever.

By Faith Bonaventura, being askt in what books he had learnt his marvellous wisdom, pointed to his crucifix.

By Faith Elizabeth of Hungary, the daughter of kings, the wife of the Duke of Thuringia, being left a widow at twenty, gave all she had to the poor, and dwelt amongst them as their servant, labouring for them, visiting them, waiting upon them, nursing them, by word and deed teaching them the love of God.

By Faith the Waldensians retired among mountain fastnesses, and dwelt in the caves of the Alps, that they might keep their religion in undefiled purity; and thus have been enabled to preserve it, like the snows around them, under all manner of persecution, through six centuries—a period seldom vouchsafed to the glory of anything earthly.

By Faith Wicliff, the morning-star of the Reformation, rose out of the darkness, and heralded the coming daylight.

By Faith Luther proclaimed his Theses against the doctrine of Indulgence. By Faith he burnt the Pope's Bull, and thereby for himself, and for thousands of millions after him, threw off the crushing yoke of Rome. By Faith he went to the diet at Worms, though warned that the fate of Huss would await him, going in the strength of Christ, despite of the gates of hell, and of the Prince of the powers of the air. By Faith, a single friendless monk, standing before the princes of the Empire, he witnest a noble confession with meekness in behalf of the truth. By Faith he translated the Bible, and received the blessed reward of being the interpreter of the word of God to his countrymen for all generations.

By Faith Rogers, the protomartyr of our Reformation, when his wife and his eleven children met him on his way to the stake, and an offer of life and pardon was brought to him in their sight, if so be he would recant, walkt on with a stout heart, and washt his hands in the flames while he was burning, rejoicing in the fiery baptism whereby he gave up his soul to God.

By Faith Ridley lookt forward with joy to the fire that awaited him, and bad his sister come to his marriage.

By Faith the aged Latimer, when stript to his

shroud, rose up on high, as though his very body had been new-strung, and cheered his own heart, and his companion's by the prophetic assurance, that on that day by God's grace they should light such a candle in England as would never be put out.

By Faith the noble Army of Martyrs mounted in their fiery chariots to heaven.

By Faith Oberlin went forth among the Vosges, and labouring in all things at the head of his people, spread the blessings of religion and civilization among the wild inhabitants.

By Faith Clarkson and Wilberforce overthrew the slave-trade: and as it is the nature of the grain of Mustard-seed to grow until it has become great among the trees of the forest, so through their Faith has slavery been already abolisht throughout the British dominions.

By Faith Simeon, preaching the word of God in this town, through a long life of persevering activity, became the instrument of sending forth zealous preachers of Christ into all parts of the country, and thus contributed, under God's blessing, more than any other man, to that revival of true religion, which has taken place of late years amongst us; and which, we hope and pray, will increase and spread, until in England at least the knowledge of God shall fill the land, as the waters cover the sea.

And what shall I say more? For the time would fail me to tell of Ignatius, and Justin, and Cyprian, and Perpetua, and Basil, and Augustin, and Patrick, and Columban, and Bede, and Anselm, and Huss, and Melanchthon, and Zwingli, and Calvin, and Knox, and

Hooper, and Rowland Taylor, and Bunyan, and George Fox, and Penn, and Baxter, and Flavel, and Wesley, and Zinzendorf, and Francis Xavier, and Eliot, the Apostle of the Indians, and Schwarz, and Hans Egede, and Howard, and Neff, and Henry Martyn, who by Faith subdued kingdoms for Christ, wrought righteousness, obtained the fulfilment of the promises, stopt the mouths of blasphemers, and filled them with hymns of praise, quencht the violence of hatred, melting it into love, out of weakness were made strong, waxt valiant in the fight against Satan, and turned armies of aliens to bow before the name of the living God. Women and maidens withstood the entreaties of their parents and children, looking with longing for the moment that was to open the gates of immortality. Children rejoiced in the thought of the glorious city to which they were going. Others, thousands upon thousands, devoted their lives to the humblest labours in the service of Him, whom they would gladly have glorified by their deaths. Wherefore, seeing, brethren, that we also are compast about with so great a Cloud of Witnesses, let us lay aside every weight, and our besetting sin, and let us run the race set before us with patience, looking to Jesus the Author and Finisher of our Faith.

And now, my young friends, before I bid you farewell, let me address a few words of affectionate exhortation more especially to you. We have been speaking of battles and of victories, of great warriors and heroes, the battles and victories, the warriors and heroes of Faith. The thoughts of battles and victories are thoughts you are most of you familiar with. There are few young men, at least in your rank of life, whose hearts have not often been moved by dreams and visions of battle and victory, under one form or other. For such thoughts are congenial to the ardent, generous spirit of youth, which magnifies and longs to devote itself to whatever attracts it. Some of you may never have risen in such thoughts beyond your sports and games. Some may have dreamt of contests and victories in the various fields of knowledge; others on the stage of civil and political life. Some,—though in times of such general peace among nations but few, —will dream of open war, of the trumpet, the plumed array, and the charge. In all such conflicts there is a stirring and joyous excitement, which braces our faculties to the utmost: and few can resist the mighty fascination that lies in the thought of victory. Such feelings are natural, are unquenchable and irrepressible: nor are they altogether to be reprehended. Our great poet, who sang how Paradise was Lost and Regained, has ventured to attribute something of the sort to the boyhood of the Saviour.

> Victorious deeds
> Flamed in his heart, heroic acts; one while
> To rescue Israel from the Roman yoke;
> Then to subdue and quell o'er all the earth
> Brute violence and proud tyrannic power,
> Till truth were freed, and equity restored.

It may be, that in this picture the human element is brought forward too strongly. This was a difficulty inherent in the subject, which no genius could surmount. Never has our Lord been represented as He was, except in the divine simplicity of the Gospels;

which thus is among the sure marks of their truth. But, as the sight of Goliath kindled the heart of David, and made it burn with desire to overthrow the giant who defied the armies of the living God, so to the noblest among the sons of men would it have been a lifegiving hope, to raise up the people of God out of their slavery, and to cast down the idolatrous dominion of Rome. In our days too there are Goliaths to be overthrown: yea, in these our days there is brute violence to be subdued, and proud tyrannic power to be quelled: there are truths to be set free, and rights to be establisht. And well may the noblest soul among you burn with desire to go forth in this great warfare. Only you must steadily bear in mind that the good of the conflict does not lie in the conflict itself, but in the end which is to be attained by it,—that you are to fight, not for fighting's sake, but in order to accomplish some purpose; and this purpose is not to be your own glory, your own distinction, your own aggrandizement, but something that will promote the glory of God, and the good of His creatures. In order that you may not misdirect your efforts, you should recognise what is the true source and meaning and object of those warlike feelings, which are so ready to flame up within you, and which, as they may be mighty auxiliaries in the cause of good, may also be terrible engines of evil. They betoken and admonish you that, so long as you are on earth, you are in a state militant, and members of a Church militant,—that you are not, and must not be at peace with the world, such as you find it, whether around you, or within you,—but that you have a post to gain and to maintain, and this cannot be done without an arduous and continuous struggle. This post can only be gained, can only be maintained by Faith. Faith must lead you to desire it: Faith must rouse you to seek it: Faith must strengthen you to conquer it: Faith must give you endurance and watchfulness to preserve it. You have a formidable enemy to battle against, Sin, in all its forms, of ignorance, and folly, and reckless desolation. You are to fight against Sin, both within your own hearts, and in the world; but above and before all within you. Nothing effectual can be achieved outwardly, no victory of any moment can be gained, until Sin is subdued and quelled within your own hearts. In each warfare Faith is to be your weapon,—your shield, as St Paul terms it, to defend you against Sin, when it assails you with any of its poisoned arrows,—your sword, to fight against Sin in the world, when it has been so far brought into subjection within you, that you may aspire to be enrolled in the army which God sends forth to wage His battles against evil. Do not invert the rightful order. Do not fancy that you can work any good in the world, until the Evil Spirit has been cast out of your own hearts. Else your very best acts will be marred by selfishness: your virtues will only be splendid vices. Strive therefore in the first place to cast out the Evil Spirit from your own hearts. Pray to God to cast it out. This is the might, and this is the difficulty of prayer, that it is altogether a work of Faith. Pray to God to strengthen that Faith in you, which will enable you to cast out, and to keep out the Evil Spirit, even the Faith in Jesus, His Eternal Incarnate Son. And then go forth on your heavenly mission to cast out Sin from the world, and to bring the world out of the miserable wilderness of unbelief into the blessed Paradise of Faith. O if such a body as I now see around me, so gifted, so fitted out with human learning and knowledge, as, unless you grievously misspend and waste your time, you may be, before you leave this University,—if such a body were to go forth with united hearts, hearts united by Faith in Christ and by the Love of God,—if you, my brethren, were to go forth in this spirit on your various missions,—then might we hope that manifold blessings would be poured down on your labours, and that the heart and soul of England would arise in freshness and joy out of the deathsleep which is lying so heavily on many parts of the land. Go forth in this spirit, my dear young friends; and may God bless you with His choicest blessings! Go forth in Faith to overcome the world, strong in the Lord, and in the power of His might: and may Christ give you, as He has promist to them that overcome, to eat of the Tree of Life, which is in the midst of the Paradise of God.

www.ingramcontent.com/pod-product-compliance
Lightning Source LLC
Chambersburg PA
CBHW020318240426
43673CB00039B/848